Free to All

THE UNIVERSITY OF CHICAGO PRESS · *Chicago and London*

FREE TO ALL

CARNEGIE LIBRARIES
& AMERICAN CULTURE
1890—1920

Abigail A. Van Slyck

Abigail Van Slyck is associate professor of architecture, of art history, and of women's studies at the University of Arizona.

Chapter 1, in a slightly different form, was originally published as "The Utmost Amount of Effectiv *(sic)* Accommodation," in the *Journal of the Society of Architectural Historians* 50 (December 1991): 359–83. Reprinted with permission of the Society of Architectural Historians (Philadelphia).

The University of Chicago Press, Chicago 60637
The University of Chicago Press, Ltd., London
© 1995 by The University of Chicago
All rights reserved. Published 1995
Printed in the United States of America

04 03 02 01 00 99 98 97 96   2 3 4 5

ISBN: 0-226-85031-5 (cloth)

Library of Congress Cataloging-in-Publication Data

Van Slyck, Abigail Ayres.
    Free to all : Carnegie libraries & American culture, 1890–1920 / Abigail A. Van Slyck.
        p.   cm.
    Includes bibliographical references (p.) and index.
        1. Library architecture—United States—History—19th century.   2. Library architecture—United States—History—20th century.   3. Public libraries—Social aspects—United States.   4. Architecture and society—United States—History—19th century.   5. Architecture and society—United States—History—20th century.   6. United States—Civilization—1865–1918.   I. Title.
    Z679.2.U54V36   1995
    727'.8'0973—dc20   95-3638
                                                                                            CIP

⊗ The paper used in this publication meets the minimum requirements of the American National Standard for Information Sciences—Permanence of Paper for Printed Library Materials, ANSI Z39.48-1984.

To M.B.R.F.

Contents

Illustrations

Graphs

Table

Acknowledgments

This project began in California, where I "discovered" Carnegie libraries in the 1980s. By a twist of geographical fate, I had never before lived where Carnegie-financed public libraries were particularly visible. I had grown up in a part of suburban Detroit that owed its full-scale expansion to the prosperity generated by the auto industry in the 1920s—*after* the Carnegie Corporation had discontinued the library building program. Indeed, the library I used as a child (as I later learned) had been designed by Marcel Breuer in 1953. My undergraduate years at Smith College did much to broaden my horizons, but New England's important role in the beginnings of the public library movement in the 1850s meant that the chances of encountering a Carnegie-financed public library there were slim; by the early years of the twentieth century, many Massachusetts towns had already constructed purpose-built public libraries (some designed by H. H. Richardson) and had no need for a Carnegie-financed building.

As a result, when I moved to California to pursue graduate studies at the University of California at Berkeley, Carnegie libraries were a revelation. As I explored towns like Petaluma, Sonoma, St. Helena, San Rafael, Healdsburg, and Eureka, I was unprepared for the frequency with which I encountered symmetrical, classical, oak-lined Carnegie libraries. Perhaps if I had been a long-time Carnegie library user, I would have found these buildings unremarkable. To my unaccustomed eyes, however, they seemed ripe for further study.

Equally important, the University of California at Berkeley also brought me into contact with a smart and savvy group of scholars—architectural historians and Americanists in related fields—who challenged me to think about the cultural landscape of the United States in new ways. Our discussions over many years shaped my ideas about the kinds of buildings that are worth serious study and about the sorts of questions we might ask about these buildings. I am indebted to these friends for their interest and encouragement in the early phases of this project, and particularly to Annmarie Adams, Mark Brack, Paul Groth, the late Spiro Kostof, Margaretta Lovell, Gülsüm Nalbantoğlu, Katharine Peterson, Christine Rosen, Bruce Thomas, and Dell Upton. Of this group, Dell Upton deserves my special thanks for his initial enthusiasm for the topic, for his constructive commentary on my dissertation, for the model of innovative scholarship he provides, and for his continued interest in my work. Throughout the process, his insight has helped me discover what I wanted this book to be.

My research on this project was a delight, in large part because it brought me into regular contact with public librarians who invariably shared my enthusiasm for the project. I have always counted myself fortunate to have worked for so many years on a building type whose permanent residents also belong to a profession that values free access to information. Indeed, I even began to take it for granted that the public librarians regularly set aside their own work to help me dig into archival material that (at least in some cases) no one had ever consulted. In recent years, I have had the chance to pursue similar research in other countries and have come to realize that American public librarians are a breed apart. Combining intellectual curiosity, an appreciation of the importance of original research, and a willingness to tackle any reference question, they constitute one of our society's most important cultural resources. My thanks go to Lyle Bowman, at the Tahlequah Public Library; Robert D. Briell, at the Warren-Trumbull County Public Library; Sharon Canter, at the River Bluffs Regional Library, St. Joseph, Missouri; Wayne Furman, at the New York Public Library; Melba Herrmann, at the George W. Norris Regional Library, McCook, Nebraska; Marilyn A. Holt, at the Carnegie Library of Pittsburgh; Betty Lloyd, at the Arthur Johnson Memorial Library, Raton, New Mexico; Kenneth B. Miller, at the Bowen Branch of the Detroit Public Library; Julie M. Overton, at the Greene County District Library, Xenia, Ohio; J. Randall Rosensteel, at the Free Library of Philadelphia; Michael Ruffing, at the Cleveland Public Library; Mary Ternes, at the District of Columbia Public Library; Noel Van Gorden, at the Detroit Public Library; Ann Woods, at the Cooke County Library, Gainesville, Texas; and especially to Virginia D. Hiatt, at the Union City (Indiana) Public Library, and Lynne Nothum, at the Lackawanna (New York) Public Library, who went out of their way to make my visits to their communities pleasant and productive. Although I never learned the names of many other library staffers who smoothed my way, I want them to know how much I admire their professionalism and how much I appreciate their help.

I would also like to acknowledge the assistance of the staff at other research libraries and archives that I visited in the course of my research, particularly Patricia Haynes, at the Carnegie Corporation of New York; Patricia Cahill, Bernard Crystal, and Brenda Hearing, at the Rare Book and Manuscript Library, Columbia University; Shana Powell, at the Cooke County Heritage Society in Gainesville, Texas; Lorna Condon, at the Society for the Preservation of New England Antiquities; Margaret Smith at the Houghton Library, Harvard University; Daniel May at the MetLife company archives; and Nancy Sherbert of the Kansas State Historical Society.

Since much of this research was completed while I was an impoverished graduate student, I would like to thank the friends and family who gave me bed and board as I traveled around the country: Chris Conklin and Jay Kistler, who established a presidential suite for me in Pittsburgh soon after they moved there; Susan Beck and Cynthia Moekle who opened their New York apartments to me; and my parents, Ann and Ellis Van Slyck, in the Detroit area. Special thanks go to David Russell for sharing with me his friends in McCook, Nebraska.

I would also like to thank those colleagues who have read and commented on my attempts to reformulate the dissertation into a better and more nuanced book. Sally McMurry and Paul Ivey each read parts of the book with great care and helped keep me from going too far astray at important points. Charley Seavey gave me a number of opportunities to present my work to his graduate library science classes at the University of Arizona, sessions which resulted in lively discussions about the social ramifications of library practice. I am also grateful to Irene d'Almeida, Joonok Huh, and Joan Jensen (my fellow Rockefeller Humanists-in-Residence at the Southwest Institute for Research on Women in the summer of 1991), and to Karen Anderson, Jan Monk, and other women's studies scholars at the University of Arizona who participated in our discussion groups that summer.

I am also happy to acknowledge the financial support that I received from a number of sources: U. C. Berkeley, for student fellowships that gave me the time to complete the research and writing of the dissertation on which this book is based; National Endowment for the Humanities, for a Travels to Collections grant that took me to New York to consult archival materials related to Melvil Dewey and the Library Bureau; Southwest Institute for Research on Women and Women's Studies Program at the University of Arizona, for a Rockefeller Humanist-in-Residence fellowship in the summer of 1991 that supported me while I wrote chapters 4 and 5; the College of Architecture at the University of Arizona, for lightening my teaching load in the fall of 1992 so that I could devote more time to writing, and for underwriting many of the illustrations in chapter 1; and to the Provost's Office at the University of Arizona, for a grant from the Author's Support Fund, which helped pay for the balance of the illustrations.

Finally, I would like to acknowledge more personal debts of gratitude to friends and family who bolstered my spirits during the low points that inevitably accompany such a lengthy project. I particularly want to thank my parents, who encouraged my scholastic bent from the start, and who are so good at helping me celebrate my successes. I have also been blessed with good friends who have shared (to a greater or lesser extent) my love for good food, red wine, and Perry Mason reruns. By reminding me to have fun, Chris Conklin, Jay Kistler, Katharine Peterson, Bruce Thomas, Nancy McMichael, Mary Graham, and David Klanderman have each played an important role in helping me finish this book. Finally, I would like to acknowledge how important Mitch Favreau has been to every step of this project—inhabiting home-improvement hell without any assistance from me for the last six years, volunteering to do more than his share of drudgery that was directly related to this project, and throughout it all, providing the certainty of a loving relationship that grounds my otherwise all too hectic existence.

Introduction

Carnegie libraries—public libraries built between 1886 and 1917 with funds provided by Andrew Carnegie—are among the most numerous public buildings in the United States. They are also as familiar as old friends. With classical colonnades supporting triangular pediments and surmounted by domes, they present a face that is immediately recognizable. Symmetrical buildings cloaked in a variety of classical styles, their dress is both conventional and easily anticipated. Located in public parks, they seem neither threatening nor eccentric. We expect neither drama nor excitement from them, and we find it comforting when they meet our expectations.

For all this familiarity, however, Carnegie libraries are not well understood. The people most closely connected with them—those who have worked in them, those who have borrowed books from them, those who have supervised their adaptation to new uses—have not seen these buildings clearly, often retelling their histories in ways that distort the past. The great physical similarities in Carnegie libraries have typically prompted one of two responses. One has been to manufacture specialness in the face of evident uniformity, emphasizing the small peculiarities of an individual building or its history. The other has been to exaggerate the formal similarities between Carnegie libraries, celebrating them as evidence of a shared national experience, and using them to invoke a golden era in which children skated on the library grounds through long, warm, summer afternoons, undisturbed by the social disruptions of our own less perfect time. Such a golden age of American unity is, of course, a myth that has appeared throughout the nineteenth and twentieth centuries, and its reappearance in recent decades says more about the United States in the 1980s and 1990s than it does about the conditions that brought Carnegie libraries into being almost a century ago.[1]

Architectural history has been slow to provide a more balanced interpretation of Carnegie libraries. Indeed, the field's traditional focus on

the avant-garde has hampered consideration of these conventionally designed buildings. More recently, a growing interest in vernacular architecture has done much to clear a space for a history of Carnegie libraries,
particularly by broadening the definition of buildings deemed worthy of
study. In many ways, however, Carnegie libraries do not yet fit comfort-
ably into vernacular architecture studies. As products of professional expertise, as buildings that draw liberally on Western traditions of architectural design, as material artifacts assembled from mass-produced
components, often shipped over long distances, Carnegie libraries do
not respond well to methodologies that have been forged to interpret
locally-produced, handcrafted buildings. Neither the innovation diffusion model of cultural geography nor the detailed examination of local
construction technologies is a useful model for studying buildings
erected in the age of mass production.[2]

In short, we have allowed Carnegie libraries (and many other buildings) to fall through the methodological gap that exists between the history of the architectural avant-garde and vernacular architecture studies.[3] In order to close this gap, we must begin by acknowledging that
the distinction between vernacular and high-style buildings is an artificial one, a social construction of the nineteenth century. Indeed, our
framework for understanding buildings is an outgrowth of an extended
campaign for professional recognition that prompted self-styled architects to emphasize the difference between their designs and the products of "mere builders."[4] In the first half of the nineteenth century, A. J.
Downing and other pattern book authors argued for the great superiority
of professional design over mere building, conveniently ignoring the
similarities between professionally-designed cottages and a wide range
of "vernacular" house forms, including the New England central chimney plan, the I house, and the Georgian plan.[5] After the Civil War, professional architects like H. H. Richardson and McKim, Mead & White
drew openly on these same sources, using the early New England house
and the Georgian house as models for their Queen Ann style vacation
homes.[6] These open and self-conscious references, however, put traditional houses on a par with the more exotic sources from which professional designers also drew their inspiration. Grouping vernacular buildings with artifacts that were either chronologically remote (like the
Tudor) or geographically remote (like the Japanese or Saracenic), late
nineteenth-century architects succeeded in isolating high-style and vernacular designs into separate and distinct cultural categories.

Even if the line that divides high-style and vernacular buildings is artificial, the question remains as to how to erode this division. How can we move smoothly from buildings designed by architects to those in which no architects were involved? Generally speaking, we need to de-emphasize our consideration of each building as a static object, the product of an individual to be judged by a universal standard of taste. Instead, we must look at all buildings as evidence of social processes in which a variety of attitudes are negotiated in specific social and cultural settings.

Such an approach depends upon widening our analytic frame of reference in order to increase our opportunities for viewing buildings from multiple perspectives. Following the lead of cultural geographers, we can begin by considering buildings as components of the larger cultural landscape. We must view buildings in their immediate surroundings, no matter how stylistically or aesthetically incongruous the resulting images seem. We may also need to reconstruct in our mind's eye what has disappeared, imagining the buildings in the physical world of which they were a part. As we adopt this wider frame, however, it is important not to ignore the details. We need to consider the material world within buildings, and to ask ourselves about the choice and arrangement of furnishings. More difficult to reconstruct because more ephemeral, these arrangements were often just as important as the buildings themselves for shaping and coloring the experience within the building.[7]

We also need to expand our chronological frame of reference. The window of time usually considered (from the moment the commission was given to the moment the building was complete) is too narrow to allow a full consideration of the entire building process. It takes for granted important questions that were answered early in the process before the architect or builder arrived on the scene: Why do we need this building? What functions should it house? How much is it worth to us to have it? What is its relationship to other institutions and activities? Where should we build it? Who do we want to use it? How do we want people to perceive it? Likewise, this narrow window of time ignores the impact that buildings have on their users after they are complete.

This expanded time frame will also allow us to acknowledge the wide range of participants involved in the making of architectural meaning. Although patronage studies are an accepted genre of the history of art and architecture, they have typically been constructed around a very narrow definition of patronage as the one-on-one interaction between client and architect. While this model works well for revealing the actions of men (and sometimes of women) of great wealth and power, it ignores the processes by which middle- and working-class men and women have shaped the cultural landscape, either by banding together in groups to pay for a design or by forgoing the aid of an architect altogether.

There is just as much to be learned from introducing users into the historical narrative. While it is possible and valid to identify the intentions of architects and their patrons, subsequent users often attached meanings to buildings that were unintended by those who determined the physical forms of those buildings.[8] Recent analyses of prescriptive literature have provided a means of discussing the idealized use of space, but attempts to describe the actual experience of architecture are still too few.[9]

Finally, we need to reframe our studies of the architectural process in relationship to other social processes that are not architectural at all. The negotiation of gender roles, the construction of class identities, the realignment of economic relations—these are all social processes that we need to take into account. After all, they help determine the range of possibilities for built forms, just as built forms affect the ways that these processes are played out in the material world. By relating the architectural process to other social processes, we can make important contributions to interdisciplinary studies.

This emphasis on the relationships between social and cultural processes is not intended to diminish the importance of studying buildings themselves. The idea of using buildings merely to illustrate social or cultural trends is anathema to the approach advocated here. The point is still to use material culture as important primary evidence, allowing it to convey something that cannot be gleaned from other sources. In order to use material culture in this way, the architectural historian must continue to develop analytical skills that are not a regular part of the social historian's training. Scholars of material culture are not just social or cultural historians with pictures in our books, but rather are those who have developed analytical frameworks that allow us to decipher meanings produced by the built environment.

Nonetheless, the approach I advocate changes the emphasis of the field in important ways. Architectural historians traditionally based their claim to professional expertise on taste. The construction of scholarly authority based on taste, a good eye, an in-born empathy with the creative process, was explicit in much of the pioneering work of the field and remains implicit in much of the scholarship that is produced today. Aesthetic judgments affect the topics we choose (as we still tend to feel we must choose pleasing buildings), the arguments we make (as we tend to demonstrate how to appreciate the visual qualities in our buildings), and the way we present the material (as we illustrate and describe buildings in loving detail). This reliance on taste has given the impression that architectural historians only talk to one another, and has severely limited the audience for architectural history scholarship. What is less often acknowledged is that this emphasis on taste has also severely limited the field itself. The emphasis on taste and the claim for professional expertise based on an aesthetic standard that is both in-born and developed at an early age were products of the social elite who forged the field; it has also had its long-term effect on making the field a welcome place for men and women who are white and middle- or upper-class, and accounts for the fact that architectural history has been less welcoming to other class, racial, and ethnic groups.[10]

The approach I advocate rejects taste as the basis for the special skills of the architectural historian. It will certainly make it possible to choose "ugly" buildings as a topic of study. It is an approach intended to demystify the process of design; in replacing taste with scholarly analytical skills that can be taught and that can be learned, it is also an approach that is intended to demystify the process of writing about design. Finally, it offers great potential for giving architectural history a wider audience—scholars in other fields and laymen alike may find something of value in this approach.

If Carnegie libraries offer an opportunity to cut across disciplinary subspecialties that maintain artificial distinctions between high-style and vernacular structures, they also highlight the methodological hazards confronting scholarly fields in transition. For instance, the sheer number of buildings involved (totaling over sixteen hundred in the United States alone) ruled out even a cursory examination of them all.[11] The archives of the Carnegie Corporation of New York preserved the correspondence that passed between the philanthropist (or his agents) and recipient towns, but did not include photographs or drawings of any sort. Even in the years when the program required design approval prior to releasing funds, the Carnegie policy was to return all drawings to recipient towns. While it might have been possible to reconstruct a comprehensive visual survey from other sources (including the Curtis Teich postcard collection), it was not clear that such an overview should be the basis of the study. After all, even an exhaustive formal analysis would not reveal the cultural and social processes that had led to the forms, nor provide a handle for reconstructing their many meanings. Instead, it seemed more useful to focus on selected examples, matching actual buildings with extensive primary research about site selection, architect choice, design, construction, and use.

Thirteen cities were chosen to serve as case studies, their selection, guided by the correspondence of the Carnegie Corporation, to represent the chronological, geographic, and demographic range of the library program. In Pennsylvania, Allegheny City and Homestead had played important roles in Carnegie's life, Allegheny City as the first American home of the Carnegie family when they immigrated from Scotland in 1848, and Homestead as the site of one of Carnegie's steel manufacturing plants. Dating from the last decades of the nineteenth century, the libraries in these towns represent the beginning and end of the first phase of Carnegie's library philanthropy when only a few towns received large grants.

The balance of the case studies date from a later period of Carnegie giving, when the lower dollar amount of individual grants was offset by a great increase in the number of cities to receive such grants. This group is further divided into those cities that received a library before Carnegie policies required a design review (namely, Union City, Indiana, St. Joseph, Missouri, Tahlequah, Oklahoma, Warren, Ohio, and McCook, Nebraska), and those that built libraries after 1908 when Carnegie's representatives took a more active interest in library design (namely, Detroit, Michigan, Gainesville, Texas, Lackawanna, New York, Raton, New Mexico, Oakland, California, and Calexico, California). In addition, these case studies cover the range of geographic regions most profoundly affected by the Carnegie program, particularly the Midwest, the Great Plains, Texas, and the far West. Together, they also cover the wide range of demographic conditions to be found in communities that participated in the Carnegie program, from Tahlequah, with a population of only 1,419, in what was then the Indian Territories, to prosperous county seats like Gainesville and Warren (with populations of 7,874 and 8,529, respectively), to St. Joseph, where stockyards workers pushed the population over 100,000, to an industrialized giant like Detroit (with a population of over 465,000). As the dollar amount of Carnegie gifts became increasingly tied to population figures, this sample also provides a means of looking at Carnegie libraries that varied in expense, from buildings that cost $10,000 in Tahlequah, Union City, and Calexico, to those that cost at least twice that amount in Warren and Lackawanna. Oakland and Detroit received substantially larger sums ($190,000 and $750,000, respectively), which were used to pay for a large downtown library and for a number of smaller neighborhood branches.

Finally, the sample also represents a wide range of social and cultural conditions, in the economic base of the communities, in their urban density, in their racial and ethnic diversity, in the age of the community and its cultural institutions, and even in their attitudes towards Carnegie's offer. While most cities welcomed the chance to use Carnegie funds to subsidize their schemes for civic beautification, Detroit's voters successfully blocked the acceptance of what they perceived as Carnegie's tainted money for nine years.

This core of cities, then, furnishes an important key to the central cultural themes and the dominant social patterns that unite all Carnegie libraries, and provides a baseline against which to assess variations. Thus, while the core cities appear with great regularity in this history, they are hardly alone. Instead, they form a historical framework flexible enough to accommodate information from the many other communities that make brief appearances in the story.

As a result, individual cases serve as the building blocks of the text, but the focus remains firmly on the processes that went into endowing these buildings with meaning. There are, of course, many processes involved in the creation of architectural meanings. In order to disentangle the strands, the book is structured to identify these processes and to investigate what Carnegie libraries meant to the various groups who became involved with these buildings.

In chapter 1, entitled "Giving," I examine Carnegie's role in the history of the libraries that so often bear his name. Putting Carnegie in the context of cultural philanthropy in nineteenth-century America, I argue that initially Carnegie's philanthropy was based on the paternalistic assumptions of his nineteenth-century predecessors, that Carnegie went on to pioneer a pattern of philanthropic behavior modeled on the corporation, and that this shift affected the forms of the library buildings endowed with Carnegie money.

In chapter 2, "Making," I look specifically at the process of designing and building the libraries themselves, focusing on the market forces that increasingly limited the range of architectural choices available in library design. The process of professionalism was an important factor, prompting both architects and librarians to articulate and codify design principles that could be taught in newly established professional schools. Other market forces also came into play. Indeed, even before the establishment of the Carnegie library program, mass-produced building products (including an increasing number manufactured specifically for library use) offered the architect the choice of high-quality materials, but also inevitably limited the aesthetic choices that were economically feasible. The Carnegie program exacerbated this tendency by encouraging the rise of architectural practitioners specializing in library design. Thus, the family resemblance among library buildings is neither a coincidence nor an indication of expressive deficiencies. Rather, it is the expression of an architecture produced in a capitalist marketplace.

In chapters 3 and 4, I examine the local response to Carnegie's program of library philanthropy, highlighting the limitations of architectural histories that treat the whole country as relatively uniform. There were, of course, several components to the local response, including choosing a site, hiring an architect, and selecting a design. Although the choice of site typically elicited the most heated local debates, siting and architectural design both signaled the role that the library was to play in the community, including the library's intended audience and its larger social function. In many ways, Carnegie's insistence on dealing only with a community's elected officials challenged existing patterns of cultural organization and transformed library building into a highly charged political issue. Indeed, as publicly-funded institutions increasingly took on the cultural functions once relegated to the home, libraries were implicated in diverse attempts to fix the shifting boundaries between public culture and private life.

In chapter 3, I focus on large cities, where library debates revolved around issues of class as public officials drawn from recent immigrant groups challenged the traditional cultural power of the native-born elite. In many respects, the differences between the two groups remained irreconcilable and resulted in the coexistence of two distinct patterns of library placement and design—the large central library placed in a cultural center adjacent to the central business district and a number of small branch libraries placed in residential neighborhoods. In chapter 4, I look at smaller towns, where the library debate was one part of a larger discussion about gender-based control of culture. Following the lead of their big-city counterparts, male elected officials sought to transform the library into a cultural institution that would play a role in the community's commercial life. Deprived by Carnegie's policies of their official voice in cultural decisions, middle-class women in small-town America campaigned for libraries that would reinforce the difference between commerce and culture, using Victorian ideas of women's sphere to maintain a voice in public affairs.

In the final two chapters, I move beyond the opening day of the library to assess the meaning of the library's form for its two newest user groups—female librarians who flooded into the profession in these years and the children who found in the Carnegie library one of the first public buildings with space consistently dedicated to their needs. This attempt to reconstruct the experiences of the largest populations to make sustained use of libraries on a regular basis is exciting, particularly since this aspect of public library history has not been examined in a systematic way. At the same time, however, first-hand accounts of library use by these groups are frustratingly rare. Indeed, to the extent that women and children are precisely the groups whose ideas and opinions were least often represented in the historical record, the chapters that address their concerns are inevitably slimmer than the portions of the book that deal with upper- and middle-class men.

The scarcity of evidence notwithstanding, "Working" (chap. 5) considers the Carnegie library as the work setting for the pioneering generation of female librarians. In this context, the efficient library design espoused by Carnegie can be read as an attempt on the part of male library leaders to maintain the prestige of their profession by circumscribing the professional activities of new female librarians. By the same token, deviations from the Carnegie ideal (particularly the emphasis on a separate children's room) reveal the range of strategies used by women to claim a more active professional role for themselves.

"Reading" (chap. 6) looks at the experience of children who made intensive use of Carnegie libraries. Despite the attempts of children's librarians, few young readers saw the children's room as a home-like setting presided over by a kindly surrogate mother. For many small-town children, the librarian was a daunting presence who guarded the entrance to a special realm of adventure and excitement. In contrast, urban library users, especially those from immigrant families, took little notice of the librarian at all. Taking for granted their right to use public space, they confounded the expectations of library officials by treating the library as an extension of the public street.

Carnegie libraries, then, stood on contested ground. Despite their strong family resemblance, they were not the unselfconscious expression of a unified American spirit. Instead, they were always cultural artifacts whose meanings varied with the intentions and experiences of a diverse group of users. This book rejects the need to choose a single interpretation for these buildings, celebrating instead the richness involved in looking at these buildings from multiple and often conflicting points of view.

GIVING

The Reform of American Library Philanthropy

ANDREW CARNEGIE OCCUPIES A CRUCIAL place in the cultural history of the United States. On the one hand, his library philanthropy was informed by general trends in late nineteenth-century American culture, particularly its widespread concern for making library facilities available to the public free of charge. At the same time, Carnegie shared the late nineteenth-century conviction that men of wealth had a moral responsibility for providing these cultural institutions. Initially at least, he also favored buildings that reinforced the paternalistic role that sustained nineteenth-century philanthropy.

On the other hand, however, Carnegie also pushed these late nineteenth-century developments in new directions. Touched by the mania for efficiency that characterized the early twentieth century, Carnegie used the metaphor of the corporation to reform the practices of American philanthropy. In the process, he redirected the course of American library design and redefined the nature of library use.

Librarians vs. Architects

In the decades before the Civil War, it is difficult to speak of an American library building type at all. Only in the 1870s and 1880s were conditions right for the invention of an American library building type. In those years, widespread passage of public library laws (at least in New England) provided the legal apparatus for creating public libraries in great numbers, while postwar prosperity and the professionalization of both librarianship and architecture ensured that these new libraries were housed in permanent, professionally designed buildings.[1]

Typically, late nineteenth-century library buildings were the product of local philanthropy, gifts of men grown wealthy during the war. While their middle-class contemporaries continued to support moral reform movements (like the YMCA) as a means of encouraging social cohesion, very wealthy men who had pulled themselves up the social ladder tended to be less enthusiastic about social constraints imposed from above.[2] Instead, these self-made millionaires were attracted to libraries and other cultural institutions as a means for promoting individual development from within. George Peabody (a London-based financier), Walter L. Newberry (a Chicago real estate and railroad promoter), and Charles Bower Winn (who inherited the small fortune that his father had accumulated in the leather trade in Massachusetts) were among the wealthy men who financed library building in the second half of the nineteenth century.[3]

Despite geographical and temporal differences, each of these nineteenth-century library builders cast himself in the role of the patriarch of an extended family, while the recipients of his gifts played the parts of dependent relations. The philanthropist nurtured this illusion by extending his benevolence only to towns with which he had some sort of personal connection. If he shared Winn's inclination, he might also choose to invest his endowment with a memorial function, inviting citizens of the recipient town to share in his grief and giving them access to a level of intimacy usually reserved for family members.[4] Although his gifts to Baltimore and to the Massachusetts towns of Danvers, North Danvers, and Newburyport did not fulfill a memorial function, Peabody expressed this familial relationship by referring to the educational mission of his gifts as "a debt due from present to future generations."[5] Recipients of these gifts also participated in the metaphor when they welcomed Peabody to town with banners that read "One Generation Shall Praise Thy Works to Another."[6]

Although paternalistic philanthropy required both benefactor and recipient to address each other with exaggerated graciousness, the kind of fatherly protection offered by Peabody and others like him exacted a heavy price. At the Danvers parade in Peabody's honor, a battalion of pupils from the Danversport Grammar School carried banners that read, "We owe him gratitude; we will not repudiate the debt," reminding all present that Peabody's gift carried with it certain obligations.[7] Nineteenth-century philanthropy, like parental love, imposed upon its recipients a debt of gratitude that they had not asked to incur and that, no matter how hard they tried, they could never adequately repay.

When it came time for these paternalistic philanthropists to house their benefactions, they consistently turned for advice to the new generation of professional architects trained either at home or abroad in the

Figure 1.1 Henry Hobson Richardson, Winn Memorial Public Library, Woburn, Massachusetts, 1876–79. Photograph by Baldwin Coolidge, Courtesy of the Society for the Preservation of New England Antiquities.

compositional principles of the Ecole des Beaux-Arts. Chief among them was Henry Hobson Richardson, who designed multipurpose cultural institutions for four cultural philanthropists in eastern Massachusetts, almost single-handedly creating a building type that met the needs of these library founders.[8]

Begun in 1876, the Winn Memorial library in Woburn, Massachusetts, is a case in point. Drawing on the approach to architectural composition that he had learned in Paris, Richardson articulated each of the building's functions separately in both plan and elevation (figs. 1.1 and 1.2). The museum, for instance, was housed in an octagonal room at one end of the building. Variations in proportion and orientation distinguished the rectangular rooms of the picture gallery, reading rooms, and library proper. These distinctions were reinforced in the elevation of the building, as Richardson varied the height, shape, and ridge orientation of the roofs over each of the major rooms in order to isolate each function within a distinct volume.

Richardson organized these functional volumes along two perpendicular axes. Aligned with the building's long axis, the museum, picture gallery, and library proper provided a monumental vista from one end of the building to the other (fig. 1.3). Their orientation and scale reveal the importance that architect and patron alike assigned to rooms devoted to the storage and display of cultural or natural artifacts. In contrast, the public reading rooms were perceived as of secondary importance; thus, they sit on the building's cross axis (fig. 1.4). Unlike their more monumental counterparts, these rooms have an almost domestic scale, thanks to their alcoves, inglenooks, and lower ceilings. At the intersection of these two axes stood the delivery desk, staffed by the librarian who mediated, both literally and figuratively, the user's experience of the books.

Finally, Richardson clothed the building in a formal vocabulary borrowed from the Romanesque. This stylistic mode had two advantages. First, it seemed appropriate to the building type, given the library's predecessors in medieval monasteries. Second, a style that often juxtaposed elements of different sizes was well suited to a building in which so many different functions would be expressed on the exterior.

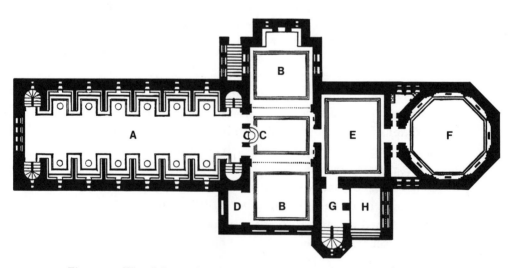

Figure 1.2 Winn Library, first-floor plan. A = book hall, B = reading rooms, C = librarian's desk, D = alcove, E = picture gallery, F = museum, G = vestibule, H = porch. Redrawn from M. G. Van Rensselaer, *Henry Hobson Richardson and His Works*, New York, 1888, 69.

Figure 1.3 Winn Library, book hall. Courtesy of the Society for the Preservation of New England Antiquities.

Yet, in the very years that Richardson was refining his library formula professional librarians emerged as another force in American library design. From the moment the American Library Association (ALA) was founded in 1876, librarians began using their collective voice to condemn the physical layout of libraries designed by architects. As early as 1879, librarian William Poole told an audience of his colleagues at the fourth annual ALA convention his rule of thumb for planning a library: "Avoid everything that pertains to the plan and arrangement of the conventional American library building."[9]

If architects took Poole's comments as a direct attack on their professional acumen, they did nothing more than interpret the spirit of his words. In fact, Poole's comments were only the opening shots of a long, intense battle between architects and librarians over which professional group should prevail in matters of library planning. By asserting their particular aptitude in this area, librarians hoped to enlarge the body of knowledge in which they could claim expertise. In doing so, they sought to advance their struggle for professional recognition, even as architects were seeking to consolidate their own hold on professional stature.

Despite its competitive nature, the debate was firmly rooted in practical considerations of library administration. While it took several decades for librarians to settle on the ideal form for a small public library, they agreed from the start on the evils of the alcoved book hall.[10] Unimpressed by a pedigree that extended back to sixteenth-century Europe, librarians complained about every aspect of this distinguished book-storage system. The alcoves, they noted, were impossible to supervise from a single vantage point, requiring libraries of this design to bar patrons from entering the book hall itself. Responsibility for retrieving books fell to a library clerk, who, in order to get a book from the upper

Figure 1.4 Winn Library, interior of reading room. Photograph by Baldwin Coolidge, Courtesy of the Society for the Preservation of New England Antiquities.

level, had to cross the length of the hall, climb a precarious spiral stair-case, locate the book at the upper level, and retrace his steps back to the librarian stationed at the delivery desk in the next room. As if ex-hausting the clerk were not bad enough, galleried book halls threatened the safety of the books as well. As librarians like Poole were quick to point out, it was impossible to heat the ground floor of a galleried book hall to a comfortable temperature without overheating the upper levels and damaging the books.[11]

In addition to these specific grievances against the book hall, librari-ans took offense at the general state of affairs in which visual effect took precedence over the requirements of easy library administration. At the 1882 ALA meeting, for instance, Poole condemned Smithmeyer and Pelz's design for the new Library of Congress, not only because of its galleried book-storage system, but also because it would "make a show building" and would be "needlessly extravagant" in its search for "what is falsely called 'architectural effect'"[12]

Despite the time and attention that librarians devoted to the question of library planning in the last decades of the nineteenth century, they rarely had a chance to put their own ideas into practice. Whether clothed in its original Romanesque mode, in the Queen Anne style, or even in classical garb, the Richardsonian type equipped with the alcoved book hall served as the model for small public libraries.[13]

The question, then, is, Why was the Richardsonian type so popular? It is tempting to explain the phenomenon as the result of a childlike innocence on the part of library trustees. After all, many towns that re-ceived library buildings in this era had neither an existing library nor a resident librarian. In many cases, the trustees did not think about hiring a librarian until after the building was under construction.

Contemporary librarians were much less generous in their assessment of the Richardsonian phenomenon. Poole himself, at yet another ALA conference, painted the typical board of library directors as a group of dullards who tended "to look around for a library building which had galleries and alcoves, and to reproduce its general plan, and as much of its details as they could pay for. They usually copied its worst fea-tures."[14] The tenor of his other comments make it clear that Poole and most of his colleagues harbored the suspicion that donors and architects alike shared a love of the monumental for its own sake.

While it is easy to imagine a donor relishing the comparison of his gift to one of the great European libraries of the past, the appeal of Richardson's library formula is more deep-seated than mere vanity.

Richardson's libraries were so popular because they were particularly successful at articulating the family metaphor that sustained nineteenth-century philanthropy. While the double-height book hall lent the building the monumental scale of a public place, the fact that users could not enter the hall reminded them that they had access to these fine library facilities only by the grace of the donor. At the same time, the reading room, with its inglenooks and its massive fireplace (typically with a portrait of the donor over the mantel), had a domestic scale and the coziness that played such an important part in the Victorian ideal of home. Library users were at once in a public institution and in the bosom of an extended family. In short, the architectural products of nineteenth-century philanthropy worked in tandem with the cultural assumptions that supported benevolent activities.

Andrew Carnegie Enters the Philanthropic Game

When asked to explain why he chose to channel his philanthropic energies into the building of public libraries, Andrew Carnegie (fig. 1.5) always told the story of Colonel James Anderson of Allegheny City, Pennsylvania. One day each week, in the years before the Civil War, Anderson had opened his personal library to the working boys of his

Figure 1.5 Andrew Carnegie. Courtesy of Carnegie Corporation Archives, and Rare Book and Manuscript Library, Columbia University. Copyright Davis & Sanford, New York.

neighborhood. As one of those boys, young Carnegie treasured the time he spent in the Colonel's library. In his *Autobiography*, he credited the library with instilling in him a love of literature, with steering him "clear of low fellowship and bad habits," and with opening to him "the precious treasures of knowledge and imagination through which youth may ascend." [15] Since Carnegie understood this ascent in both spiritual and material terms, he felt he owed a great part of his undeniable material success to the education that Colonel Anderson's library had afforded him.

Carnegie's anecdotal explanation is often repeated, in large part because it fits so closely with the Carnegie myth. Propagated by Carnegie himself and perpetuated by a host of subsequent writers, the Carnegie myth closely resembles Horatio Alger's rags-to-riches tales. Starting with Carnegie's birth in Scotland in 1835, the myth emphasizes the dire straits of the linen weaver's family impoverished by the advent of the power loom. It follows thirteen-year-old Andrew's immigration to the United States with his family in 1848, and it stresses the inexorable quality of his rise to greatness. His promotions from bobbin boy in a textile factory to telegraph operator to railroad supervisor to millionaire steel manufacturer are presented as plausible and inevitable. In most accounts, the rags-to-riches myth ends in 1901, when Carnegie sold his steel company for $480,000,000 to J. P. Morgan, who thereupon congratulated his long-time rival on becoming "the richest man in the world." [16]

The Carnegie myth is history of a highly subjective sort, the facts of Carnegie's biography manipulated in order to serve the story's rhetorical logic. The immigrant boy's poverty, for instance, is exaggerated in order to throw the steel manufacturer's wealth into bolder relief. At the same time, by attributing Carnegie's meteoric rise to his strength of character, the myth obscures Carnegie's considerable contributions to American business practices. One must read business history to discover that Carnegie invented cost accounting, pioneering the practice on the railroad and later using it in steel manufacturing to undersell his competitors without undercutting his profit margin.[17]

Despite these manipulations, the Carnegie myth is based on fact, and the young Scot's early interest in philanthropy is borne out by the historical evidence. Indeed, Carnegie was a young man of thirty-three when he first expressed his intention to use his surplus wealth for charitable purposes. An inveterate planner, Carnegie sketched out in writing a future for himself that included a few years' study at Oxford, followed by a well-ordered existence in London, "taking a part in public matters especially those connected with education & improvement of the poorer classes." [18]

In fact, Carnegie's future did not correspond directly with this 1868 daydream. His study sojourn in Oxford never materialized, and he delayed another eighteen years before taking up philanthropy in earnest. Yet the date of the daydream, its London locale, and its educational emphasis are indicative of Carnegie's familiarity with and respect for a man like George Peabody. Although Carnegie brought ideas of his own to his career in benevolence, his earliest philanthropic efforts were informed by the example of postwar philanthropists of Peabody's sort.

Carnegie's mature ideas about benevolence were first presented for public consumption in two articles published in the *North American Review* in 1889, "Wealth" and "The Best Fields for Philanthropy." [19] Aimed at the educated readership of the *Review*, these articles outlined lessons that Carnegie hoped his fellow millionaires would take to heart. In Carnegie's own words:

> The main consideration should be to help those who will help themselves; to provide part of the means by which those who desire to improve may do so; to give those who desire to rise the aids by which they may rise; to assist, but rarely or never to do all. [20]

In short, Carnegie warned the philanthropist to protect himself against the risk of throwing away his money on someone without the strength of character to make the best use of it.

Going on to explain that "neither the race nor the individual is improved by almsgiving," Carnegie hinted at the terrible results of an ill-spent philanthropic dollar. Not only did it risk the ruin of individuals, but it also threatened the inevitable progress of the age. The danger was particularly dire at the individual level, where indiscriminate charity would certainly "sap the foundation of manly independence" of the not-yet-deserving poor and destroy his chance of reaching the requisite stage of deservedness. [21]

Inherent in Carnegie's statement was the contradictory idea that only those who did not need help were eligible to receive it. In Carnegie's defense, he did not manufacture this contradiction; but inherited it from a long tradition of Protestant liberalism. Like his predecessors, Carnegie believed that wealth was a clear sign of the intellectual and moral capacity of the wealthy, whose natural role was to act as the stewards of their wealth for the good of the community. [22]

If Carnegie's concern with distinguishing the deserving poor from their undeserving fellows would have been familiar to any of his nineteenth-century predecessors, his actions would have seemed equally conventional. Like Peabody and others, Carnegie began his philanthropic career by extending gifts only to towns with which he had some sort of personal connection. An 1881 gift to Dunfermline, Scotland, gave the poor weaver's son a chance to flaunt his millions to the residents of his hometown. Over the next twenty years, Carnegie included the United States in his library benefactions, offering relatively large cash gifts to a handful of towns on both sides of the Atlantic. Five of the six American towns to receive Carnegie gifts in this period had played a significant role in the donor's life.[23] Allegheny City, Pennsylvania, had been Carnegie's first home in the United States, and in 1886 it became the first American city to receive a Carnegie library gift. The next gift went to Pittsburgh, the city just across the Allegheny River and the site of the headquarters of Carnegie's steel empire. Subsequent gifts went to three other Pennsylvania towns: Johnstown, near the South Fork Fishing and Hunting Club, to which Carnegie belonged, Braddock, and Homestead, both sites of Carnegie steel works.[24]

Having patterned his initial forays into philanthropy on the paternalistic model of the late nineteenth century, Carnegie adopted a similar attitude toward the architectural form of the libraries as well. This attitude is particularly apparent at the Carnegie Library of Allegheny City. There, responsibility for the building fell to a library commission comprising six members, half appointed by Carnegie and half appointed by the city. Fixing upon a competition as the best means of securing plans for the building, the commission invited seven architectural firms to compete.[25] Two of those firms had Richardsonian connections: Shepley, Rutan and Coolidge was Richardson's successor firm, and C. L. Eidlitz had served as Richardson's collaborator on the New York State Capitol in Albany. Their appearance on the list of invitees reveals the extent to which the library commission acknowledged Richardson's town library designs as appropriate models for Allegheny City.

Another firm invited to compete was Smithmeyer and Pelz, whose principals were still involved in the design of the Library of Congress. This choice not only confirms the commission's pretensions to grandeur; it is also revealing in what it says about the board's attitude toward the library design controversy that was raging about them in the late 1880s. Perhaps the commissioners did not recognize librarians' complaints about the book hall as an indictment of Richardson's elegant buildings. It is impossible, however, to imagine that they misread Poole's unequivocal condemnation of Smithmeyer and Pelz's Library of Congress design, published four years earlier in the ALA's *Library Journal*.

Was this a deliberate snub to librarians, or merely a product of the commissioners' ignorance about the current debate? Existing information about the program devised as a guide for the competitors suggests some of each. The program originally sent to competing architects in July 1886 no longer exists, but the requirements were murky enough to

Figure 1.6 Smithmeyer and Pelz, Carnegie Library and Music Hall, Allegheny City (now Pittsburgh), Pennsylvania, 1886–90. Courtesy of Carnegie Library, Pittsburgh.

prompt a number of competitors to write for clarification.[26] In response, the commission resolved that "plans may provide for placing of books in alcoves or stacks, in whole or in part."[27] The imprecise nature of the original program suggests that the commissioners were ignorant of the importance that librarians attached to the choice of a book-storage system. Their clarification, however, continued to allow the use of alcoves, mentioning stacks almost as an afterthought. The commissioners, it seems, were fundamentally unconcerned about the issues involved.

Despite lavish praise in the professional press for the "refined" French Gothic design submitted by the local architect W. S. Fraser, Smithmeyer and Pelz's design (figs. 1.6–1.10) received the unanimous approval of the building committee, and Carnegie's approval as well, in December of 1886.[28] As built, the building was an asymmetrical mass dominated by a clock tower and cloaked in a medieval vocabulary (see fig. 1.6). The entrance to the library proper was on the building's western side, facing Federal Street (see figs. 1.6 and 1.7). It gave directly onto the lobby dominated by a large marble stair (see fig. 1.9). To the south of the lobby, the small, square trustees' room enjoyed a prominent location in the base of the clock tower. To the east of the lobby lay the delivery room, the library's organizational core (see fig. 1.10). As originally planned, the rooms north of the delivery room were off limits to the public. On axis with the delivery room, the largest of these staff rooms was the bibliographic room, which gave access to three stack rooms and a repair room to the west.

Figure 1.7 Carnegie Library, Allegheny City, first-floor plan. A = music hall, B = lobby, C = librarian's office, D = men's toilet, E = women's toilet, F = ladies' reading room, G = bibliographic room, H = delivery room, I = reading room, J = repair room, K, L, M = stack rooms, N = lobby, O = trustees' room. Redrawn from *Library Journal* 18 (August 1893): 289.

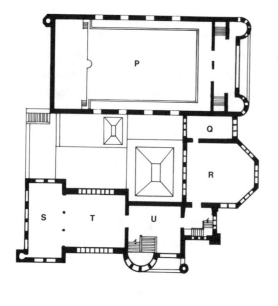

Figure 1.8 Carnegie Library, Allegheny City, second-floor plan. P = upper part of music hall, Q = apparatus room, R = lecture room, S = print room, T = art gallery, U = stair hall. Reconstructed from *Library Journal* 18 (August 1893): 289.

Figure 1.9 Carnegie Library, Allegheny City, lobby. Courtesy of Carnegie Library, Pittsburgh.

Figure 1.10 Carnegie Library, Allegheny City, delivery room. Although omitted from the original design, a delivery desk was installed soon after the building was opened and was in place by 1893. Courtesy of Carnegie Library, Pittsburgh.

The main reading room, ending with an octagonal bay, was south of the delivery room and on axis with it and with the bibliographic room. East of the reading room was the much smaller ladies' reading room, from which opened the ladies' toilet. East of the delivery room were the men's toilet and librarian's office. Since both the library commission and the architects assumed that librarianship would remain a male profession, these last two rooms communicated directly with one another, as well as with the delivery room.

The usable area of the library's second floor was limited by the skylight that illuminated the first-floor delivery room (see fig. 1.8). The principal rooms on the second level were north of the stair hall and included the art gallery (above the stack rooms) and print gallery (above the repair room). The area above the bibliographic room, not interior space when the building was first completed, was left available for subsequent expansion. South of the stair hall, above the trustees' room, another stair in the clock tower led up to a room designated for scientific lectures (above the main reading room) and another set aside for the storage of chemical apparatus used during lectures (above the ladies' reading room).

Without interior communication with the library, the music hall had a separate entrance on Ohio Street. The lobby, with cloak room and ticket office, led into the music hall proper, where an organ (paid for by an additional Carnegie gift of $10,000) loomed over the stage in the far wall. Cantilevered galleries provided a second level of seating, reached from stairs on either side of the lobby.

Despite the commissioners' initial nonchalance about library administration, the building constructed under their aegis corrected many of the worst errors of conventional nineteenth-century library design. Gone were the alcoved book halls dear to Richardson's heart. In their place, single-height stack rooms mitigated the damaging effects of central heating and saved the steps of library assistants sent to retrieve requested volumes. Even the official response of the professional library community, published in 1893 in the *Library Journal,* avoided the vituperative attack that many other library buildings elicited from librarians.[29]

Credit for incorporating these innovations into the building belongs to Smithmeyer and Pelz, whose Library of Congress experience made them uniquely and acutely aware of Poole's ideas on library planning. Indeed, there are many similarities between the Allegheny City plan and an ideal plan for a small library that Poole had published in the *Library Journal* just nine months before the Allegheny City competition was announced (fig. 1.11).[30] In both schemes, the user came first into a lobby that gave access to the trustees' room and staircase. In both, the entrance was on the building's short axis, while the book-storage room, the delivery room, and the largest reading room (in Poole's plan, identified as the periodical and newspaper room) were organized on the long axis.[31] In both, the delivery room was located at the intersection of these two axes. Finally, both Poole's scheme and the Allegheny City plan maintained the practice of gender segregation.[32]

Despite these planning similarities, the Smithmeyer and Pelz plan departed from Poole's ideal in tone and character. In order to accommodate the complex relationship between the donor and the user, the Allegheny City library was more monumental than Poole's ideal. In the real building, for instance, an imposing stairway dominated the lobby (see fig. 1.9), instead of hiding demurely in a stair tower that would have

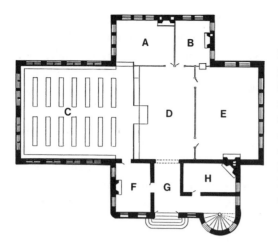

Figure 1.11 William Poole's plan of a small library building, 1885. A = reference room, B = ladies' reference room, C = book room, D = delivery room, E = periodical and newspaper room, F = librarian's office, G = lobby, H = directors' room. Redrawn from *Library Journal* 10 (September–October 1885): 253.

been all but invisible to anyone entering Poole's hypothetical plan. Likewise, the delivery room at Allegheny City was an imposing room with a high ceiling and ample proportions (see fig. 1.10); at thirty-six feet by forty feet, it was more than twice the size of Poole's. In addition, each surface was elaborately decorated: overhead was a skylight of stained glass; under foot were mosaic floors covered in "chaste arabesques surrounding the words . . . 'Carnegie Free Library,'" and on the walls was a friezelike blind arcade inscribed with the names of twenty-five American authors.[33] While Poole's delivery room was a void at the center of a centrifugally organized collection of rooms, the delivery room of the Allegheny City library focused inward on a massive fireplace. Above its mantel a portrait of Carnegie, donated by the commissioners from their personal funds, invited library users to pause and ponder their debt to Carnegie's liberality.

At the same time, the Smithmeyer and Pelz building was also more intimate and inviting than Poole's ideal. In the real building, the entrance to the delivery room from a door in the corner mitigated the ritualistic quality that might have resulted from a more formal, axial approach. The specially shaped reading room and the alcove that served as the ladies' reading room were also important physical reminders of domesticity, intended to convey a sense of hominess to the readers.

As built, the Allegheny City library reminded library users that they were near the bottom of a library hierarchy that started with Carnegie and descended through the trustees, to the male librarian, to the female library clerks, and only then to the library users. Even here, the social and spatial hierarchy favored male readers over female ones. Yet, at the same time, the homey touches encouraged readers to think that the hierarchy was sustained not just by economic power but also by mutual love and respect, as in an extended family. Library users might then look upon Carnegie as a rich uncle, who deserved respect, obedience, and affection, and whose affection in return precluded any class resentment.

An anonymous article that appeared in the *Pittsburgh Bulletin* at the time of the library dedication reveals that contemporary observers interpreted the building's meaning in just this way. Although the bulk of the article is a straightforward description of the new building, scattered comments reveal the author's precise understanding of the building's spatial and social hierarchy. The trustees' room, for example, he described as "a high-wainscoted, dignified-looking apartment sacred to the one which its name implies," a room that "the light enters . . . in a dim religious way, through stained glass windows high above the floor." Likewise, when the writer called the book stacks "the Holy of Holies in this literary temple," he used religious terms to articulate the message that the building's design conveyed to users: mere mortals were not welcome in every part of this cultural institution.[34]

The monumentality of the two main public spaces was not lost on the reporter from the *Bulletin*. He noted, for instance, that "the main staircase claims notice for its graceful sweep as well as its solidity and beauty." In the same vein, the delivery room (he calls it the "reception room") seemed to him "a lofty apartment, its ample skylight reaching from wall to wall."[35] From the even tone of the article, it is clear that the writer found these monumental elements completely appropriate to this type of public building.

Yet the writer used the same approving tone to comment on the library's cozy touches—the comfortable chairs, the electrical and gas fittings, the sanitary conveniences—that "make the place an ideal one for the enjoyment of a favorite author." In short, the writer was undisturbed that a public institution should also offer its patrons the "forgetfulness of care" that was usually relegated to the domestic sphere in the late nineteenth century. Commenting matter-of-factly that the open fireplace "greet[s] the visitor right cheerily from the base of a monster mantelpiece," the writer was evidently undisturbed by the brutal juxtaposition of monumental and domestic imagery. Deprived of its functional purpose by the building's system of central heating, the fireplace played a largely symbolic role; a shrine to the donor, it was the only appropriate spot for Carnegie's portrait, "an object that must, on opening day and thereafter, attract the most roving attention."[36]

By the end of this imaginary tour of the building, it seems clear that part of the article's purpose was instructive; the writer hoped to teach his readers how to think and behave appropriately in their new public library. Referring to the city with feminine pronouns, the writer closed his piece with an admonition. The building, he noted,

is something to assuredly make her hold in perpetual gratitude the man whose liberality has been so fittingly and nobly embodied. . . . Her people, as one man, must hope for the munificent donor, long years of health and prosperity, and the opening ceremonies must serve to give voice to this feeling, while the years to come must fail to dim the memory of the man whose heart prompted the gift, and fail to eradicate or weaken the sense of obligation which [Allegheny City] must feel toward Andrew Carnegie.[37]

For this anonymous writer, the building was a success. More than a warehouse for books, it served to remind the citizens of Allegheny City of their undying, unpayable debt of gratitude, affection, and respect for the philanthropist who made it possible.

Carnegie's Reform of American Philanthropy

Within a few years of the library dedication in Allegheny City, institutional endowments came under close scrutiny as the popular press began to publish debates about the moral dimensions of accepting philanthropic gifts. The controversy began with "Tainted Money," an article in the *Outlook* written by Washington Gladden, the minister of the First Congregational Church in Columbus, Ohio.[38] Gladden's theme was a simple one. By accepting money which had been earned by illegal or unethical means, institutions of cultural and moral enlightenment "condoned the wrongs by which they [such funds] were obtained." Compelled "simply by the dictate of ordinary decency to refrain from criticizing the financial methods of the donor," the recipient church or "Christian" college completely dismantled both its authority and its ability to shape the moral consciousness of its members. In short, by accepting tainted money, such institutions undermined their raison d'être.

Although it was less than two pages long, Gladden's article brought about a fundamental shift in the terms in which philanthropy was discussed in the public arena. Philanthropy, of course, had been a topic of discussion for some decades, but such writings (including Carnegie's own article "Wealth") had always focused on the giver of the gift. Starting from the assumption that the poor would take any money offered them and always ask for more, these earlier writings had usually addressed the problems of "indiscriminate charity," and never considered the possibility that a gift might be refused. By approaching the issue from the opposite direction, by looking at it from the receiver's point of view, Gladden paved the way for the first fully articulated attack on philanthropic paternalism.

In many ways, Gladden's ideas were simply part of the distrust of big business that fueled many Progressive-era reforms and that brought about the transformation of American culture in the decades around the turn of the century. Indeed, Progressive reform movements provided both the personnel and the public forums in which the tainted-money controversy was addressed. Gladden himself had first begun to think out loud about this issue at the National Conference of Charities and Corrections in 1893.[39] Seven years later, Vida Scudder investigated the same theme in "Ill-Gotten Gifts to Colleges," an article published in the *Atlantic Monthly.* Cofounder of Hull House with Jane Addams, Scudder shared Gladden's apprehension about the moral implications of tainted money, but her settlement house experience prompted her to add a more pragmatic caveat: the acceptance of tainted money only served to undermine the public's confidence in "the integrity of [our] academic life," and to increase "the difficulty of understanding between class and class."[40] Graham Taylor, the editor of the Progressive magazine *The Commons,* disagreed with Gladden's conclusions. Yet, even as he argued that rejecting tainted money only served to create "vested funds for perpetuating wrong," Taylor discussed philanthropy in the very terms established by Gladden.[41]

Although neither Gladden nor Scudder mentioned Carnegie by name, his gifts were implicitly included in their attacks on tainted money. Indeed, Scudder's disdainful description of "Christian institutions of the land, which gratefully accept [tainted money] and rise to chant the paean of democracy triumphant," is only a thinly veiled reference to Carnegie's 1886 book, *Triumphant Democracy.*[42]

More direct jabs at Carnegie and his philanthropic motives were delivered in a variety of other ways. Chicago-born journalist Finley Peter Dunne, for instance, used his fictitious Irishman, Mr. Dooley, to voice his criticism of Carnegie. According to Mr. Dooley, "The way to abolish poverty an' bust crime is to put up a brown-stone buildin' in ivry town in the counthry with me name over it."[43]

Carnegie also came under attack at the grass-roots level, as prospective recipients of his gifts cited moral reasons for declining his library offers. Detroit is a case in point. Although the city eventually accepted a sizable Carnegie gift (as we shall see in chap. 3), pressure from the Detroit Trades Council made it politically inexpedient for city officials to accept Carnegie's money when it was first offered in 1903.[44] Local headlines, like the *Detroit Evening News*' "DETROIT SPURNS CARNEGIE'S GOLD—Aldermen Couldn't Bring Themselves to Accept 'Tainted Money,'" make it clear that Gladden's campaign had an effect beyond the realm of mere ideas.[45]

Carnegie's reaction to the tainted money controversy was two-fold. First, in 1901, he published a book entitled *The Gospel of Wealth and Other Timely Essays*.[46] Although the book included essays on subjects as diverse as "An Employer's View of the Labor Question" and "Democracy in England," the title piece of the collection was a reissue of his two earlier articles on philanthropy from the *North American Review*. Combined into a single article, these earlier essays were substantially unchanged from their first manifestation. Their appearance in 1900 is best interpreted as Carnegie's reassertion of the basic assumptions that supported his earliest endeavors in philanthropy. Rather than backing away from the idea that wealth (no matter how accumulated) marked a man as morally superior to his poorer neighbors, Carnegie argued that "superior wisdom, experience, and ability to administer" made the man of wealth the ideal "agent for his poorer brethren, . . . doing for them better than they would or could do for themselves."[47] At the same time, by retitling the essay, he called attention to the biblical rhetoric that had always been a part of the text.[48] In this way, Carnegie used Gladden's vocabulary of Protestant morality to present his own point of view.

Second, the tainted money controversy helped create the social climate which prompted Carnegie to take a critical look at the way philanthropy was practiced in the United States. In fact, Carnegie himself had long voiced serious objections to indiscriminate charity, warning particularly against the pauperizing effect of almsgiving. In a vivid demonstration of paternalism's failure to ease tensions between labor and capital, workers who lived in George Pullman's model town struck his Pullman Palace Car Company in 1894. Contemporary events such as this forced Carnegie to extend his censure to other methods of philanthropic practice as well.

Although he could not agree with all of Gladden's complaints, the criticism Gladden's article aroused stung Carnegie, who was particularly sensitive about his public image. In the late 1890s, it must have been hard for him to look at his philanthropic activities without acknowledging that he himself was guilty of the indiscriminate charity he abhorred. From that time on, Carnegie devoted what would become the second phase of his philanthropic career to reforming the methods which he and other millionaires could use to ease the burden of the stewardship of wealth.

By the turn of the century, Carnegie had taken steps to shift the direction of his own philanthropic activities. The most noticeable aspect of this shift was a huge increase in the number of Carnegie library gifts. In 1899 alone, Carnegie promised libraries to 26 cities, more than twice the total number of Carnegie-financed buildings built in the previous thirteen years. The numbers continued to grow, the peak coming in 1903 when Carnegie offered libraries to 204 towns. By 1917, Carnegie had promised 1,679 libraries to 1,412 towns at a cost of well over $41 million.[49]

Certainly, Carnegie had moved beyond the local level of giving that was characteristic of his nineteenth-century predecessors. In fact, throughout the second phase of his philanthropic career, Carnegie's approach to his charitable endeavors would have seemed strange indeed to a George Peabody or a Charles Bower Winn. In contrast to Peabody's sporadic method of philanthropy that depended so much on the patron's whim, Carnegie instituted clearly defined procedures that gave his dealings with individual towns the formality of a contractual agreement. For his part, Carnegie would give a library to any town with a population of at least one thousand, the amount of the gift usually set at two dollars per capita. Recipient towns were required to provide a site for the library building and to tax themselves at an annual rate of 10 percent of the total gift, the funds to be used to maintain the building, to buy books, and to pay the salaries of the library staff.[50]

The advantages of this kind of philanthropic contract were numerous, at least from Carnegie's point of view. First, it helped assure him that the recipients of his gifts were willing to do their part toward supporting the library, or in the terms he himself had used in "Wealth," that he was helping only those who helped themselves. Second, it provided clear-cut policies for administering the library program, allowing Carnegie to turn over the drudgery of the day-to-day paperwork to his personal secretary, James Bertram.[51]

Indeed, Bertram seems to have been responsible for introducing many refinements to Carnegie's system of library philanthropy. Over the years, he put into place an easily administered procedure for dealing with requests. Upon receiving an inquiry, Bertram sent a schedule of questions to be answered by the town's officials. This form asked for the town's population and for information on the existing library (if any), including the number of books in its collection and the previous year's circulation statistics. It also asked how the library was housed (including the number and measurements of the rooms and their uses) and the state of the library's finances (including a breakdown of its receipts and expenditures). Finally, it asked the amount the town council was willing to pledge for annual maintenance if the town should receive a library, whether there was a site available, and the amount of money collected toward the new building.[52]

If the population was large enough, the annual appropriation high enough, and the existing library facilities poor enough, the town had a good chance of securing a library offer from Carnegie. Bertram then sent a form letter, making an offer and stating that the funds would be available as soon as the recipient town submitted a copy of the resolution of council promising an annual tax levy for library purposes.[53] Once the resolution was in hand, Bertram contacted Robert Franks, treasurer of the Carnegie Steel Company, who established an account in the name of the town. Recipient towns received their Carnegie grants in installments, only after sending Franks an architect's certificate verifying that the sum requested corresponded with completed work.

These procedural changes reveal much about Carnegie's attitude toward his philanthropic activities in this period. Jettisoning the family model that had supported his earliest benefactions, Carnegie embraced the corporation as the driving metaphor for the entire philanthropic enterprise. Applying the principles of efficiency that he had developed for his railroad and manufacturing concerns, Carnegie centralized decision making, regularized procedures, and limited the possibilities for making mistakes. Instead of becoming personally involved with the administration of his philanthropies, Carnegie established procedures that allowed others to carry out his policies. Abstract, quantitative criteria (which could be applied by anyone) replaced subjective judgments (which could be made only by the philanthropist himself). What is more, these procedures included checks and balances that distributed responsibility and ensured that the smooth functioning of the system depended on no single person.

Figure 1.12 First Meeting of the Carnegie Corporation, 1911. *Standing, left to right:* Henry S. Pritchett, James Bertram, Charles L. Taylor, Robert A. Franks. *Seated, left to right:* William N. Frew, Robert S. Woodward, Elihu Root, Andrew Carnegie, Margaret Carnegie, Louise Whitfield Carnegie. Courtesy of Carnegie Corporation Archives, and Rare Book and Manuscript Library, Columbia University.

The legal acknowledgment of the corporate nature of Carnegie's philanthropic reforms came in 1911. In that year, in the music room of his Fifth Avenue mansion, in the presence of his wife and daughter, he presided over the first meeting of the Carnegie Corporation, the corporate body chartered to administer the library program (fig. 1.12). The date is less significant than the name. After all, Carnegie began reorganizing his philanthropic activities around 1899, and in the intervening years he had merely refined the system with Bertram's help. In establishing one of the first modern foundations, however, Carnegie did not have a term to distinguish a corporate body whose purpose was to make money from one whose purpose was to give it away. Thus, it was, and remains, the Carnegie Corporation.

Defining "The Modern Library Idea"

This reform of American library philanthropy virtually guaranteed that the Carnegie libraries built in the twentieth century would differ from their nineteenth-century predecessors. The corporate metaphor that sustained the new philanthropy was fundamentally at odds with the family imagery of nineteenth-century libraries influenced by Richardson's designs. What is more, Carnegie's philanthropic reforms, and particularly his insistence on public support for his gifts, changed the perception of these buildings in important ways. Elaborate structures were fine for a library built and supported by private funding, but a library maintained with funds drawn from public coffers had to convey its fiscal responsibility in its smaller size and more modest demeanor. The new formula for determining the dollar amount of each gift ensured that this new generation of Carnegie buildings would be smaller and less elaborate than their predecessors, while Carnegie's new program requirements (limiting the building's facilities to library functions and a small lecture hall) were also intended to help recipient towns stay within their more conservative budgets.

The timing of Carnegie's reforms is also significant in that it coincided with independent changes in the basic philosophy of library administration. The traditional understanding of the library as a treasure house, protecting its books from untrustworthy readers, was falling out of currency. Increasingly, the library profession sought to use the public library to bring readers and books together, rather than to keep them apart. According to librarian Arthur E. Bostwick, "the modern library idea" was characterized by public support, open shelves, work with children, cooperation with schools, branch libraries, traveling libraries, and library advertising.[54]

Service to children was the first feature of "the modern library idea" to receive serious consideration. As early as 1876, librarian William I. Fletcher pointed out the inconsistencies between the library's claim to an educational function and the usual practice of barring children under twelve from public library use. Concern for the safety of the books, however, continued to outweigh the educational mission of the library for another ten years. Even in the 1880s, experiments in this area met with limited success. In New York City, a children's library established in 1885 was closed in the early 1890s when adult readers complained about the noise that children made as they climbed the stairs to their third-floor reading room.[55] The provision for free access to book shelves got an even slower start. Condemned outright by Melvil Dewey in 1877, the practice was still the subject of lively debate at professional meetings a decade later.[56]

The 1890s were the turning point in both these developments. Although an 1893 survey of 126 public libraries revealed that over 70 percent maintained a threshold of at least twelve years of age, the libraries that admitted children often made a special attempt to provide a place for them. The Hartford (Connecticut) Public Library established a corner of the main reading room for children's use in the early 1890s, while in Pawtucket, Rhode Island, a children's corner was specially fitted with low tables and chairs.[57] By 1897, a survey conducted by the editors of *Public Libraries* revealed that libraries in Boston, Brookline, and Cambridge, Massachusetts, Brooklyn and Buffalo, New York, Pittsburgh, Pennsylvania, Detroit and Kalamazoo, Michigan, and Denver, Colorado, all provided separate children's rooms for their young readers; in at least four cases, these rooms had been opened within the previous two years.[58] By the turn of the century, most librarians regarded a separate children's room as a necessary component of the public library.[59]

Although the question of free access to books was still hotly debated in the 1890s, large urban libraries joined the ranks of those institutions experimenting with open shelves. Of particular note was the Cleveland [Ohio] Public Library, which offered unrestricted access to all books at all hours beginning in 1890. Allaying fears about the wholesale theft of books, librarian William Howard Brett reported to the ALA that the practice had served to increase the library's circulation.[60]

By the end of the decade, other writers expanded explicitly upon this theme. In 1897, John Cotton Dana argued that the substantial decrease in the cost of modern books made obsolete the conventional definition of the library as "simply a storehouse of treasures." Instead of using the delivery counter as a physical and symbolic barrier between the reader and the books, the new library should allow the reader to move among the shelves, to enjoy "the touch of the books themselves, the joy of their immediate presence." Comparing book selection to shopping, Dana implored his colleagues to treat readers with the same consideration and trust that ready-made clothing stores extended to their customers. The pleasure involved in the open library, Dana argued, would not only bring in more readers; it would also encourage "reading of a higher grade." Far from subverting the educational aims of the public library, open shelves would facilitate their implementation.[61]

Dana realized that his comparison of cultural and commercial institutions constituted an abrupt departure from conventional ideas of library administration. Indeed, he emphasized the radical nature of this shift in his language, referring to the modern public library as "a book laboratory." At the same time, he drew on this analogy from the industrial world to suggest changes in library design. Moving beyond what had become a standard critique of "architectural effects, . . . imposing halls, charming vistas, and opportunities for decoration," Dana also explicitly rejected "the palace, the temple, the cathedral, the memorial hall, or the mortuary pile" as appropriate paradigms for library design. Dana suggested looking instead to "the workshop, the factory [and] the office building" as better models: for "the book laboratory." The attraction is easy to see: the architectural expression of these buildings was not based on older building types; it had been developed in conjunction with modern functional requirements. More forcefully than any of his contemporaries, Dana called for the modern library to break with the architectural traditions previously established for the building type.[62]

Dana's more specific suggestions, however, point to the difficulty of forging new planning solutions, while rejecting what came before. Although Dana admired the exterior forms of industrial and commercial buildings, his ideal library did not follow the principles of open planning that characterized their interiors. Holding fast to the conventional idea of the library as a series of functionally specialized rooms, he called for a delivery room (with a delivery desk, information desk, and access to toilets and cloak rooms), a catalogue room, book rooms, a children's room with open shelves, a reference room, and the librarian's office, all in close proximity to one another. In addition, there were to be resting rooms for assistants, class rooms, mending and binding rooms, and periodical and newspaper rooms. Although these rooms could be situated farther from the delivery room, they were to be located near the reference room.[63] Since no illustrations accompanied his article, it is impossible to know how Dana would have arranged these rooms to meet his demands for efficiency. Dana's progressive ideas may indeed have made the library more responsive to the public's need; yet, in expanding the range of services offered by the modern library, his ideas also exacerbated the problems of library design.

Designing the Modern Library

The debates of the 1890s affected library architecture at the turn of the century. Whether financed with Carnegie funds, with money donated

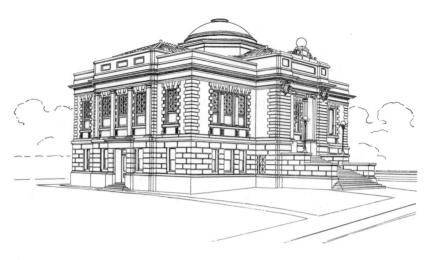

Figure 1.13 Smith and Gutterson, Carnegie Library, Ottumwa, Iowa, opened 1902. *Architectural Review* 9 (January 1902): 30.

by philanthropists working on the paternalistic model, or from public coffers, American public libraries reflected the unresolved conflicts over the function of the public library.

In general, public libraries of this era were stylistically more consistent (fig. 1.13; and see figs. 1.14, 1.16, and 1.18 below). In the *Architectural Review*'s 1902 compilation of the best modern library design, a full fifty-seven of the sixty-seven public libraries included were classically detailed, while only five employed the Romanesque mode popularized by Richardson.[64] Dana and subsequent writers on library design attributed this wholesale shift to classicism to the influence of the Ecole des Beaux-Arts and the World's Columbian Exposition in Chicago.[65] While many eminent library architects were trained in the principles of the Ecole, that training was chiefly concerned with an approach to planning and composition; it did not promote classicism per se. Richardson's Romanesque Revival library designs, for instance, were the product of the Ecole's teaching. The shift toward classicism is more accurately explained as the Ecole des Beaux-Arts response to the new emphasis on the public nature of the library. Classical elements had long been part of the Ecole's means of expressing the *caractère* of a public building and had enjoyed an early association with such pioneering public libraries as the Bibliothèque Ste.-Geneviève in Paris and the Boston Public Library (see fig. 3.1 below). The classical mode also offered more specific symbolic opportunities; many classical libraries were graced with a dome that literally and figuratively transformed the centrally placed delivery desk into the locus of public enlightenment.

Even in buildings with similar classical detailing, however, library planning was anything but consistent. At the Parsons Memorial Library in Alfred, Maine, for instance, the perfect symmetry of the front facade disguised the fact that the interior arrangements were essentially those of a Richardson library; the delivery desk served to keep readers out of the double-height, alcoved book hall, while the reference area with its fireplace and flanking window seats provided a cozy reading space distinct from the large reading room (figs. 1.14 and 1.15).

Other plan types proved more adaptable to new ideas. The Reyerson

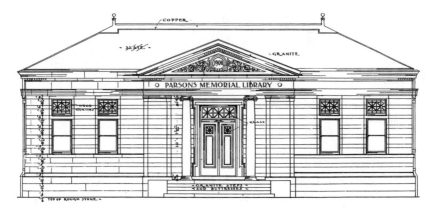

Figure 1.14 Hartwell, Richardson, and Driver, Parsons Memorial Library, Alfred, Maine, opened 1903. *Architectural Review* 9 (January 1902): 54.

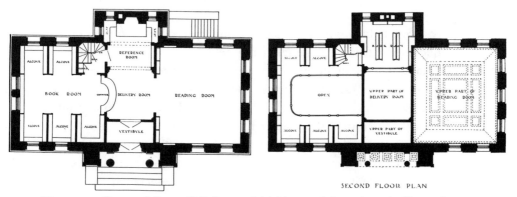

Figure 1.15 Parsons Library, (*left*) first- and (*right*) second-floor plans. *Architectural Review* 9 (January 1902): 54.

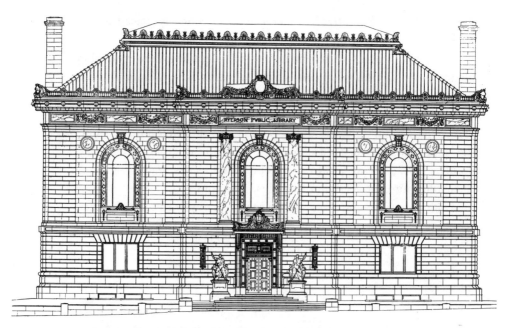

1.16 Shepley, Rutan and Coolidge, Ryerson Public Library, Grand Rapids, Michigan, opened 1904. *Architectural Review* 9 (January 1902): 45.

Public Library in Grand Rapids, Michigan, for instance, was planned around a central hall that led to reading rooms on either side and to a small stack room at the rear (figs. 1.16 and 1.17). Although the T-shaped arrangement had been popular since the 1880s, Shepley, Rutan and Coolidge used it in the Grand Rapids Library with greater sensitivity to current library debates, including a children's reading room equal in size to the periodical reading room.[66] Juvenile readers, however, did not have free access to books; like their adult counterparts, they were required to request their reading material at the delivery desk opposite the main entrance. A variation of this scheme replaced the rectangular book storage room with a radially arranged, open shelving area, allowing readers supervised access to books (figs. 1.18 and 1.19). Designers of many other libraries at the turn of the century followed no established type, experimenting instead with unique planning solutions (fig. 1.20).

The variety of approaches to library planning illustrated in these examples is evident in American public libraries generally at the turn of the century.[67] To be sure, late nineteenth-century debates had made some impact on library design; over 85 percent of the public library plans included in the *Architectural Review* survey followed Bostwick's ad-

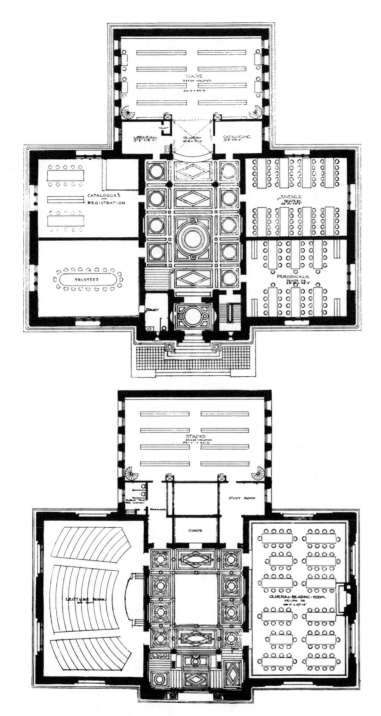

Figure 1.17 Ryerson Library, (*upper*) first- and (*lower*) second-floor plans. *Architectural Review* 9 (January 1902), 45.

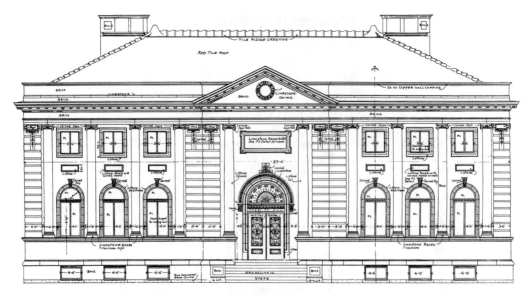

Figure 1.18 Penn Varney, Free Public Library, Schenectady, New York, opened 1903. *Architectural Review* 9 (January 1902): 34.

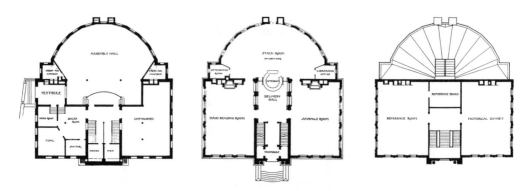

Figure 1.19 Public Library, Schenectady, (*left*) basement, (*center*) first- and (*right*) second-floor plans. *Architectural Review* 9 (January 1902):34.

vice and provided reading rooms for specialized materials (including newspapers, maps, historical literature, and other unspecified special collections), and over 75 percent included a fully-fitted children's room. Yet the debates of the 1890s had resulted in consensus on few other planning issues. The question of public access to books remained particularly problematic at the turn of the century. Only about a quarter of the libraries surveyed followed Dana's call for completely open access to their book collections. Over half of the sample maintained completely

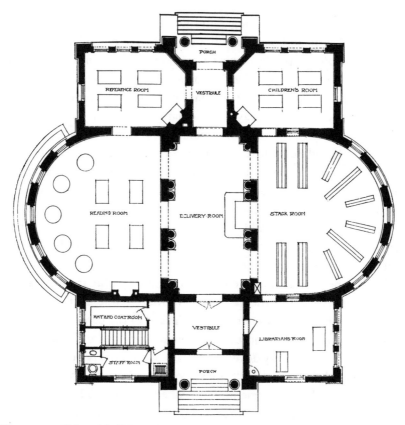

Figure 1.20 Edward L. Tilton, Carnegie Library, Mt. Vernon, New York, 1903, first-floor plan. *Library Journal* 29 (July 1904): frontispiece.

closed stacks, while another 15 percent provided open access to only a small portion of their collections. There was also no agreement about the use of separate rooms for reference reading, for cataloguing and for trustees' meetings: only 58 percent of the libraries surveyed included these rooms. Other room types catering to uses not directly associated with the book collection (rooms for group study, exhibition rooms, lecture halls, and club rooms) appeared in fewer than a third of the libraries in the sample.

Carnegie's Reform of American Library Architecture

This somewhat confusing pattern of library design holds true for Carnegie libraries as well. Indeed, since Carnegie libraries account for over 40 percent of the 1902 *Architectural Review* sample, they played a significant role in defining the general tendencies outlined above.[68] A direct comparison of the plans of Carnegie and non-Carnegie libraries, however, reveals that Carnegie-financed buildings tended to put greater emphasis on rooms devoted to public service. Carnegie libraries, for instance, were more likely to include children's rooms, reference rooms, and lecture halls, and less likely to reserve a room for the use of their trustees than libraries funded in other ways. Particularly interesting is the issue of public access to their books. Like libraries funded from other sources, more Carnegie libraries had closed stacks than had open access to all books; yet the preference was statistically very small, with only 44 percent using closed stacks, while 40 percent allowed open access. In comparison, a true majority (68 percent) of non-Carnegie libraries maintained closed stacks. All told, the Carnegie libraries in the 1902 survey were 25 percent more likely to provide free access to the books than their non-Carnegie contemporaries.

Despite these progressive tendencies in Carnegie libraries at the turn of the century, a clearly articulated policy toward Carnegie library design developed only gradually over the first decade of the century. Ironically, the original impetus behind these developments had to do more with economy than with a fully developed sense of public service. As Bertram later described the situation, "almost every community which received a donation from Mr. Carnegie in years gone by to erect a library bilding, came back with the plea that they had used the mony in the bilding and had no mony left to purchase bookstacks and furniture."[69] Additional gifts to cover such exigencies had, of course, been a regular part of American philanthropy when donors had thought of their relationship with their beneficiaries in familial terms. Under the tightly defined rules of corporate philanthropy, however, such requests constituted a breach of the new philanthropic contract. Starting about 1904, Bertram began reviewing the plans for buildings that ran over budget.[70] By 1908, Bertram's approval was required on the plans of all buildings constructed with Carnegie money.[71]

The advice that Bertram passed on to the recipients of Carnegie's gifts was hardly new, and certainly not of his own devising. Rather, it was based directly on ideas about library administration that librarians had espoused in the previous twenty years. Drawing on the writings of Poole, Dana, and others, as well as on his conversations with Cleveland's librarian, William Howard Brett, Bertram began to see that cost overruns were the result of inefficient library planning, rather than the product of inept financial management. The planning principles espoused by the library profession became Bertram's catechism, and the spread of what he called "effectiv library accommodation," his holy mission.[72]

With the intensity of a religious convert, Bertram internalized not only the librarians' dogma but also their prejudices. Long considered the natural enemy of the librarian, the architect became Bertram's personal *bête noire*. With Poole's admonition to "avoid everything that pertains to the plan and construction of the conventional American library building" ringing in his ears, Bertram suspected even the best-intentioned architects of leading their clients astray in matters of library planning. Bertram's attitude was succinctly expressed by Mrs. Percival Sneed, the librarian of the Carnegie Library in Atlanta, who did her best to explain the situation to the editor of the *Ocala (Florida) Banner*. As Sneed put it,

I would like to straighten out the complete misunderstanding as to the attitude of the Carnegie Corporation in the matter of plans. . . . The whole matter of plans with them hinges on the fact that they wish the towns to get the best value for their money and they know, as all trained librarians know, that there are almost no architects who are competent to draw the interior of a library so that its administration will be easy and economical, unless the architect has the advice of an active librarian. . . . It is impossible that any person whould [*sic*] have a grasp of what the plan should be unless that person has actually administered a library and has done work in it. This fact is unquestionable and perfectly well known to all members of the library profession.[73]

Sneed left no doubt that Bertram had decided to put Carnegie's support behind librarians in their battle with the architecture profession.

At first, Bertram spread the gospel of "effectiv library accommodation" on a case-by-case basis, but eventually he took steps to circumvent the inefficiency of this system. In 1911, in the same year that the Carnegie Corporation was chartered, Bertram compiled the collective wisdom on progressive library planning into a pamphlet entitled "Notes on the Erection of Library Bildings." Repeatedly revised and expanded over the next eight years, the "Notes" grew from a single page of text, to a version that included one and one-half pages of text and four schematic plans, to a version that included two pages of text and six schematic plans.[74] In fact, the production and printing history of this pamphlet is somewhat murky; architect Edward L. Tilton, a New York architect specializing in library design, may have had a hand in producing the schematic plans, while a number of librarians were invited to critique both plans and text before the pamphlet was issued.[75] In its various forms, the "Notes" accompanied all formal offers of library gifts from 1911 on.[76]

In its six-plan version, two of the pamphlet's four pages were given over to text. Mustering what tact he could, Bertram began by explaining why the pamphlet was necessary. Library committees were ill prepared to select an appropriate library design, he explained, because they "ar frequently composed of busy men who [lack] time or opportunity to obtain a knowledge of library planning." Architects, he warned, were equally unreliable since they "ar liable, unconsciously, no dout, to aim at architectural features and to subordinate useful accommodation." Library boards and their architects would do well to remember the following rule of thumb: "Small libraries should be pland so that one librarian can oversee the entire library from a central position."[77]

The text goes on to explain how the Carnegie Corporation determined the amount of the gift, with the admonition that "there wil be either a shortage of accommodation or of money if this primary purpose is not kept in view, viz.: TO OBTAIN FOR THE MONEY THE UTMOST AMOUNT OF EFFECTIV ACCOMMODATION, CONSISTENT WITH GOOD TASTE IN BILDING." According to the text, the usual mistakes stemmed from giving too much space to the entrance area, delivery room, cloak rooms, toilets, and stairs.[78] The new philanthropy encouraged neither the large expenditure nor the complex symbolism that served to impress Allegheny City's library users with the donor's generosity.

Conspicuously lacking in Bertram's "Notes" is any mention of style or any discussion of beauty—in short, any of the traditional concerns of the architect. True, the insistent symmetry of the plans and the reference to "good taste in bilding" suggest that Bertram may have had in mind a restrained version of the classicism that had been popular in public libraries since the turn of the century. At the same time, one of Bertram's major reasons for writing the pamphlet was to pressure communities into forgoing the high domes, classical porticoes, and monumental stairs that had graced those earlier buildings. After years of struggling with architects who encouraged their clients to go over budget, Bertram had understandably begun to equate architecture with extravagance. In the pamphlet's single paragraph on the design of library exteriors Bertram acknowledged the need for "the community and architect [to] express their individuality," but he immediately warned against "aiming at such exterior effects as may make impossible an effectiv and economical layout of the interior."[79] Architecture, Bertram implied, was most apt to get in the way of effective library planning and could be avoided completely with no ill effects.[80]

By maintaining this distinction between *architecture* as the expressive, stylistic elements on the exterior of a building, and *building* as the practical accommodation of heating, lighting, and structural soundness, Bertram revealed that his ideas about architecture were highly conventional. Bertram, however, reversed the usual nineteenth-century hierarchy that assigned greater importance to the expressive qualities of *architecture*. Echoing the *Library Journals*'s 1891 statement that "it is far better that a library should be plain or even ugly, than that it should be inconvenient," Bertram insisted that practical matters take precedence over artistic expression.[81]

The planning ideas Bertram espoused were presented in the "Notes" both in text and in schematic drawings. The ideal Carnegie library was a one-story rectangular building with a small vestibule leading directly to a single large room; where necessary, this room was subdivided by low bookcases that supplemented the bookshelves placed around its perimeter to hold the library's collection. In addition to book storage, this room provided reading areas for adults and children and facilities for the distribution of books. The basement had a lecture room, a heating plant, and "conveniences" for staff and patrons. Bertram even went so far as to suggest ceiling heights (nine to ten feet in the basement; twelve to fifteen feet on the first floor) and the placement of windows (six feet from the floor, to allow for shelving beneath).

Six plans accompanied the final version of the text (figs. 1.21 and 1.22). Diagrammatic in nature, they gave no indication of wall thicknesses or window placement. Although Bertram claimed that these plans were "suggestiv rather than mandatory," he warned in the same breath that "those responsible for bilding projects should paus before aiming at radical departures."[82] Variations in the plans accommodated differences in size and site. Plans A and B were closest to Bertram's ideal—a simple rectangular building with a central entrance on the long side. The next two responded to unusual sites. Plan C was meant for a site that was deeper than it was wide, while Plan D sought to adapt the same arrangements to a corner lot. Plans E and F used an off-center entrance and a single reading room to provide accommodations for very small libraries. Despite these differences, each plan followed Bertram's planning rule of thumb, allowing a single librarian to oversee the entire library.

These plans are telling of Bertram's debt to late nineteenth-century

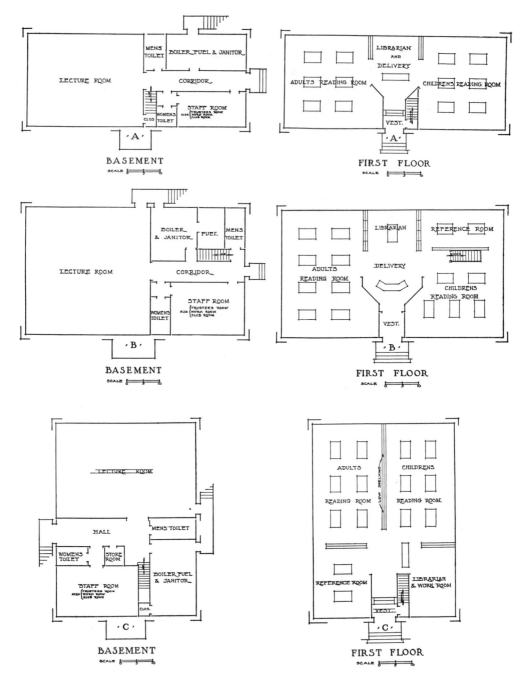

Figure 1.21 [James Bertram], "Notes on the Erection of Library Bildings," version 3, c. 1915, schematic plans A, B, and C. Courtesy of Carnegie Corporation Archives, and Rare Book and Manuscript Library, Columbia University. Copyright Davis & Sanford, New York.

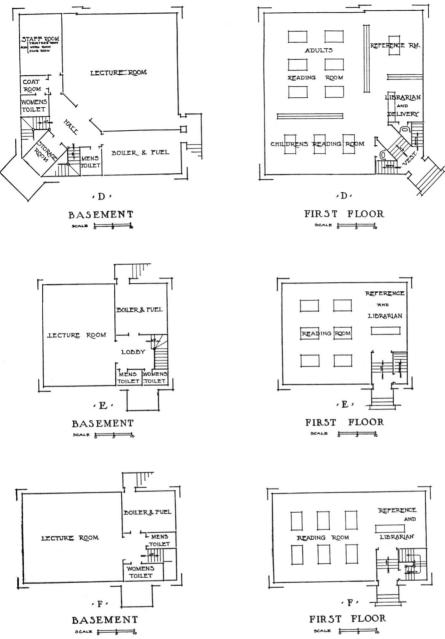

Figure 1.22 [James Bertram], "Notes on the Erection of Library Bildings," schematic plans D, E, and F. Original caption: Elevations of plans submitted for approval should clearly sho the floor and ceiling lines of basement and main floor, and the natural and artificial grade lines. Floor plans should sho, clearly designated, all roof supports and similar obstructions of the accommodation. Courtesy of Carnegie Corporation Archives, and Rare Book and Manuscript Library, Columbia University. Copyright Davis & Sanford, New York.

debates about library planning. The unwavering commitment to open access to all the books in the collection and the emphasis on a children's reading room equal or nearly equal in size to the reading room for adults were, after all, ideas first employed in the 1890s. Perhaps the greatest contribution of the "Notes" was to translate the rhetoric of the 1890s into graphic forms that could be adapted to a wide variety of circumstances.

At the same time, however, Bertram's pamphlet went beyond the writings that inspired it, pursuing the implications for planning that were left unexplored in the library literature of the 1890s. In 1897, Dana had suggested the factory and the office building as appropriate models for the modern public library building. Although Dana hoped for a similarly fresh approach to library design, his more conventional understanding of planning prevented him from advocating any radical changes in the arrangement of library interiors. Only in 1911 did Bertram and the others involved in writing the "Notes" apply Dana's analogy to the realm of planning. Subdivided only by low bookcases, with glass partitions to buffer sound without interfering with visual command of the interior space, the six plans included in the "Notes" all used open plans like those already in place in department stores, factories, and skyscrapers. Having already made the connection between philanthropy and corporate organization, those associated with the Carnegie program were in a good position to see a similar connection between library design and the buildings designed for corporate, commercial, and industrial use.

Redefining the Nature of Library Use

The architectural forms advocated by the Carnegie Corporation were intended to improve library efficiency. Yet they also suggested fundamental changes in the way that people experienced the library, whether they were librarians, library board members, or readers. Through these plans, Carnegie, the corporate philanthropist, encouraged activities different from the ones encouraged by Carnegie, the paternalistic philanthropist. In the paternalistic library, the donor himself had occupied the apex of a pyramidal social structure, followed by the trustees, the librarian, and the library assistants, with male and female library users at the very bottom. Bertram's ideal plans reveal a different set of priorities. They offered a spatial blueprint for a re-sorted social hierarchy that minimized the differences among the several parties.

In the reformed library, for instance, the donor's presence was substantially less palpable. Unlike their predecessors in Allegheny City, later recipients of Carnegie gifts were not required to inscribe the donor's name on the building's exterior.[83] When recipients did opt to acknowledge Carnegie's contribution, they typically chose to include his name in an inscription in the building's classical frieze. Set in a classical framework high overhead, these words provided only the most abstract reminder of Carnegie's role in library affairs. Inside the library, the donor was all but invisible. By deleting all fireplaces from his ideal plans, Bertram neatly removed the temptation to transform the hearth into a shrine to the benefactor.[84] In the reformed library, there was no donor's portrait, gazing intently down on the reader.

As the donor's lieutenants, the trustees were also made less visible. Deprived of a separate room reserved exclusively for their use, the trustees were obliged to meet in a room that did quadruple duty, serving as a work room, a staff room, and club room as well. In contrast to the place of honor the trustees' room had received in Allegheny City, the basement location of this room was a literal translation of the trustees' figurative drop in the library's social scale.

The librarian (by 1911, more likely to be a woman than a man) found herself in an ambiguous position. The open plan offered her a spatial situation comparable to that of the manager of a factory or an office building. From her post at the delivery desk, the librarian was at the center of library activities. Not only did she survey the entire first floor, but she herself was always in view as well. In their basement meeting room, the library board maintained a central role in establishing library policy, but the librarian upstairs personified the institution for most library users on a daily basis.

Despite the librarian's rise in status relative to the library trustees, these gains were undercut by other aspects of the Carnegie Corporation's ideal plans. The basement location of the staff room, for instance, suggests that the library staff had dropped lower in the library hierarchy, with respect to library users, both physically and symbolically—a demotion that was reinforced by the multipurpose nature of the staff room. Instead of reigning over an inner sanctum of their own, members of the library staff had to share their room with the trustees and local clubs.

For library patrons, male and female, young and old, the new library offered a pleasant surprise. From the outside, the emphasis on symmetry helped identify the building as a public one; readers could enter freely, secure in the knowledge that they were welcome. Inside, the architectural experience had been evened out. Ceilings were of a uniform height, and rectangular rooms were evenly lit from windows that started six feet from the floor. Gone were the specially shaped reading rooms with their aura of Victorian domesticity. Gone were monumental vistas into large public rooms. If the experience was less dramatic, it was also less intimidating.

Library users were confronted with neither a glimpse of a sumptuous trustees' room nor a shrine to the donor. The physical boundaries that in earlier libraries separated them from the library staff had disappeared. Most important, they were allowed to fetch their own books directly from the shelves lining the walls that surrounded them. They had entered into a relationship of trust with those in power.

For women and children, the new library offered unfamiliar freedom. Women were no longer segregated into ladies' reading rooms, or treated differently from their male contemporaries. And, whereas earlier libraries had been exclusively adult affairs only the smallest of the new libraries failed to provide a special reading room for the use of children. Young readers found in the children's reading room a portion of the public landscape that catered directly to their needs.

Conclusion

The changes that Carnegie wrought in the direction of American philanthropy and American library design were mutually supportive. Old-style philanthropy that cast the recipients of the gift in the role of perpetually grateful dependent relations found its parallel in unreformed libraries where users were forever reminded of their place at the bottom of the library's social hierarchy. The reformed library, a single room dominated by a centrally placed circulation desk and lined with book shelves, was the physical embodiment of the contractual arrangement between the philanthropist and the beneficiaries of his gifts, an agreement that specified and limited the recipients' obligations.

If Carnegie was confident that his reforms had improved the quality of American library design, the other actors in the library-building process were often less enthusiastic about them. Sometimes differing social agendas were at issue. Indeed, the middle-class people who served on local library boards were often more interested in providing urban amenities for their own class than they were in aiding the aspiring poor. Professional librarians of a Progressive bent were more sympathetic to Carnegie's goals, but rarely shared his deep-seated distrust of working-class readers. Thus, they were often eager to provide buildings that would encourage readers to feel more at home.

At other times, the question hinged on different attitudes toward the design process itself. As we will see in the next chapter, the challenge of designing a library that could accommodate divergent social agendas prompted many professional architects to organize their businesses in new ways.

In short, Carnegie did not succeed in dictating a new library type for American society; there were simply too many other forces at work. Nonetheless, his library philanthropy did prompt various groups to articulate their opinions about libraries and their proper use. Ultimately, Carnegie's importance lay in initiating substantive discussion about the role that culture should play in modern America.

MAKING
The Marketing of Library Design

FOR AMERICAN ARCHITECTS PRACTICING at the turn of the century, the Carnegie library program was an unexpected boon. Indeed, in an economy still recovering from the depression of the 1890s, an infusion of hundreds of thousands of dollars in new construction was a welcome boost to the building industry.

Better yet, the public nature of the buildings offered suitably dignified commissions to those practitioners who were concerned that house design lowered the prestige of an occupation still struggling for professional status. At the same time, a Carnegie commission for a small public library offered many architects the chance to follow in the footsteps of H. H. Richardson, who was still widely acknowledged as the greatest American architect of the previous generation.[1]

These benefits notwithstanding, a Carnegie commission often involved the architect in a complex and difficult design process. Ostensibly, Carnegie supported the idea of "home-rule." Locals were expected to select their own architect and to act as the client for the building's design. This ideal of local autonomy, however, was undermined by Carnegie's financial control over the project, particularly after 1908, when his secretary, James Bertram, refused to release funds for design that failed to meet his stringent planning guidelines. As a result, architects found themselves in the awkward situation of answering to clients who did not control their own purse strings, and were hard put to reconcile the advice of their architect, the directives of their benefactor, and their own ideas of appropriate library form.

Under these conditions, the great formal similarities among hundreds of Carnegie-financed library buildings are perplexing. What accounts for the striking similarities between buildings whose only common denominator is the source of their funding? The obvious answer—that Carnegie (or his agents) dictated the use of a symmetrical domed building with a temple-front motif framing the entrance—is wrong on a number of counts. As we have seen, Bertram did not begin to review designs until after 1908, and then focused on issues of planning. Yet, the now familiar temple-fronted library type had appeared in dozens of Carnegie libraries built before that date, and in dozens of other libraries funded from other sources (see figs. 1.14, 1.18, 4.8, 4.9, and 6.1). What is more, the implication that Carnegie imposed this design on reluctant beneficiaries is not supported by archival evidence. Indeed, the dome and temple-front type was the favorite of local decision-makers who often went to great lengths to secure such design over Bertram's objections (see chap. 4).

In reality, library design under the Carnegie program was affected by a broad range of social, cultural, and economic trends at the turn of the century. A widespread cultural interest in the ideas of efficiency fostered a popular faith that there was one best solution to a given planning problem. The professionalization of architecture and library science was another factor. Indeed, in both fields, ideas of library design became part of the body of knowledge imparted by means of a standardized professional education. Mass production and mass marketing also played an important role, as the ready availability of architectural products designed specifically for library use made it easy and cost-effective to adopt nationally-consistent forms of architectural expression.

To be sure, the Carnegie library program did not remain aloof from these changes. As we shall see, Carnegie's policies paralleled many of these changes and in some cases intensified their impact. Yet, we must be careful not to endow Carnegie with a power that he never possessed. The typical "Carnegie" library was not the product of the philanthropist's dictates, but the result of a multifaceted process that narrowed the range of architectural expression in the early years of the twentieth century.

The Culture of Professionalism

If architects working at the turn of the century inherited an interest in library design from their nineteenth-century predecessors, they worked in a fundamentally different professional context. In the decades after the Civil War, for instance, the intensity of the debate about library architecture was the outgrowth of fledgling campaigns for professional status in both architecture and librarianship, and the result of professional jealousy that developed when each group tried to support an exclusive claim to expertise in library planning.[2] The difficulty in reaching a consensus about library design was also related to issues of professional identity. As long as architects based their claims for professional status on the artistic aspect of their work, there would be no easy compromise with librarians who defined themselves as guardians of knowledge. By the late 1890s, however, the professions of librarianship and architecture began to move in parallel directions as each group independently began to adopt aspects of the culture of professionalism that had been pioneered in law and medicine. Clearly standards for professional competence became very important, and both groups increasingly embraced efficiency as the standard against which this competence could be measured. Without actively seeking reconciliation, architects and librarians who joined the culture of professionalism began to share a similar outlook.[3]

Equally important, both groups turned to professional education as a means of providing institutional recognition of clearly articulated standards for theoretical knowledge and professional conduct. The first professional school of library science was established in 1887 at Columbia College under the direction of Melvil Dewey.[4] Although the trustees closed the school in 1888 (primarily because Dewey had not consulted them about his decision to admit female students—the first on the Columbia campus), the school reopened the next year under the aegis of the New York State Library at Albany.[5] In addition to teaching the skills required in cataloguing and reference work, the professional curriculum emphasized work with children, cooperation with schools, branch libraries, and traveling libraries.[6] Library education advocated the constellation of library policies that librarians soon came to call "the modern library idea," and played a central role in the promotion of public service as a measure of professional competence.[7]

In architecture, there was a similar connection between professional education and developing standards of professional achievement. Although there had been schools of architecture at MIT, Cornell, and the University of Illinois since at least 1873, professional education was given greater importance at the end of the century, in part at least to serve the cause of "scientific eclecticism," a late nineteenth-century concern with reforming mid-century excesses.[8] The large number of architecture schools established in the 1890s vastly increased the availability of architectural education, just as the American Institute of Architects (AIA) moved to make a degree from an accredited school of architecture the primary requirement for membership.[9] This new emphasis on a standardized architectural knowledge base was reinforced through state licensing, first established in Illinois in 1897, and implemented in thirteen other states by 1918.[10]

These mechanisms were aimed primarily at securing the profession's right to define the legal and economic conditions of architectural practice. Yet, by institutionalizing the profession's right to define professional competence, these mechanisms inevitably had an impact on architectural production as well. To the extent that teaching design in a classroom setting or assessing design on licensing exams was predicated on a well-articulated set of acceptable formal characteristics, professionalization itself favored a limited range of architectural solutions. Under these conditions, a wholesale shift toward classicism in professional design was not inevitable, but it was logically consistent. After all, the classical orders and the written rules governing their requisite components, proper proportions, and appropriate deployment provided a theoretical baseline against which professionals could assess one another's designs.[11]

The Library Bureau and the Modern Library

If turn-of-the-century architects found that they had more in common with librarians than had their predecessors, they also found that librarians had developed more persuasive means to convey their ideas of library design. No longer content simply to describe their ideas of library design, they began to translate their ideas into material form. Starting with small pieces of library equipment, librarians steadily increased the size of the library fittings with which they shaped their work environments.[12]

The central figure in this history is again Melvil Dewey, whose interest in introducing efficiency into library work prompted him to serve as the secretary of the ALA's Co-operation Committee that was formed in 1877. In addition to evaluating available library supplies, the committee was also a clearing house, buying supplies in bulk and passing on the savings to small libraries. Realizing the enormous commercial potential of the committee's work, Dewey soon divorced the supply business from the ALA, establishing the Readers and Writers Economy Company in 1879, with himself as president and treasurer. Despite periodic business failures, Dewey continued to pursue the supply company idea throughout the 1880s, and in 1888 established the Library Bureau. This new company proved to be a phenomenal success, supplementing its headquarters in Boston with branches in New York, Chicago, London, and Paris before its purchase by the Rand Kardex Company in 1926.[13]

Dewey's active participation in the Library Bureau ended in 1901. Nonetheless, the company's approach was strongly influenced by Dewey's professional concern for improving library efficiency, and by his conviction that the design of every piece of library equipment was important to achieving that goal. As late as 1906, a Library Bureau ad reminded librarians that "technically correct equipment may cost a little more in the beginning, but it pays for itself every day in administrative result."[14] In this view, standardization was not just a means of making equipment cheaper to produce, it also had a normative value, in that approved library principles were built into the designs available for purchase. Thus by describing the proper use of their products, Library Bureau catalogues were teaching tools that spread the lessons of modern library administration far beyond the confines of the professional library school classroom.

No object was too insignificant for the Library Bureau to handle, and indeed the company came to pride itself on being able to provide a library with "everything except the books." Catalogue cards were the Bureau's first important product, and one that remained its biggest money-maker, especially after the cards were adopted by banks, insurance companies, and other businesses as a flexible means of maintaining customer records. In addition, the Bureau sold other large durable goods (like furniture and book stacks), consumable goods (like date stamps, rubber bands, and paper clips), professional advice (in the form of classification manuals and journal subscriptions), and even librarians (in the sense that they maintained an employment department "to get the right man for the right place").[15]

Dedicated to the idea that approved professional practice could be built into the library environment and interested in consolidating their corporate reputation as a comprehensive supply house, the Library Bureau also positioned itself as a center for disseminating professionally-sanctioned ideas about the design of library buildings. Initially, this involvement was limited to the activity of the consultation department, which offered professional advice on every aspect of library activity, and which by 1902, specifically advertised its eagerness "to confer with architects concerning details of heating, lighting, ventilation and fixtures as applied to special needs of libraries."[16] The Bureau may have found that architects simply ignored these offers of advice.[17] Certainly, throughout the 1890s the company introduced products and services that could shape a library's large-scale interior arrangements with or without the architect's cooperation. In 1897, the Bureau introduced the Furniture Department, whose task was "to take the library building from the general contractor, its exterior walls completed, its interior walls and floors and partitions done, and equip it with all other fixed and movable furniture," evidently from stock items. The same catalogue also advertised the Bureau's willingness to undertake custom interior woodwork, either from architect's drawings, or from sketches supplied by their own draughting department.[18]

The degree to which architects availed themselves of the Library Bureau's services during the design process is an open question, since no corporate records exist from this period. The Bureau's corporate officers liked to suggest that "the best architects of the country . . . have learned to call us in for preliminary advice and suggestions in the layout and arrangement of departments."[19] Yet, such assertions, made in this case at a 1908 salesmen's dinner in Boston, seem calculated to fuel future marketing efforts, and cannot necessarily serve as accurate reports of past performance. Indeed, lectures on "Handling committees and architects" in the training course for salesmen suggest that long-standing tensions between architects and librarians (as represented by the Library Bureau) had not completely dissipated, and may have prevented architects from seeking out the company's expertise.[20]

Subsequent editions of the annual catalogue specifically mention donors and trustees as clients for their consultation and custom woodworking services, a change which suggests that the Bureau was hoping to get the most powerful players in the library process to force architects to consult with them. During the same years, the introduction of illustrations of products in place allowed trustees and librarians alike a tool for communicating their preferences to their architects (fig. 2.1). Although the earliest of these illustrations identified the library without naming the architect responsible, by 1909 catalogue captions included the firm name, giving the architect free advertising in a nation-wide market (fig. 2.2). This was, of course, a great boon for firms marketing themselves as library specialists, and may represent the Bureau's attempt to reward architects who used their services.

If architects gradually became more willing to use the Library Bureau services, it may also be because they saw that the Bureau's products and marketing increasingly took into consideration developments in architectural theory and design. The process of change was gradual indeed, with catalogues issued between 1890 and 1896 taking little account of

Figure 2.1 Illustration from an 1899 Library Bureau catalogue, showing reference room furniture designed and made by Library Bureau. Library Bureau, *Classified Illustrated Catalog* (1899), 25.

contemporary trends in architectural design. In those years, reading room and desk chairs, for instance, were all derived from the bentwood office chairs popular in Victorian offices (fig. 2.3). The earliest indication of the Bureau's recognition of recent artistic trends came in 1897, with the introduction of the Windsor chair, a design doubly sanctioned by the English Arts and Crafts movement and by the revival of American colonial styles (fig. 2.4).[21] Within two years, the Bureau had shifted toward an Arts and Crafts aesthetic, discontinuing the bentwood chairs, offering many of their stock items only in an antique oak finish, and depicting whole Arts and Crafts interiors, like the unidentified staff room with furniture designed and made by the Library Bureau shown in figure 2.5.

After the turn of the century, Library Bureau catalogues also began to address aesthetic issues that they had previously ignored. Instead of insisting on the company's "particular attention . . . to mechanical points

Figure 2.2 Illustration from a 1909 Library Bureau catalogue, identifying the building and its architect. This library was erected with funds from a Carnegie grant offered in 1903. Library Bureau, *Library Catalog* (1909), 14.

of construction" (as had the 1897 catalog), sales literature increasingly adopted the rhetoric of the Arts and Crafts movement, with lofty statements about "purity of design, structural excellence and perfect finish ... free from any form of fantastic ornament." The choice of the Arts and Crafts aesthetic is telling in this context in that it allowed the Bureau to bridge the gap between librarianship's emphasis on functional design and architecture's growing interest in classicism. Thus, when they described Bureau furniture as "beyond the influence of changing taste," or noted its "simplicity of design, correct proportions, and perfect finish," Bureau sales catalogues asserted a basic congruity between the Arts and Crafts aesthetic and classical styles, a formal harmony demonstrated in their products (fig. 2.6). Bases for card catalogues and file cabinets, for instance, had massive square legs with three wide flutes, and could fit easily into a classically-detailed library without offending an Arts and Crafts sensibility.[22]

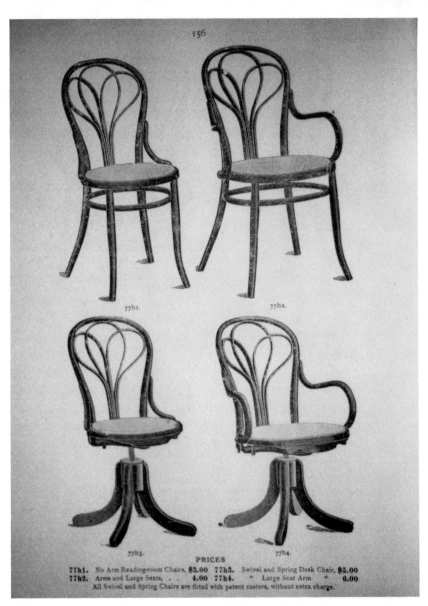

Figure 2.3 Illustration from an 1893 Library Bureau catalogue, showing bentwood chairs common in late Victorian office environments. Library Bureau, *Classified Illustrated Catalog* (1893), 156.

This willingness to admit that aesthetic issues played a role in library design was new in the library world; after all, an earlier generation of librarians had felt that aesthetic concerns had led architects to ignore the needs of library function. Thus, it may have been Dewey's departure from the Library Bureau in 1901 that freed the company officials to

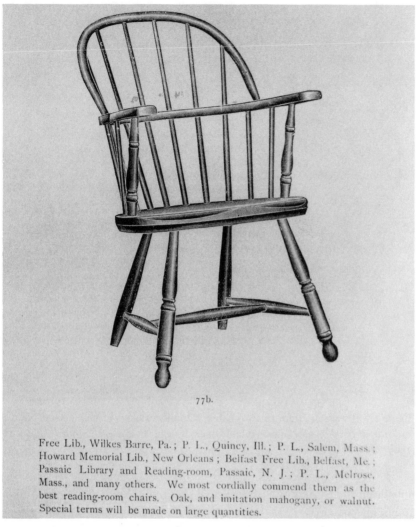

77b.

Free Lib., Wilkes Barre, Pa.; P. L., Quincy, Ill.; P. L., Salem, Mass.;
Howard Memorial Lib., New Orleans; Belfast Free Lib., Belfast, Me.;
Passaic Library and Reading-room, Passaic, N. J.; P. L., Melrose,
Mass., and many others. We most cordially commend them as the
best reading-room chairs. Oak, and imitation mahogany, or walnut.
Special terms will be made on large quantities.

Figure 2.4 The Library Bureau's Windsor chair, first offered for sale in 1897. Library Bureau, *Classified Illustrated Catalog* (1897), 124.

forge new ties with the architecture profession. Certainly, the signs of a
new cooperative spirit were increasingly pervasive after the turn of the
century. In 1902, for instance, the Bureau began to espouse total design,
arguing that custom design had "the double advantage of bringing [library furniture] into perfect accord with the surroundings, and at the
same time adapting it in size and form to the space it is to occupy."[23] In
this way, the Bureau reiterated an argument that architects were using
in the same years to support their own campaign for professional status,

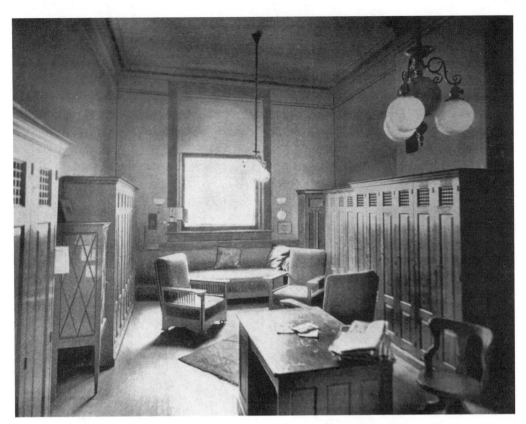

Figure 2.5 Illustration from an 1899 Library Bureau catalogue, showing staff-room furniture in the Arts and Crafts style. Library Bureau, *Classified Illustrated Catalog* (1899), 28.

bolstering the careers of a professional group that had once seemed like an enemy.

In short, librarians and architects approached library design from different directions—architects using the example of previous buildings to define the building envelope, librarians using their various tasks to define an interior work environment. Yet, their thinking about library design brought them closer together than either group admitted openly. While both groups continued to claim a special expertise in library design, professional education and the need to define and codify standards of professional practice narrowed the range of library designs approved by each group. At the same time, the realities of selling their ideas and services in a capitalist market made both groups realize that their professional goals could be mutually supportive.

Figure 2.6 Illustration from a Library Bureau advertisement, showing a file cabinet in the simplified classical style favored by the Bureau at the turn of the century. *Public Libraries* 7 (January 1902): 44.

The Impact of the Carnegie Library Program

The Carnegie library program interacted with these trends toward standardization in complex ways. On one hand, many of the forces affecting library design arose independently of Carnegie and had already begun to make an impact when the philanthropist shifted to the retail phase of his library giving. Nonetheless, the Carnegie program accelerated the movement toward library standardization by financing the building boom that librarians and architects used as a laboratory in which to experiment, adjust, and eventually reconcile their different approaches to library design.[24]

Carnegie policies also reinforced existing trends toward library standardization by limiting the pool of acceptable library designers. From the beginning of the second phase of library giving, Bertram consistently used the term "architect" to refer to those who could be trusted with library design. Yet, not just any architect would do, and Bertram increasingly chastised grant recipients who failed "to enlist the cooperation of an architect who had successfully designed library buildings," or asked them to defend the designer's qualifications by listing "what other library plans your proposed architect has drawn satisfactory to the principals."[25] Some library boards reacted to Bertram's insinuations by defending the expertise of the chosen architect, others by dismissing their architect and hiring another. All of them, however, understood the importance that the Carnegie program attached to experience in library design.

The cumulative effect of Bertram's pressure to hire architects with a background in library design was to encourage the practice of architectural specialization. This was hardly a new trend, of course; since the first half of the nineteenth century architectural designers with professional aspirations had marketed themselves as experts in the design of particular building types, as Robert Mills did with government office buildings, as A. J. Davis did with domestic architecture, and as Richard Upjohn and John Notman did with church design.[26] Nonetheless, the Carnegie library program fueled the preexisting trend toward architectural specialization both directly and indirectly. Direct pressure came in the form of advice, issued repeatedly to grant recipients, to fire architects inexperienced in library design and to hire only those with previous library experience. Bertram's rigorous review provided an indirect but even more effective pressure. As Bertram's expectations became more exacting, and as his reputation became more wide spread, architectural firms that could claim expertise in the design of *Carnegie* libraries became extremely attractive to other towns with Carnegie grants. Although there are countless examples of local architects who built Carnegie libraries, Carnegie library commissions increasingly tended to be consolidated in the hands of a relatively small number of firms that gained at least regional prominence in designing these library buildings.

Some of these firms continued to follow older patterns of practice, entering prestigious design competitions for large-budget projects in larger cities. Cass Gilbert, for instance, won competitions for Carnegie-financed buildings in both St. Louis and Detroit (see figs. 3.14–3.21). The New York firm of Ackerman and Ross was particularly active in pursuing library commissions in this way, winning competitions for Carnegie buildings in Atlanta, Washington, D.C., Nashville, and San Diego, and competing unsuccessfully for Carnegie commissions in Schenectady, N.Y., and Davenport, Iowa (see figs. 3.26–3.31 and 4.10 below).[27] The firm also competed for non-Carnegie library commissions in Galveston, Texas, Trenton, New Jersey, and Utica, New York. At Ottumwa and Schenectady, Ackerman and Ross competed against F. R. Comstock, another New York architect who pursued the competition route with somewhat less success.

As the dollar amount of Carnegie grants fell steadily over the course of the program, however, such costly architectural competitions became less popular as a mode of selecting an architect. More important, Carnegie's criticism of central library facilities reduced the opportunities for an architect to earn a substantial fee for the design of a single, large building. In order to tap the full potential of Carnegie patronage, architects had to be ready to take on a much larger number of projects, each of which represented only a fairly small fee.

One of the architects who was most successful at adjusting to these new conditions was Edward L. Tilton.[28] Like many of his late nineteenth-century contemporaries, Tilton had received his initial architectural education on the job, in the office of McKim, Mead & White, before traveling to Paris in 1887 to study at the Ecole des Beaux-Arts. Returning to New York in 1890, he worked briefly with McKim, Mead & White before opening his own office in partnership with his fellow draftsman, William A. Boring. For the next decade, Boring and Tilton enjoyed a steady rise in the competitive world of New York architecture. Within ten years they had won the competition to design the U.S. Immigration Station on Ellis Island, a plum commission that also brought them international recognition in the form of a Gold Medal Award at the Paris Exposition of 1900. Other medals followed at the expositions in Buffalo in 1901 and in St. Louis in 1904. By that time, both men had served terms as president of the Society of Beaux-Arts Architects, a group that they had helped found, and that served as a confirmation of their prestigious architectural education.

By the early years of the twentieth century, however, a personal friendship with James Bertram helped transform Tilton's general expertise in the design of classically-detailed public buildings into a more specific interest in library architecture. Carrying Bertram's personal letters of introduction, Tilton received a warm welcome from local officials entrusted with securing library designs. Warren, Ohio, is a case in point. The library board in this county seat had already met with an architect who had designed two other Carnegie library buildings in Ohio. Yet, their minutes record that they felt compelled to consider Tilton, "a personal friend of Mr. Carnegie's secretary." They not only invited Tilton to meet with them within the week, but offered him the commission on the day of their meeting.[29]

As interesting as the Warren case is for revealing Bertram's personal subversion of Carnegie's official policy of home rule, it is even more telling of the impact that Carnegie commissions had on the practice of architecture. As Tilton explained in a letter to the library board, he could not advocate the use of an architectural competition; this accepted form of securing a high-quality and artistic design was "a source of constant worry and annoyance to the building committee," and tended to result in designs that were difficult to build within the appropriation. Instead, Tilton offered what he felt was a fool-proof method of bringing a Carnegie library to successful completion. "By this method," he wrote,

> I shall undertake to design the building within the appropriation; to furnish all usual plans, working drawings, details and specifications, and to associate with me a local architect whom your committee can recommend as being competent, and who will be constantly on the spot to superintend the construction, and whom I shall pay out of my 5% commission according to the schedule of the American Institute of Architects.
>
> I shall further undertake to furnish a responsible firm of contractors, Messrs. Hoggson Bros. of New York, who will give you a guarantee and bond to construct the building complete, including furniture and fittings, within the amount of the appropriation; and who will employ your local contractors and mechanics for all parts of the work which can be done by them, such as Masonry, Carpentry, Plumbing, etc., and providing they are competent and responsible.[30]

Although this evidence of a close and on-going working relationship with the Hoggson brothers reversed the general trend of the time for architects to divorce themselves from the construction process, it allowed Tilton to offer his clients a finished product at a guaranteed price.

Tilton's methods required substantial changes in the nature of his practice. For instance, Tilton dissolved his partnership with Boring in 1904, at the height of their success together. Since the two men continued to share office space, staff, and equipment, the dissolution does not seem to have been precipitated by either personal or professional animosities.[31] Rather, it is more likely that the former partners preferred to pursue different professional strategies. Boring followed a more conventional route, seeking to build a reputation on the basis of a small number of prestigious and costly commissions.[32] In contrast, Tilton's specialty in the design of Carnegie libraries allowed him to win a large number of comparatively modest commissions. After a decade in which financial fluctuations increased the difficulty of securing larger commissions, this must have seemed like a reasonable strategy for professional survival.

To succeed at this alternative strategy, Tilton experimented with new means for marketing his growing expertise in library design. Recognizing that the Carnegie program had given professional librarians a greater say in planning decisions, Tilton increasingly addressed himself directly to librarians, as well as to the boards who paid their salaries. In September of 1911, for instance, he attended the convention of Ohio and Michigan librarians at Cedar Point, Ohio, where he read a paper on the architecture of the small library. Opening with a condemnation of his own profession for having "conspired" with building committees to design impractical libraries, his paper covered everything from the siting of branch libraries to the details of lighting and heating, from the choice of stylistic vocabulary to rules of thumb for calculating the size and cost of a building based on the number of volumes it was to house.[33] Tilton eventually developed this last topic into a series of formulas for determining the construction costs, square footage, building height, collection size, the amount of shelving needed, and the square footage of corridors, lecture room, staff quarters, and reading rooms. Published in the American Library Association's *Library Journal*, "Scientific Library Planning" revealed the extent to which Tilton abandoned the professional persona of the architect-as-artist in order to pursue professional connections with the library world.[34]

The evidence suggests that Tilton's methods worked. Indeed, Tilton consistently completed his Carnegie commissions under budget, a fact that he was careful to advertise, both to prospective clients and to his friend Bertram. By the spring of 1905, he was able to report to Bertram that he had completed public libraries at Mt. Vernon (New York), Bayonne (New Jersey), Winston-Salem (North Carolina), and Cleveland (Ohio), and a college library at Smith College in Northampton (Massachusetts), all within their Carnegie appropriations.[35] Significantly, the library board at Warren had hired Tilton without following his fool-proof method, and thus became one of the exceptions in Tilton's impressive record.[36] Bertram eventually rewarded this record of fiscal responsibility directly, mentioning to grant recipients that Tilton was an architect who had successfully completed Carnegie libraries in the past.[37] Although it is difficult to get an accurate count, Tilton designed enough Carnegie libraries to establish himself as a specialist in the library field, eventually designing more than sixty libraries in World War I Army camps.

Perhaps one of the most interesting implications of the Tilton story is the suggestion that the usual sort of professional prestige did not ensure success at designing Carnegie libraries. Indeed, by de-emphasizing the art of architecture, the Carnegie library program helped open the field of library design to architects beyond the circle of the Eastern elite who swelled the membership of professional societies and whose work filled the pages of architectural journals. Architects who enjoyed none of the conventional signs of professional prestige found they could build solid reputations on library design. In Indiana, for instance, architect Clifford Shopbell of Evansville dominated the field; first in partnership with Will A. Harris, and then on his own, Shopbell designed at least fifteen of that state's Carnegie libraries between 1902 and 1917.[38] Wilson B. Parker of Indianapolis designed at least ten other Carnegie libraries in Indiana, while the Fort Wayne firm of Wing and Mahurin enjoyed a more moderate success with the building type.[39] In California, W. H. Weeks used his experience in school design as his entree into the realm of library planning, eventually designing twenty-one Carnegie libraries in northern California.[40] F. E. Wetherell (alone and in partnership) designed at least seven of Iowa's Carnegie libraries, while C. S. Haire of Helena, Montana, designed four of the Carnegie libraries in his state.[41]

Perhaps the best example of the sort of firm that flourished under the Carnegie library program was the firm of Patton & Miller of Chicago. In many ways, the partners were exemplars of the new American architect. Educated at new American schools of architecture (Normand S. Patton at MIT, Grant C. Miller at the University of Illinois), they were introduced to the principles of Beaux-Arts composition without gaining the patina of European travel. From their offices in Chicago, they established a thriving practice, designing over three hundred buildings in the course of their fifteen-year partnership. Working frequently for bureaucratic clients (notably the Chicago Board of Education), they played a substantial role in the growth of the Midwest. Recognizing that libraries were becoming an increasingly important building type, and one in which few Midwestern firms could claim any expertise, Patton & Miller traded on their experience with school design to present themselves as specialists in library architecture. Coinciding as it did with the beginning of Carnegie's library giving on a national scale, the firm's interest in library design was fortuitous; by the time the partnership was dissolved in 1912, over one-third of the firm's three hundred buildings were libraries, most of them built with Carnegie funds.[42]

More important, correspondence with their clients reveals that Patton & Miller went to some effort to make themselves experts in the design of *Carnegie* libraries. They identified the priorities of the Carnegie program, and offered their clients accurate advice on Bertram's reactions to certain kinds of designs and certain kinds of requests. In 1906, a letter on the firm's letterhead to Mr. Hewlett of Kewanee, Illinois, intimated that their professional services extended beyond architectural design. The wrier stated:

Our Mr. Miller in talking with the board advised against asking Mr. Carnegie for an additional appropriation stating that we had received definite instructions from Mr. Bertram that Mr. Carnegie was opposed to being requested to increase his appropriation.

Mr. Miller also stated that we were unwilling to proceed with plans in any uncertainty as to the amount of the appropriation and that the amount must be settled before we began work.[43]

The firm clearly understood that the first priority in designing a Carnegie library was to keep the budget limit firmly in mind from the start. They also understood that requesting additional funds could do much more harm than good in the town's relationship with Bertram. Although their clients in Kewanee did not heed it, Patton & Miller offered sound advice on dealing with a corporate philanthropist.

Like Tilton, Patton & Miller also recognized that their success as architects of Carnegie libraries also depended upon winning and maintaining Bertram's trust. Thus, they were careful to anticipate and forestall any criticism that might make its way to Carnegie via Bertram. As they explained to Mr. Hewlett,

the board in dealing with Mr. Carnegie ought, in justice to us, to state clearly that the directions were given to us in preparing the plans so as not to injure our reputation by intimating that we had represented that these plans could be built for $20,000. We do not like to write to Mr. Carnegie direct for fear that this would seem disrespectful to the library board and therefore we make this appeal that in correspondence with Mr. Carnegie our position shall be fairly stated.[44]

From the Carnegie point-of-view, Patton & Miller demonstrated exemplary professional behavior, combining library design experience with close attention to the bottom line and sincere respect for the principle of home rule.

The benefits of tailoring business practices to Carnegie's priorities were substantial, and Patton & Miller soon began to enjoy many of the advantages that Bertram extended to his old friend Edward Tilton. By at least 1908, Bertram had begun to mention the pair to recipient towns as a firm that "might" provide suitable plans. In the next few years, Bertram seems to have allowed a geographical line to determine his answer to direct inquiries about architects. He suggested Tilton (and sometimes Carnegie's brother-in-law, Henry D. Whitfield) to towns in eastern states, while his recommendations to recipients in western states helped extend Patton & Miller's practice from Illinois and the adjacent states into Kansas, Texas, and other states.[45]

The Patton & Miller story is equally interesting for suggesting the fragile nature of a good relationship with the Carnegie organization. In 1911, the firm's reputation as Carnegie specialists was at its height. Indeed, at the end of the year Patton was one of the architects with whom Bertram discussed standardizing library plans.[46] Yet, the fortunes of each partner after the split-up of the firm in 1912 demonstrate that such trust was difficult to maintain. As senior partner in Normand S. Patton, Holmes & Flinn, Patton succeeded in winning a number of Carnegie library commissions, but he still felt compelled to protect his reputation with Bertram when misunderstandings arose with his local clients.[47] In contrast, Miller's new firm of Miller, Fullenwider & Dowling abandoned the policy of advising clients to stay within their appropriation. Indeed, when Henry Sanborn, the secretary of Indiana's Public Library Commission, investigated the cause of budget overruns in Albion, Indiana, he reported to Bertram that he had "conclusive proof that this firm of architects [Miller, Fullenwider & Dowling] tries to lead boards to deceive the Carnegie Corporation. One of the letters very openly boasted of spending more than the required amount on another Indiana library and it said that 'the less Mr. Bertam knew the better.'"[48] Bertram was incensed, but since the Albion library board was unable (or unwilling) to hand over the incriminating letter, he could take no action. Instead, he urged Sanborn to encourage other communities to "[stand] up for their rights with professional men, who ar sometimes prone to disregard the wishes of those employing them and paying them."[49] In short, Miller's actions seem to have confirmed Bertram's suspicions about architects and their uncertain dedication to the cause of efficient library design. They certainly reveal that expertise with the Carnegie system could cut two ways.

Conclusion

The place of architects in the Carnegie library program was complex indeed. As a group, they never enjoyed Bertram's confidence and trust in the same way that librarians did. Despite their success at finding a common ground with librarians in the culture of professionalism, architects remained for Bertram the enemies of good library design. Even those architects who worked in good faith to follow the Carnegie guidelines found it difficult to win Bertram's unqualified approval. As late as

1910, when reviewing Albert Randolph Ross's design for a library branch in Nashville, Tennessee, Bertram could complain that he had "rarely seen a set of plans where space was so wasted." [50]

This antagonism notwithstanding, architects remained an integral part in the making of Carnegie libraries. However much Bertram continued to see librarians and architects as belonging to opposite camps, both groups embraced ideals of efficiency as part of their professional ethos, and even Bertram required an architect's involvement as an important means of reinforcing professional standards in library design. Equally telling, the aesthetic theories that had developed hand in hand with professionalism had a decisive impact on the Carnegie library ideal, as expressed in the "Notes on the Erection of Library Bildings." Indeed, despite Bertram's critique of the temple fronts and elaborate domes that professional architects used to define the building type, the insistent symmetry of the sample plans reveals the strength of the link between the small public library and classicism by 1911.

In many ways, architects often found it easier to accept the design standards of the Carnegie program than their clients did. The prospect of further Carnegie commissions was reason enough for many architects to heed Bertram's advice, and professional demands for creative autonomy were rare. In contrast, locals were concerned only with the one library at hand, and interpreted it as a means of achieving social and cultural agendas that were more complex than simply distributing books in an efficient way. This difference in interpretation fueled most debates over the siting and form of Carnegie libraries.

TAKING

Libraries and Cultural Politics

Part I

THE SUCCESS OF THE CARNEGIE LIBRARY program was due in large part to the prompt, widespread, and enthusiastic response of American communities eager for purpose built library buildings at the turn of the century. Carefully framed to avoid the perception that he was forcing his gifts onto unwilling communities, Carnegie's policies ensured that the library program would thrive only to the extent that recipient towns were receptive.

Yet, it is wrong to take the local response for granted. Communities did not flock to the Carnegie program simply because it was there. Their enthusiasm is rather an indication of the degree to which Carnegie's offer coincided with a new interest in building urban amenities that, it was hoped, would restore some balance to their social life and physical appearance, a balance that seemed to have been upset by an unchecked pursuit of commercial prosperity.[1] What is more, thanks to the implementation of conservative fiscal policies in the 1880s and 1890s, municipal governments at the turn of the century were in a better position to finance these amenities than they had been at any time since the Civil War.[2]

It is also wrong to assume that a Carnegie library meant to local communities what it meant to Carnegie, or even that the Carnegie library meant the same thing for all elements of a given community. In large city and small town alike, the Carnegie library was rarely the product of a spontaneous, universal, community spirit. Rather, Carnegie's requirement that elected representatives lend official approval and tax-financed support to each library inadvertently forced confrontations between groups with divergent attitudes toward culture and its role in American life. The specific nature of the grant—a library—focused the attention of the community, at least for a time, on questions of culture, while the potential infusion of capital sharpened that focus. As a result, Americans of all sorts found themselves debating the place of culture in their communities with an intensity previously unknown. Was culture a necessity or a luxury? Who was the intended audience for the community's cultural life? What was the proper relationship between the culture, generally defined, and the cultural institutions built to house it? What was the relationship between a town's social reality and its physical landscape? Who should be empowered to make these decisions?

In large cities, the confrontation was between local cultural philanthropists drawn from an older, native-born elite (men who throughout the last quarter of the nineteenth century had donated their time as library trustees) and municipal officials drawn from more recent immigrant populations. In spite of pressure to make the library serve the entire city, library trustees clung to the nineteenth-century ideal of culture as the province of the economic elite, an attitude revealed in the placement of large central libraries in City Beautiful settings at some distance from downtown, often in buildings modeled on the Boston Public Library (a building already fifteen years old at the turn of the century).[3]

The trustees' conservatism was somewhat tempered by the rise of Progressive attitudes, especially among professional librarians who campaigned for the establishment of branch libraries in slum neighborhoods. To the extent that this movement brought libraries close to the homes of working-class readers, this decentralization coincided with Carnegie's wishes. Yet, Progressive educational theory and its faith in the importance of play often undercut Carnegie's original intention that the library help create a disciplined work force.[4]

As we shall see in chapter 4, the library confrontation in smaller towns was based on gender rather than class. Middle-class women who had organized into literary study clubs in the last quarter of the nineteenth century found their central role in library affairs threatened by Carnegie's insistence on dealing directly with elected officials. Interpreting the library as a source of "home influence" and as a force for morality in their towns, club women who wanted to place the library near residential areas found themselves in conflict with their husbands and brothers who preferred central locations where the library might attract prospective investors to town.[5]

By prompting men and women to articulate their different ideas of culture, of culture's role in their community, and ultimately of the community itself, the Carnegie program also forced them to articulate their sense of themselves, their conception of the gender system in which they lived, and their idea of how the physical environment could support or subvert the daily experience of that gender system. The study of this interaction of gender and space is important for understanding the processes that created the physical environment of the nineteenth century; it is equally important for understanding how Americans negotiated the ideology of separate spheres in their everyday lives, and particularly how women interpreted the difference between the idea of women's place and the reality of women's space.[6]

Cultural Politics in Larger Cities

In the last quarter of the nineteenth century, the public library became an increasingly common fixture in the urban landscape of larger American cities. Along with picturesque parks, museums, auditoriums, and even department stores, libraries were part of an explosion in the number of urban settings designed to soften the sharper edges of daily life. Taken as a whole, these institutions transformed the face of American cities by providing public (and semipublic) spaces that were devoted primarily to middle-class users, meeting middle-class demands for leisure-time activities and requiring all users to adopt middle-class standards for genteel behavior.[7]

In contrast to many of these middle-class urban institutions, however, libraries remained closely associated with their elite roots. Indeed, many public libraries were direct descendants of private libraries or athenaeums first established in the antebellum era. Even when there was no direct connection, public library trustees still tended to be drawn from the ranks of the native-born social elite that had dominated the boards of those earlier institutions.[8] Like their predecessors, this generation of trustees embraced the Romantic tradition that viewed culture as the key to a transcendent state, the pursuit of which they also tended to agree was primarily an upper-class activity. Their opinions varied, however, on whether the "general public" (that is, the working class) could or should share in this endeavor. Would exposure to culture teach taste and refinement, or were these qualities in-born prerequisites to the appreciation of culture?[9]

There seemed no obvious answer to this question, and even the most liberal trustees remained ambivalent about the public nature of the institutions over which they presided. Throughout most of the nineteenth century, library policies were remarkably conservative. Some policies (like limited evening hours) actually served to discourage working-class readers from using the library, while others (like prohibiting public access to the stacks) reveal the trustees' deep-seated distrust of the reading public. To the extent that these library boards were either appointed or self-perpetuating, trustees were insulated from public, municipal, and professional pressure for liberalization. As a result, even publicly supported libraries continued to function as elite institutions throughout the last quarter of the nineteenth century.[10]

The large urban library buildings erected in this era reflected the tension that trustees felt between the urge to protect culture from the contamination of the working class and the desire to use culture to redeem the "general public." On the one hand, these monumental buildings typically worked within the classical tradition to create an exterior image that made appropriate allusions to the library's public function. On the other hand, they were often expensive and even luxurious buildings prominently sited in upper-class neighborhoods. Their massive interior spaces also served an elite view of culture, by creating a rarified atmosphere in which culture seemed to belong to a special, almost mystical realm. The two most influential examples of the type were the Boston Public Library, begun in 1888 to the designs of McKim, Mead & White, and the New York Public Library by Carrère & Hastings, begun ten years later. Together they represent two ends of a narrow range of architectural solutions aimed at reconciling the tension between the library's public function and its role in preserving an elite view of culture.[11]

The more conservative of the two examples is the Boston Public Library (figs. 3.1–3.4). Located on Copley Square in the heart of the city's elegant residential Back Bay neighborhood, it originally stood directly adjacent to the Art Museum (another institution dedicated to the elite view of culture), and still stands across the square from Trinity Church, whose Episcopal congregation included many of Boston's social elite.[12]

The building itself combined a variety of historical precedents that shared similar exterior forms. In what William Jordy aptly dubbed "the thrice-sanctioned front," the building's Copley Square facade (fig. 3.1) referred to H. H. Richardson's Marshall Field Wholesale Store (and through this design, to the palazzo form characteristic of Renaissance Florence), to the Tempio Malatestiano in Rimini, to the Bibliothèque Ste.-Geneviève, and even to the medieval libraries housed in the cloisters of Italian monasteries.[13] This range of references allowed the building to trigger associations that were both specific and appropriate to what the trustees perceived as the library's dual function. The building presented itself as a direct descendent of the first great public library of the modern world, even as it offered a flattering comparison between

Figure 3.1 McKim, Mead & White, Boston Public Library, Boston, 1888–95. *Monograph of the Work of McKim, Mead & White, 1879–1915*, 1914–20.

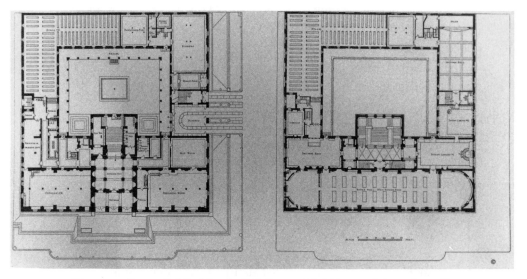

Figure 3.2 Boston Public Library, (*left*) first- and (*right*) second-floor plans. *Monograph of the Work of McKim, Mead & White, 1879–1915*, 1914–20.

Boston's cultural elite and the men of wealth who supported the rebirth of culture in fifteenth-century Italy.

If the Boston Public Library successfully conveyed the double nature of the late nineteenth-century public library, it also brought together historical precedents with largely incompatible plans (see fig. 3.2). The

Figure 3.3 Boston Public Library, entrance hall. *Monograph of the Work of McKim, Mead & White, 1879–1915*, 1914–20.

combination of a central court and a second-floor reading room on the front of the building proved to be a liability from the view of library function. Indeed, design decisions made with an eye to exterior expression limited the flexibility of the plan and thwarted the rational arrangement of functionally related spaces. Despite the technological advances introduced by librarian Justin Winsor, the original layout failed to meet the functional requirements of the modern public library, and was never used precisely as planned.[14]

Figure 3.4 Boston Public Library, delivery room. *Monograph of the Work of McKim, Mead & White, 1879–1915*, 1914–20.

The forced combination of incompatible plans also affected the reader's experience of the Boston Public Library. True, the Boston building was comparable to the Bibliothèque Ste.-Geneviève at ground level (figs. 3.5–3.7). In both cases, the public space on the ground floor was limited to a relatively dark, single-height entrance hall on the building's transverse axis (see figs. 3.2 and 3.5). At the far side of the hall, light from second-story windows illuminated the grand stairway leading to the second-story reading room (see fig. 3.3). Read as Romantic symbols, both buildings imply that the benefits of culture are not automatically open to everyone. Instead, the journey toward enlightenment requires conscious effort on the part of readers. Enlightenment is a struggle, but a struggle that redeems the uncultured and makes them worthy to receive culture's benefits. Yet, at the Bibliothèque Ste.-Geneviève, the stairs led directly to the reading room which filled the entire second floor of the building's simple rectangular footprint (see figs. 3.6 and 3.7).

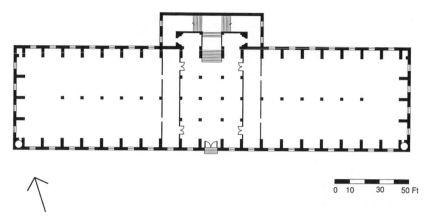

Figure 3.5 Henri Labrouste, Bibliothèque Ste.-Geneviève, Paris, 1844–50, ground-floor plan. Redrawn from Arthur Drexler, ed., *The Architecture of the Ecole des Beaux-Arts*, New York, 1977, 336.

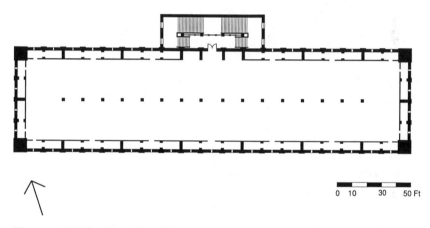

Figure 3.6 Bibliothèque Ste.-Geneviève, second-floor plan. Redrawn from Arthur Drexler, ed., *The Architecture of the Ecole des Beaux-Arts*, New York, 1977, 337.

A light, airy room, its ceiling vaults supported on delicate, exposed iron members, the reading room in Paris was a satisfying culmination of the journey from darkness and ignorance to light and enlightenment. At Boston, the arrival on the second floor was distinctly anticlimactic, interrupted by the hallway needed to bring users and staff to the rooms surrounding the open court. In this case, the figural arts helped compensate for architectural deficiencies. Edwin Austin Abbey's murals of the Legend of the Holy Grail reintroduced the theme of struggle and redemption and were particularly appropriate in the delivery room where readers waited to receive their books (see fig. 3.4).[15]

Figure 3.7 Bibliothèque Ste.-Geneviève, stair hall. Courtesy of James Austin.

Ten years later, subtle differences in planning and exterior imagery revealed a somewhat different attitude to this issue of the journey toward enlightenment at the New York Public Library (fig. 3.8). Like the Boston building, the New York library also made references to Renaissance forms and to nineteenth-century French buildings, but its exterior image was less specific and the associations it called up less precise. The five-part facade, for instance, had its roots in the *palais* of Renaissance

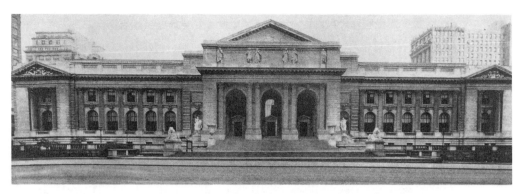

Figure 3.8 Carrère & Hastings, New York Public Library, New York, 1897–1911. Courtesy of Archives of The New York Public Library, Astor, Lenox and Tilden Foundations.

and Baroque France, and had been used throughout the nineteenth century in buildings designed according to the principles of the Ecole des Beaux-Arts. In its recent manifestations, it had served for a wide variety of public building types, and had not been associated specifically with library buildings. The same is true of the triumphal arch motif of the building's central entrance pavilion, which was drawn not from another library building, but from Richard Morris Hunt's design for the facade of the Metropolitan Museum of Art, just forty blocks north. Less related to the specific function of the building as a library, this image was arguably better suited to expressing the building's public nature. In contrast to the private origins of the palazzo, the triumphal arch was a ritual gateway that celebrated and invited movement within the urban realm; with its gigantic order, it gave the New York Public Library a monumentality long used in the classical tradition to designate public space.[16]

The counterpart to this more generalized exterior image was greater planning flexibility. Indeed, the five-part facade of the French *palais* appealed to Ecole des Beaux-Arts architects precisely because the designer could adapt the type to a wide variety of functions, simply by adding or subtracting bays between the central and end pavilions. At the New York Public Library, this flexibility allowed Carrère & Hastings to achieve effective functional zoning, both vertically and horizontally. In the basement and on the first and second floors, the rear of the building was devoted to a closed bookstack, while staff areas were grouped toward the south end of the building and public areas to the north (fig. 3.9). At each succeeding level, the area devoted to public use increased, until the entire third floor was open to the public (fig. 3.10). In a reversal

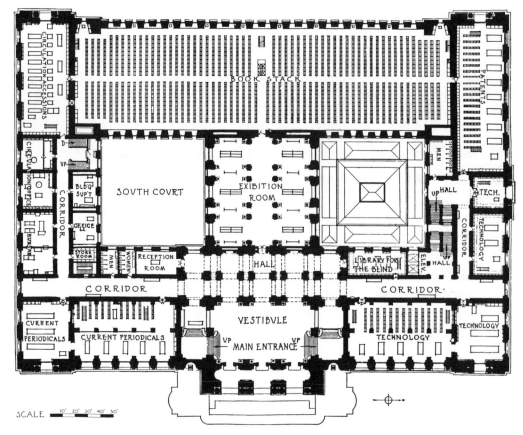

Figure 3.9 New York Public Library, first-floor plan. *Library Planning*, Jersey City, New Jersey, 1915, 141.

of Boston's practice, New York's general reading room was placed with an eye to function rather than to image. Located at the rear of the building on the third floor, it was both isolated from the street noise of Fifth Avenue and in close proximity to the closed bookstacks on the three floors directly below.[17]

For New York's readers, the drama of the library experience was immediate. The double-height entrance hall flanked on either side by stairways was brilliantly lit from windows above the doors and thus behind entering readers. All the elements of the Boston entry sequence are here—light, monumental stairs, visual connection with the library's upper floors—but now presented simultaneously. If the Boston Public Library offered readers architectural incentives to strive forward in the gradual progression from the everyday realm of Copley Square toward light and knowledge, the New York Public Library took a more active role, transporting the reader immediately into a realm far removed from the bustle of Fifth Avenue.

More important, the building's interior arrangements coincided with its exterior image as a public building. Inside, the public catalogue room was given pride of place at the building's core. The importance of the room's function—to bring readers and books together through the medium of the card catalogue—was further reinforced by the room's generous proportions, square shape, and ample natural lighting. By the time they had moved into the main reading room to await delivery of their books, readers had also traversed the entire building, moving from bottom to top, and from front to back. Having moved through the building, the public (at least symbolically) possessed it.

The perceived role of the public library was hardly static in the last decades of the nineteenth century. Indeed, the public library figured

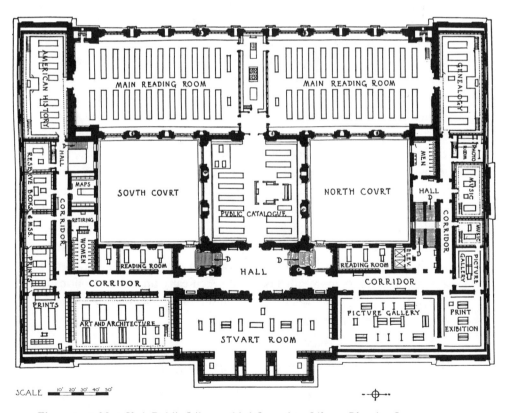

Figure 3.10 New York Public Library, third-floor plan. *Library Planning*, Jersey City, 1915, 143.

prominently in several, sometimes conflicting, versions of what American culture was, and where it was going. A native-born social elite continued to claim library building as their special ken. If anything, the steady erosion of their political power made them cling to culture as an important tool for preserving their influence in the public sphere. Marching under the banner of the American Renaissance, they identified themselves as the "saving remnant" of American culture, dedicated to protecting art and literature from the contaminating influence of commercialism and popular taste, while using art to maintain class distinctions that were being eroded in the modern world.[18]

In the same years, Progressives were attracted to the library for very different reasons. They were not interested in preserving culture from the taint of social change, but rather regarded culture and learning as immensely important tools for shaping the course of that change. Instead of attempting to use culture to highlight distinctions of class, religion, and ethnicity, the Progressive agenda focused on the library's potential to promote acculturation and its capacity to lessen social tensions by fostering a common culture based on middle-class values.[19]

Another important, but less often recognized function of public libraries at the turn of the century was the role they played in the labor agenda. Progressive assessments about immigrant illiteracy were unnecessarily bleak, based as they were on narrow definitions of reading that comprised only books in English. In fact, illiteracy rates in the United States dropped dramatically between 1890 and 1910, just as the immigration of non-English speakers rose substantially. What is more, many recent immigrants arrived in the United States as experienced library users and eager readers, particularly of literature, newspapers, and political pamphlets in their own languages.[20] Yet, their reading preferences rarely coincided with Progressive definitions of "self-improvement." So, while Progressive educational programs in the workplace provided ample reading material, this was typically technical information aimed at making workers more efficient, and specifically precluded politically motivated writing. For workers, the public library seemed to promise access to written information of all kinds.[21]

The Impact of the Carnegie Library Program

This widespread interest in public libraries helps explain the eagerness with which American municipalities sought Carnegie grants. There were also financial motives for accepting the terms of Carnegie's new philanthropic contract. Brought to the brink of financial ruin by the bust of the 1870s, many American cities had used conservative fiscal policies in the 1880s and 1890s to rebuild their financial stability. By 1900, municipal governments were in a better position to move forward on new ventures, but were still fiscally conservative enough to welcome the savings represented by Carnegie's gift of an expensive library building.[22]

If the building itself was a welcome addition, the conditions of a Carnegie grant were more problematic, particularly for library boards who were accustomed to treating the library as a proprietary preserve. Carnegie's requirement that elected officials involve themselves in library matters shifted the politics of culture. Being now more dependent on the good will of municipal officials, who were more susceptible to public pressure, library boards found it increasingly difficult to ignore working-class users. Since siting had a great deal to do with identifying the library's intended audience, Carnegie's insistence that the city provide the library site only intensified existing local conflicts about the library's role in the community.

The local political debate sparked by the Carnegie program is particularly clear in the case of Detroit. In 1901, Carnegie offered the city $750,000, specifying that half the sum was to be devoted to a central library, while the remainder was to be used for neighborhood branches. When the library commission moved to meet the usual requirements for library sites and an annual maintenance fund, the vehemence of public opposition prevented the council of aldermen from ratifying the commission's actions until 1910. Although the city aldermen borrowed the terminology of the "Tainted Money" controversy to suggest that the issue hinged on Carnegie's national reputation, cartoons that appeared in local papers revealed that the library offer touched sensitive chords closer to home. In "Joy on the Golf Links," Carnegie was depicted in full highland dress, approaching the walls of the city with a library building in hand (fig. 3.11). While the response of Detroit's taxpayers is not shown, Carnegie's arrival prompts four of Detroit's millionaires (one of whom bears a strong resemblance to Henry Ford) to dance with glee near their suburban estates. The implication is clear; the animosity towards Carnegie's offer was fueled by concerns that the institution would be shaped by the cultural agenda of the elite.[23]

In the months that followed, these local issues were depicted with growing specificity. In a cartoon published at the end of 1902, Carnegie (again in Highland dress) appears only as a small figure in the background, while the cartoon focuses on the figures representing the library

JOY ON THE GOLF LINKS.

"HURRAH! WHAT'S MORE APPROPRIATE FOR A BICENTENARY MEMORIAL THAN A NEW PUBLIC LIBRARY?"

Figure 3.11 Editorial cartoon critical of Carnegie's offer to finance library construction in Detroit. *Detroit News*, 2 July 1901.

commission and the city, facing one another across a pile of library buildings (fig. 3.12). These two main figures differ in every respect; the library commission is presented as a man, dressed in the dark top coat of an earlier era and stooped with age, while Detroit appears as a young woman, dressed in white, and bending under an enormous burden labeled "Taxes." The contrast not only suggests the extent of the gulf that existed between the ideas of the library commission and those of the city more generally, but it also roots that division in elite attempts to use the library to reassert lost power.

In their characterizations of Carnegie's intentions, the Detroit cartoons are only partially accurate. True, in the early years of the twentieth century, Carnegie had willingly financed the sort of large elaborate libraries cherished by the "saving remnant" as a means of preserving elite culture. In Detroit, St. Louis, and other cities, he had actually specified devoting half of the grant money to such a central library building. Yet, such gifts were relatively short-lived. After all, the preservation of elite culture had never been the primary purpose of this weaver's son, who was more interested in assisting other poor boys in pulling themselves up the ladder of commercial success. To bring philanthropic practice more in line with this goal (the same process that lead first to design review and later to the publication of the "Notes"), Carnegie ceased funding large central libraries by about 1908. Focusing instead on the building of branch libraries that brought books "close to the homes of the people," the Carnegie program encouraged the sort of institutional decentralization favored by Progressive librarians and municipal officials who drew their support from newly arrived immigrant populations.[24]

In short, the Carnegie program complicated the already complex politics of running cultural institutions in larger American cities, changing the dynamics of decision making without attempting to enforce a resolution between conflicting opinions. Indeed, most library boards were unwilling simply to abandon their commitment to the idea of the library as an elite preserve. Thus, their response to political pressure was not to reinvent the grand central library to make it more welcoming to working-class users. Instead, they embraced a two-tiered system of library facilities: a grand central library (built with or without Carnegie's financial help) in a City Beautiful setting, and more modest branches erected in working-class neighborhoods. In fact, the striking formal differences between the two kinds of urban libraries are material evidence of the continued tension between class-based ideas about library use specifically, and about urban amenities generally.

THE LIBRARY COM'N—"SURELY YOU OUGHT TO BE WILLING TO ADD THESE TO YOUR BURDEN, TO HELP ANDY BUILD ONE OF HIS MONUMENTS."

Figure 3.12 Editorial cartoon commenting on the conditions attached to a Carnegie grant. *Detroit Journal*, 10 December 1902.

Building the Central Library

Throughout the first decades of the twentieth century, the central library was the board's primary concern, the project on which they lavished money, time, and attention to detail. That combination could have resulted in innovative library designs. Indeed, since these urban library boards had ready access to professional expertise in both architectural and library matters, they were in the best position to translate "the modern library idea" into built form. Yet, in reality, they commissioned remarkably conservative library buildings, whose siting and design were informed by conservative, even reactionary, attitudes toward the library's role in urban life.

Whether built with Carnegie funds or not, central libraries were rarely located in the center of downtown. In a shift from the regular practice in the last quarter of the nineteenth century, the new central library building was typically affected by City Beautiful planning ideas: they were isolated from the city's existing commercial center either by physical distance, by their inclusion in new formally planned cultural centers, by open-lot siting, or by some combination of these factors. In Detroit, for instance, the Carnegie-financed central library was located two miles north of downtown, on an open lot, directly across the street from the new building for the Detroit Institute of Arts (fig. 3.13). Likewise, San Francisco's Carnegie-funded central library was part of a 1912 City Beautiful civic center scheme planned for a site one mile southwest of the city's central business district at Montgomery and Market Streets. Even Oakland, San Francisco's smaller neighbor, chose a central library site at Grove and 14th Streets, at the outer edge of the city's original nineteenth-century grid. In St. Louis, the central library was located on Olive Street, thirteen blocks from the Mississippi River and its commercial development, and distinguished from downtown by an open lot site that included a city park.[25]

To a certain extent, the library's appearance in these City Beautiful schemes reflects a new self-consciousness about the role of culture in the city. While the boosters and builders of late Victorian cities had acknowledged the value of culture in general terms, they had been content to erect stylistically distinct cultural institutions on individual sites dispersed throughout the urban grid. In contrast, their turn-of-the-century counterparts approached these issues with a new sense of urgency. Concerned about the physical and spiritual impact of the city's pursuit of material wealth, many Americans felt the need to reestablish

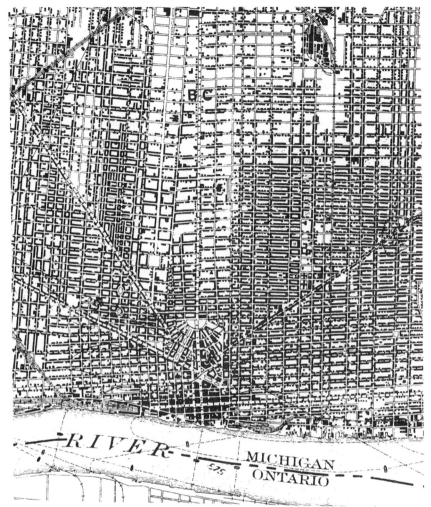

Figure 3.13 Plan of Detroit, showing (A) the location of the Detroit Public Library before Carnegie offer, (B) the location of the Carnegie-financed central building of the Detroit Public Library, dedicated in 1921, and (C) the location of the Detroit Institute of Arts, housed in a building designed by Paul Cret and dedicated in 1927. USGS map, 1917.

a balance between the interests of commerce and those of culture. To the extent that commercial development ultimately underwrote cultural activities, commerce was seen as a means to a higher purpose, just as cultural institutions were recognized "as part of a commercial strategy to win new residents and investments." [26] The physical balance of commerce and culture, however, seemed impossible to achieve in an urban core dominated by the vertical expansion of a great number of commercial skyscrapers. For many urbanites, the solution seemed to lie in City Beautiful schemes, which cleared urban space at some distance from the older urban grid and allowed for a grouping and coordination of civic and cultural buildings that expanded horizontally "to seize the ground," even as other aspects of these plans rationalized transportation and communication networks that facilitated commercial development.[27]

If these City Beautiful settings indicate a more self-conscious treatment of cultural institutions than ever before, they also reveal that the definition of culture and its intended audience had changed very little. City Beautiful cultural centers may have provided new urban space for cultural institutions, but their distance from the city suggests an ongoing concern with the sullying influence of the city. Located at a distance from the central business district and sometimes in close proximity to elite residential neighborhoods, the City Beautiful cultural center required most prospective patrons to make a special trip to reach it, reinforcing Victorian ideas of culture as its own special realm. To the extent that the central library site was remote from the hub of public transportation, it further limited library use by the city's working people, and helped preserve the library as an institution devoted to an elite audience. Although the open practice of racial discrimination was limited to Southern cities, cities throughout the country used physical distance as a means of filtering central library users by class.

This conservative conviction that the central library should be reserved for the use of the elite affected library design as well. Indeed, the majority of Carnegie-financed central libraries recall the great urban libraries built in the prosperous decades after the Civil War, when elite control over cultural matters went unchallenged. Eager to recapture these happier days and to prolong the vision of city life that they supported, the elite who dominated urban library boards were deliberately and proudly retrograde in their design decisions.

To begin the process, most big-city library boards settled upon an architectural competition as the best means for securing an appropriate design. Of the nineteen cities that received Carnegie funds for a central library and two or more branches, at least nine cities sponsored design competitions for the main building.[28]

At first glance, the decision to sponsor a competition was hardly noteworthy. Competitions for large public buildings, after all, had become commonplace by the end of the nineteenth century. Although they were more costly than other means of selecting an architect, competitions offered clients the chance to review a wide variety of formal solutions, a particularly important factor in the late nineteenth century when so many public building types were new or being dramatically redefined. By the early years of the twentieth century, however, competitions were falling out of favor. A tendency to conflate efficiency and economy prompted many clients to use less costly methods for selecting an architect. As we shall see, competitions were quickly becoming outmoded for library design in smaller towns and for urban branch libraries. The continued use of architectural competitions for central libraries in urban settings, therefore, was a deliberate anachronism.

Even more telling were the organizational strategies that library boards used to affect the outcome of these competitions. Competitions with invitational phases, for instance, gave boards the opportunity to include the designers of buildings that they particularly admired. When AIA guidelines called for professional advisors, board members had an added opportunity to select an architect-advisor whose ideas of library design paralleled their own, and to give him a role that wielded great influence over the final product. Thus, without fixing the competition per se, library boards ensured that the winning design would fall within a narrow range of formal solutions.

Detroit provides a particularly clear example of this process. There, when it came time to secure a building design in 1912, three of the library commissioners joined the librarian and deputy librarian on a Carnegie-financed fact-finding tour of libraries in Springfield (Massachusetts), Brooklyn, New York City, Newark, Philadelphia, Washington, D.C. (both the Library of Congress and the Carnegie-funded public library), Pittsburgh, and St. Louis.[29] This last building, designed by Cass Gilbert, impressed them particularly (figs. 3.14 and 3.15). Concerned that the library should serve to help the city maintain its reputation "as one of the foremost cities of the land," the delegation insisted "that Detroit cannot afford to stand for anything mean or picayunish." Thus, despite the fact that Gilbert's design had cost almost five times the amount of Detroit's appropriation, the delegation specified the St. Louis library as "of about the right character and size for Detroit." Accordingly, the commission substantially revised its requirements for Detroit's central library building. Convinced that the city should "make up its mind to furnish a considerable addition to the $375,000 offered by Mr. Carnegie," the commission began to envision a library of at least 750,000 volumes to accommodate a city with twice Detroit's existing population.[30]

In addition to rewriting the program requirements, the Detroit library

Figure 3.14 Cass Gilbert, St. Louis Public Library, St. Louis, 1907–12. Postcard from author's collection.

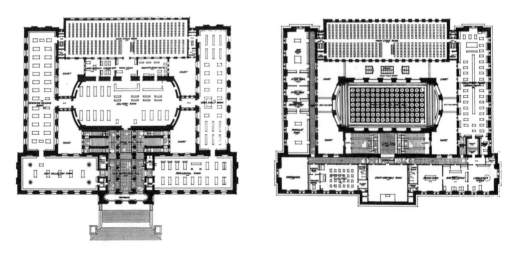

Figure 3.15 St. Louis Public Library, (*left*) first- and (*right*) second-floor plans. *American Architect* 101 (13 March 1912).

commissioners then organized a competition in order to secure a design like the St. Louis library. To begin with, they hired Frank Miles Day to act as professional advisor for the competition.[31] A past president of the AIA whose Philadelphia firm had designed buildings at Princeton, Cornell, and the University of Pennsylvania, Day had also served on the jury that had selected Gilbert to design the St. Louis library. On Day's advice, the commissioners agreed to a two-phase competition, which allowed invited architects to circumvent the highly competitive initial stage. Thus, Gilbert and other classically-minded architects from out of town (including McKim, Mead & White; Carrère & Hastings; and H. Van Buren Magonigle) proceeded directly to the final judging.[32] Finally, the commissioners' choice of jurors helped slant the competition in the direction they wanted. The three-man jury included Paul Cret, who had already been hired as the architect of the Detroit Art Museum, Herbert Putnam, the Librarian of Congress, and J. Lawrence Mauran, an architect and a member of the Public Library Board of St. Louis. Thus, when the commission upheld the jury's choice of project number three, it was little surprise that the anonymous project turned out to be that of Cass Gilbert (figs. 3.16–3.21).[33]

Notable here is the absence of Bertram's planning advice. In truth, Carnegie-funded central library buildings were the least affected by their status as Carnegie libraries. Even after 1908, when design review was a required part of the funding process, central libraries continued to reflect a concern with monumentality that went quite against the principles of efficiency that Bertram espoused so forcefully for other library

Figure 3.16 Cass Gilbert, Detroit Public Library, Detroit, 1913–21. Courtesy of the Burton Historical Collection of the Detroit Public Library.

types. An important part of the explanation is that the library profession was unable to resolve opposing philosophies of the arrangement of large urban libraries that had first been articulated in the 1870s and 1880s. One school supported the idea of centralizing all books in stacks, a solution that maximized book storage capabilities but that also required staff time to fetch books for readers, who were forced to wait in the delivery area. The opposing camp preferred a room system, with books stored in a series of rooms, organized by subject and fitted with shelves open to the reading public. By the turn of the century, most central urban libraries were an uneasy combination of the two types, and Bertram was left

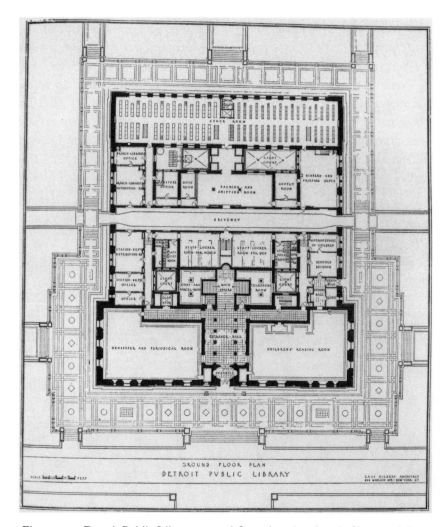

Figure 3.17 Detroit Public Library, ground-floor plan. *American Architect* 120 (28 September 1921).

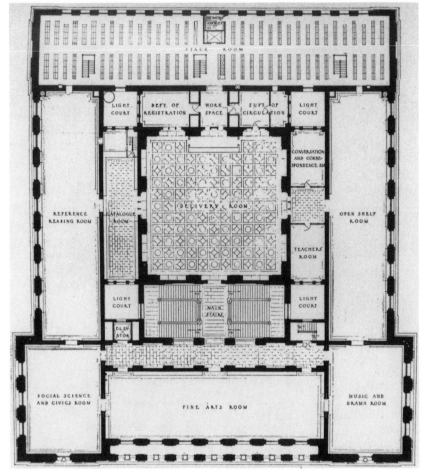

Figure 3.18 Detroit Public Library, second-floor plan. *American Architect* 120 (28 September 1921).

without a clear-cut model upon which to build an unshakable body of planning advice.[34]

Worse yet, from Bertram's point of view, the leaders of the library profession found it difficult to attack the monumentality of central libraries. Dependent upon the good will of the library boards who employed them, librarians were sensitive to the importance that these groups attached to an imposing public library building. At the same time, many librarians were increasingly aware that the grand spaces and private offices of the nineteenth-century library offered architectural reinforcement for their own professional status, just at the time that it was threatened by a sharp increase in the number of female librarians.

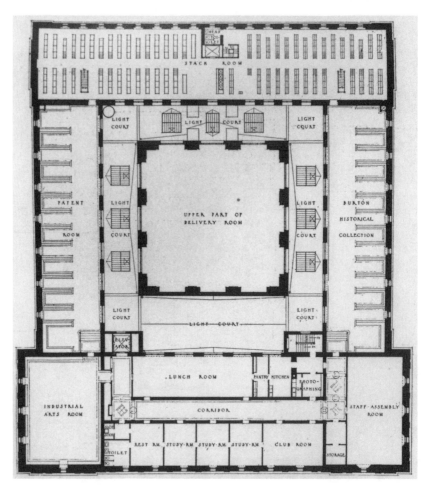

Figure 3.19 Detroit Public Library, third-floor plan. *American Architect* 120 (28 September 1921).

The difficulty in evaluating the design of central library buildings is evident in the thinking of Cleveland's librarian, William Brett. A staunch advocate of efficiency in library design and one of the librarians to whom Bertram turned for support and professional expertise, Brett waffled when confronted with Gilbert's plans for the Detroit library (see figs. 3.17–3.19). Although several elements of the plan (particularly a central delivery area and monumental stairways) would have been unacceptable in the design of small libraries, Brett refrained from condemning them outright, stating instead, "Personally, I do not regard any of these things as necessary, but I am aware that a majority of architects and librarians would so regard them. If I accept these as a consensus of opinion, I can heartily commend the details of the plan, for the architect and the librarian seem to have worked together to provide rooms adequate in the main and conveniently arranged for the work of the library." In contrast with the detailed comments on branch libraries that he had given Bertram in the past, Brett's only firmly held opinion on Gilbert's plan was that a single elevator would be insufficient for the patrons' use. Even when his convictions that library plans should be strictly functional led him back to the issue of the monumental stairs and delivery area, Brett again admitted that the architect "followed accepted ideas of library construction." [35] Without the accustomed support of professional opinion, Bertram was unwilling or unable to enforce his own well-developed antipathy to monumentality in library design. He approved Gilbert's plans for Detroit without requiring a single revision, despite an estimated budget that was over three times the size of the Carnegie

Figure 3.20 Detroit Public Library, delivery room. Courtesy of the Burton Historical Collection of the Detroit Public Library.

Figure 3.21 Detroit Public Library, children's room. Courtesy of the Burton Historical Collection of the Detroit Public Library.

grant. In a compromise that became increasingly common in dealing with central library buildings, Bertram allowed the city to make up the difference between the amount of the Carnegie grant and the amount they wanted to spend.[36]

Designed and built independently of the planning principles usually advocated by the Carnegie program, central libraries in urban centers reflected local priorities and desires more directly than other library types constructed with Carnegie money. Yet, local autonomy did not lead to a wide variety of design solutions, and geographical, cultural, and social differences between regions are not immediately apparent in these large central libraries. Indeed, whether we look at Washington, D.C., Atlanta, Detroit, St. Louis, San Francisco, or the handful of other cities that used Carnegie monies for a central library, the buildings fall within a remarkably narrow range. Large, rectangular blocks of granite or marble, articulated with monumental classical elements, central libraries in the early twentieth century were modeled on the great cultural institutions of a previous generation. Their forms reveal the extent to which elite library boards accepted definitions of culture and cultural expression that had been forged in the Northeast in the last decades of the nineteenth century.

In their exterior images, virtually all of these central libraries reveal the influence of either the Boston Public Library or the New York Public Library. Detroit, Elizabeth (New Jersey), Springfield (Massachusetts), San Francisco (California), and others adopted the Italian palazzo formula, suggesting that Boston's nineteenth-century leadership in cultural matters was still respected in many circles (figs. 3.22–3.25). Yet, this reputation cut two ways, for Boston's twenty-year-old building could equally well suggest cultural parochialism and stodginess. In Southern cities, old rivalries with New England offered even less incentive to follow Boston's example. In contrast, New York's library building was much newer (it was under construction until 1911) and seemed to match that city's more cosmopolitan reputation. Atlanta, Washington, D.C., Nashville, and St. Louis were among the cities that chose to emu-

Figure 3.22 Edward L. Tilton, Elizabeth Public Library, Elizabeth, New Jersey, opened 1912. *Library Journal* 37 (September 1912): opp. 489.

late New York's triumphal arch motif, which soon emerged as the clear favorite (figs. 3.26–3.30).[37]

Exterior image and interior organization, however, were not identical. Indeed, library boards rarely followed the example of Boston or New York consistently inside and out. Instead, they faced the issues of exte-

Figure 3.23 Edward L. Tilton, Springfield Public Library, Springfield, Massachusetts, 1907–12. *Public Libraries* 17 (March 1912): frontispiece.

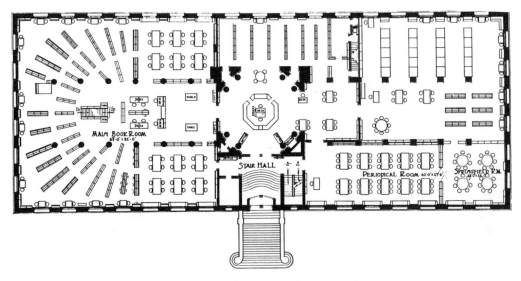

Figure 3.24 Springfield Public Library, first-floor plan. *Library Planning*, Jersey City, 1915, 203.

Figure 3.25 George K. Kelham, San Francisco Public Library, central building, opened 1917. Postcard from author's collection.

rior image, planning, and the user's experience of the library as a set of independent variables, to be combined freely to meet the needs of the modern library in their own communities.

Cass Gilbert's library design career makes the independence of image and plan evident. His 1907 design for the St. Louis Public Library was modeled loosely but consistently on the New York Public Library. Indeed, a simplified version of New York's triumphal arch graced the entrance pavilion, while the interior also followed the New York example with a public catalogue centrally located in a brilliantly lit delivery room (see figs. 3.14 and 3.15). Six years later, Gilbert designed the Detroit Public Library with a remarkably similar plan (see figs. 3.18–3.20), but gave the building an exterior image modeled directly on Boston's example (see fig. 3.16).

As telling as it is about Gilbert's approach to library planning, the similarity between the St. Louis and Detroit plans also reflects the priorities of his patrons. That Detroit's library commissioners had expressed their admiration of the St. Louis building, that they had organized a competition which all but guaranteed Gilbert's success, and that they then selected a design with a very different exterior image—together these facts suggest that the members of this library board made their

Figure 3.26 Ackerman and Ross, Atlanta Public Library, central building, Atlanta, Georgia, opened 1902 (demolished). Koch, *Book of Carnegie Libraries* (1917).

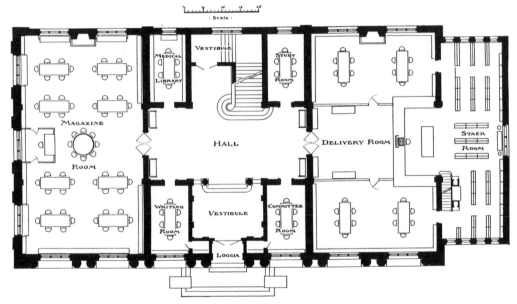

Figure 3.27 Atlanta Public Library, central building, first-floor plan. Koch, *Book of Carnegie Libraries* (1917).

selection specifically on the basis of planning, and placed less importance on the facade alone. What is more, a review of many comparable institutions suggests that Detroit's commissioners were not alone. Like them, many urban library boards selected designs that incorporated the outward symbols of public service, even as they provided architectural screens that helped reserve the majority of the library for middle-class use.

To begin with, new central libraries tended to emulate New York's focus on delivery and public catalogue areas. Gilbert's designs for St. Louis and Detroit followed New York's very closely. In both cases, the location of the closed stack at the rear of the building is modeled on the innovations introduced in New York, as is the central location of the public catalogue in a square delivery room amply lit by high windows on three sides (see fig. 3.20). Although the lateral reference room and open shelf room are not modeled directly on either Boston or New York, the fact that Gilbert used a narrow band of circulation space and staff rooms to insulate these quiet rooms from the bustle of the delivery area suggests an appreciation for New York's functional zoning and attention to noise control.

Many other central libraries emulated New York's planning priorities, even if they did not use its specific forms directly. Competitions for central libraries in Washington, D.C. (1899), and Louisville, Kentucky (1902), both resulted in winning plans with footprints in the shape of an inverted T—the stem devoted to staff areas and closed stacks, with the crosspiece reserved for public rooms (see fig. 3.29). As the room where staff, books, and patrons interacted with greatest regularity, the delivery

Figure 3.28 Ackerman and Ross, Washington, D.C., Public Library, central building, Washington, D.C., 1901–3. Courtesy of Washingtoniana Division, D.C. Public Library.

room was located at the point of intersection for functional reasons. At the same time, its central location on the primary axis of each building gave it a symbolic prominence considered appropriate for public libraries.[38]

New standards of library service soon rendered stacks obsolete and transformed the delivery room into a charging area, but central libraries still clung to nineteenth-century architectural conventions for expressing the library's role in public enlightenment. In the new libraries in Nashville, Tennessee (designed by Ackerman and Ross in 1904), and Elizabeth, New Jersey (designed by Edward L. Tilton in 1912), the charging areas were top-lit, double-height spaces that reinforced the symbolic importance of their central locations (fig. 3.31). Tilton's 1912 design for the central library in Springfield, Massachusetts, was perhaps the most radical central library plan built with Carnegie funds (see fig. 3.24). Indeed, its Italian palazzo image disguised a first-floor plan that

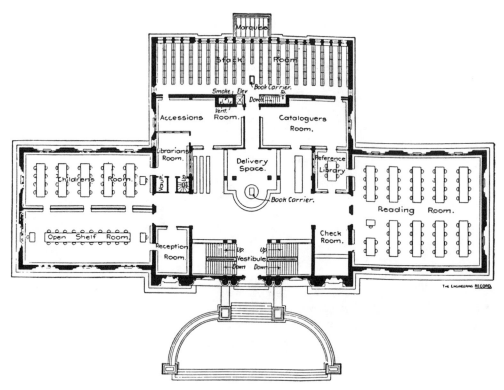

Figure 3.29 Washington, D.C., Public Library, central building, first-floor plan. Koch, *Book of Carnegie Libraries* (1917).

Figure 3.30 Ackerman and Ross, Nashville Carnegie Library, central building, Nashville, Tennessee, opened 1904. *Book of Carnegie Libraries* (1917).

was completely open to public use, and almost without interior partitions. Yet, even here, the delivery desk stood in a double-height space bathed in "a beautiful mellow light" from an amber-tinted glass dome.[39]

At the same time, these elaborate architectural symbols of the central library's public mission were precisely that—symbols. The Springfield example aside, central libraries were the least responsive to the planning implications of the modern library idea, and were particularly slow to allow the public open access to books. In truth, book stacks were a functional necessity, allowing central libraries to store their substantial collections in a relatively small space. For the most part, however, these stacks remained off limits to readers. In Atlanta, the library continued the practice of the 1880s, requiring readers to request books at a delivery counter that physically barred their access to the book storage area (see fig. 3.27). St. Louis, Detroit, Washington, and Louisville followed the more common pattern of maintaining a small open-shelf room, while storing the majority of th book collection in closed stacks (see figs. 3.15, 3.18, and 3.29). In the rare cases where readers were allowed to enter the stacks, their movements were regulated either by architectural fittings or library policy. In Nashville, turnstiles controlled the entrance to

Figure 3.31 Nashville Carnegie Library, central building, lobby. Koch, *Book of Carnegie Libraries* (1917).

the stacks, while in Elizabeth readers were barred from the upper floors of the stacks where they could not be monitored from the delivery desk.

Even in public areas, central libraries did not welcome all readers with equal enthusiasm. Indeed, most library boards (and the head librarians whom they employed) expressed their sense that the public was divided into two groups, serious readers, or "scholars," and casual visitors. Their written descriptions further reveal that the difference between these two groups was not the frequency with which they used the library, but the sort of reading they did there. Serious readers were those who consulted reference materials and read nonfiction books, whether in the arts and humanities or the fields of science and technology, while casual visitors came to the library with "no particular book or subjects in mind." By this definition, serious readers tended to be middle-class city-dwellers, searching for ways to enhance their business concerns, or using their leisure time in the pursuit of highbrow culture.

In contrast, "casual" reading coincided with working-class reading habits (like reading the daily newspaper in the library), or with middle-class assumptions about working-class reading habits (like a preference for fiction). What was left unsaid was that library boards actively reinforced this class-based hierarchy of readers by commissioning buildings that isolated middle-class users from both the messy realities of library service and the less genteel library users.[40]

How did this spatial segregation work? In Detroit, for instance, those spaces most closely associated with middle-class readers were given the most prominent locations (see fig. 3.18). The fine arts room stood behind the grand arcade of the street facade, while flanking rooms devoted to social science and civics, and to music and drama were articulated on the exterior by projecting pavilions and classical urns. Inside, these rooms also stood at the culmination of the building's impressive ceremonial entry sequence.

In contrast, working areas for the library staff were removed as much as possible from the magnificent hall on the ground floor. Although three-quarters of the ground floor was devoted to service spaces, they were carefully hidden from view, reached only through small doors at the end of the lateral hallways which extended away from the entrance hall (see fig. 3.17). A mezzanine level between the ground and second floors was devoted exclusively to service areas, while the staff assembly and lunch rooms were relegated to the third floor (see fig. 3.19). To encourage the separation of staff and user areas, a distinct service stair allowed the library staff to move between floors without recourse to the main stair.

Like staff areas, rooms designed for working-class users were located so as to minimize their connections to the grand entrance hall and first floor. The newspaper and periodical room, for instance, was located on the ground floor (see fig. 3.17). Its door in the southeast corner of the entrance hall was as close as possible to the front door, which allowed library users who intended only to read the daily paper to slip in and out of the library without traversing the entrance hall or mounting the monumental stairs. The industrial arts room and the patent room, on the other hand, were hidden from view on the top floor, near staff assembly and lunch rooms (see fig. 3.19). Since the main stair did not give access to this floor, the users of these collections were required to use the elevator, which was located conveniently near the back door of the newspaper room.

Surprisingly enough, children were given only a slightly warmer welcome. Located just across the hall from the newspaper room, the children's room provided its young patrons with a fireplace flanked by reading benches (see fig. 3.21). The only fireplace in the building, it was decorated with art tiles from Detroit's Pewabic Pottery depicting classic children's stories, including Hansel and Gretel, Alice in Wonderland, Tar Baby and Br'er Rabbit, Pocahontas, and Robinson Crusoe. Despite these homey touches, the children's room was not fully integrated into the library proper. Instead, it had an outside door and entrance hall on the north side of the building, completely separate from the Woodward Avenue entrance. The purpose, as librarian Strohm reminded Gilbert in 1913, was to give the children "no chance of over-flowing into the other part of the building." Without the separate entrance, Strohm noted, "I am sure it would be difficult to keep them away from other departments."[41] The idea was not to protect children from other library users, but to ensure that the genteel library user enjoyed the illusion of ordered and serene opulence that the architect, librarian, and library commissioners had worked to create in the stage set that they thought of as the real library.

Not every central library shared Detroit's highly developed plan. Yet, even less elaborate buildings followed a similar principle of spatial segregation. In St. Louis, basement rooms catered to the needs of children and "casual" newspaper readers, who could reach this lower level directly through a number of ground level entrances, without ever mounting the grand exterior stairs. In Atlanta, Washington, and Nashville, children were likewise relegated to the basement, and encouraged to use direct, street-level doors. The central library in Louisville also housed newspaper readers in the basement and provided them with an exterior door beneath the main entrance pavilion. Here, the children's room shared the second floor with a classroom and a teacher's room, and did not interfere with the quiet reading of their elders.

Central libraries, then, were complex buildings. Indeed, for all their references to the art of the past, they were also buildings informed with the modern concern for engineering. This engineering controlled the flow of books, of course; but, it also channeled the flow of people as well. Siphoned off at the door, "casual" reachers were not encouraged to experience either the full extent of the building or the full range of its symbolism. Inscriptions carved in stone over their doors might identify them as Universities for the People, but in reality central libraries catered only to a narrow segment of the city's population.

Building Branch Libraries

If grand central libraries did not cater to working-class readers, other library facilities did. In the last years of the nineteenth century, branch libraries became a regular part of the public service offered by libraries in larger cities. Philadelphia, Chicago, Cleveland, Cincinnati, and St. Louis are just a few examples of cities that maintained either storefront branch libraries or more modest book deposit stations (often on the shelves of drug stores) prior to 1900. Part of a Progressive-era drive for decentralization aimed at bringing parks, playgrounds, and other urban amenities into slum neighborhoods, this explosion of library facilities was fueled by middle-class settlement workers and their willingness to experiment with unconventional means for disseminating culture. By the first decade of the twentieth century, working-class readers could satisfy a yen to read in a wide range of settings throughout the city, including home libraries, reading clubs, special children's rooms, school libraries, and libraries established at summer playgrounds.[42]

Although the practice of decentralizing cultural institutions did not originate with Carnegie, his library philanthropy certainly contributed to the process. Sizable cash gifts could enable municipal library boards to implement innovative library service programs that might have gone unexecuted under other circumstances. More important, by providing funds for purpose-built branch libraries, Carnegie funds formalized the practice of decentralized library service and gave it a more permanent presence.[43]

Branch libraries, however, remained controversial institutions. Debates about their proper social role and architectural form were common, and reveal much about the contrasting attitudes toward workers as a class. To the extent that he interpreted poverty as the outward sign of inner failings, Carnegie remained wary of most working-class readers. Nonetheless, he maintained his faith in the library's ability to help worthy individuals toward self-improvement. The social elite who tended to dominate library boards certainly shared Carnegie's suspicions of working-class readers. Yet, having already experienced the erosion of their leadership roles in municipal affairs, they were less enthusiastic about seeing working-class library users get ahead. Library leaders who advised these boards did not necessarily share these opinions. Indeed, to the extent that they linked their professional status to the library's social usefulness, librarians had a vested interest in emphasizing the library's power to change lives. Designed in response to these conflicts, the library branches built between 1895 and 1920 reveal the evolution of these attitudes, the shifting power of the groups involved, and the points of tangency in their attitudes.

Pittsburgh: Andrew Carnegie and the Branch Library

Carnegie's support for branch libraries began in the first phase of his philanthropic career. As early as 1887, he offered to donate one million dollars to the city of Pittsburgh, three hundred thousand of which he anticipated for the construction of branch libraries. In the second phase of his library program, Carnegie's interest in branch libraries became even more pronounced. Indeed, the library grant that marked the dramatic change in Carnegie's library philanthropy was his 1899 gift of over five million dollars to New York City, specifically to build sixty-six branch library buildings to supplement the work of the central library. Carnegie continued to specify that large cities use a portion of his gift for branch buildings until 1908. At that time, Carnegie's interest in "bringing books close to the homes of the people" prompted him to discontinue the funding of large central libraries altogether in favor of branch libraries.[44]

Carnegie's enthusiasm for branch libraries, however, was hardly the same as enthusiasm for working-class readers. Indeed, Carnegie's distrust of American workers had been sharpened by the labor actions that rocked American industry at the end of the century, and particularly by the violent strike at the Carnegie steel works in Homestead in 1892 that erupted when management ousted the union and lowered the minimum pay threshold on the sliding scale that linked wages to the price of steel. Rather than question his own actions as an employer, Carnegie interpreted the strike as an indication of the low caliber of the workmen employed by the plant's previous corporate owner.[45] At the same time, Carnegie refused to see the strike as a response to systemic inequalities that affected an entire class, focusing instead on the issue of individual character. Lacking a class analysis, Carnegie's understanding of social reform pulled his library philanthropy in contradictory directions: he felt branch libraries were necessary to give individuals the opportunity to improve themselves, yet, as only a small number of workers had sufficient strength of character, Carnegie also assumed that many branch library users simply could not be trusted.

Carnegie's contradictory attitudes about the role of branch libraries had their greatest impact on the design of Pittsburgh's branches. Although Carnegie had made the offer in 1887 (before the Homestead strike), the city did not act on the offer until 1890, when the Carnegie-appointed board of trustees began work on the main library. A subcommittee on branch libraries was appointed four years later, and had six branches well under way when Carnegie hired James Bertram as his personal secretary in 1897. As a result, Pittsburgh's earliest Carnegie-financed branches remained largely independent of the professional library advice that Bertram later introduced into discussions of library design.[46]

The choice of architect suggests that Carnegie's views were well represented in Pittsburgh's branches. Frank E. Alden had originally come to Pittsburgh in 1885 as supervising architect of H. H. Richardson's Allegheny County Courthouse. His own firm of Longfellow, Alden & Harlow won the competition for the design of Pittsburgh's main library, and impressed Carnegie with their close attention to that project's budget. Alden carried on a cordial correspondence with the philanthropist throughout the 1890s, and may have been responsible for securing commissions for a number of Carnegie-funded projects built by his firm in the Pittsburgh area, including the Carnegie Library in Homestead (1896–98) and the addition to the Carnegie Library in Braddock (1893). Indeed, Carnegie's patronage facilitated the cordial dissolution of the firm in 1896; newly independent from their Boston-based partner, the firm of Alden & Harlow did a thriving business in Carnegie-financed projects, designing the massive extension to Pittsburgh's Carnegie Institute, as well as all eight library branches in Pittsburgh.[47]

An important issue for the architects to face was that of exterior image. How was the branch library to communicate to its working-class neighbors that this was a library specifically for their use? After all, the palazzo format of the Boston Public Library and the monumental triumphal arch of the New York Public Library did not always seem welcoming to working-class readers. Alden & Harlow's response to the problem was to develop an exterior expression that revealed the building's function, independent from analogies to other functional types. As Alden knew from his earlier professional experience, this procedure had been used by Richardson in the 1870s and 1880s to create small-town libraries, recognizable on the exterior by the combination of a tower, an arch, and a group of windows placed high in the wall of the book wing (fig. 3.32). Indeed, the Pittsburgh branches drew very specifically on two of these three elements. Four of the six original Carnegie branches had arched doorways, while the high-set grouped windows were used with

Figure 3.32 Henry Hobson Richardson, Oliver Ames Memorial Library, North Easton, Massachusetts, 1877–78. Courtesy of the Department of Printing and Graphic Arts, The Houghton Library, Harvard University.

increasing emphasis in all six (figs. 3.33–3.38). Reminiscent of the pronounced gable that graced the entry of Richardson's mature library designs, a classical pediment broke the eave line in each of the Pittsburgh branches.[48]

Richardson's example, however, was only a starting point for Alden & Harlow, who manipulated their model to meet the special requirements of the Pittsburgh commission. To begin with, they rendered Richardson's library elements in a variety of classical vocabularies and ordered them in a strictly symmetrical system. In this way, Carnegie's architects divested their libraries of the domestic connotations that had appealed to the paternalistic philanthropist of 1880, and allowed the buildings to convey their public nature to prospective readers. Opting against the stone they had used on the city's main library building, Alden & Harlow specified brick as the dominant building material, fitting their branch buildings into the existing fabric of their neighborhoods.

Figure 3.33 Alden & Harlow, Carnegie Library of Pittsburgh, Lawrenceville Branch, Pittsburgh, opened 1898. Courtesy of Carnegie Library, Pittsburgh.

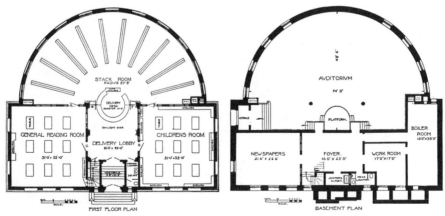

Figure 3.34 Carnegie Library of Pittsburgh, Lawrenceville Branch, (*left*) first-floor and (*right*) basement plans. Koch, *Book of Carnegie Libraries* (1917).

Inside, Carnegie's Pittsburgh branches offered prospective readers facilities that were lacking in the main library. For instance, Longfellow, Alden & Harlow's winning design for Pittsburgh's main library made no special accommodation for young readers in 1890; only in 1896 was a room adapted for their use. Yet, beginning in 1894, the same architects working for a subset of the same client group incorporated children's rooms into the designs of all working-class branches (figs. 3.39 and 3.40; and see figs. 3.34 and 3.36). In part, the difference is the product of developments in ideas about library planning in general. Yet, the prominence of children's rooms in branch libraries also reflect Anglo-Americans' special anxiety about the influx of immigrants from eastern and southern Europe. Noting the ease with which the young learned new languages, Anglo-Americans hoped that immigrant children could be easily Americanized through contact with English-language literature, even when their parents held on to familiar cultural traditions with great tenacity.[49]

Faith in books' transformative power led to the adoption of an open-shelf policy in all of Pittsburgh's branches. Yet, Carnegie's ambivalence toward working-class readers also prompted the use of architectural devices to control the interaction between the reader and the book. The

Figure 3.35 Alden & Harlow, Carnegie Library of Pittsburgh, Hazelwood Branch, Pittsburgh, 1899–1900. Courtesy of Carnegie Library, Pittsburgh.

first of Pittsburgh's branch buildings, the Lawrenceville branch, demonstrates the range of such devices (see fig. 3.34). Open stacks allowed readers the freedom to retrieve their own books, yet the radial placement of the shelves meant that the librarian at the circulation desk could monitor this freedom. Reading rooms were separated from the delivery lobby only by low partitions, which extended surveillance to these areas as well. Indeed, so important was this visual surveillance that the desk itself was circular in form, allowing the librarian to conduct her clerical and supervisory roles simultaneously, and suggesting an all-seeing presence, even when temporarily unstaffed.[50]

At the Lawrenceville branch, visual supervision was reinforced with actual physical control of the reader's movements. Although doors led directly from the delivery lobby into both reading rooms, these doors were kept closed. Since the only other doors to these rooms were in the stack room, each reader was compelled to navigate the narrow passages directly adjacent to the circulation desk, where one-way turnstiles slowed traffic and increased the librarian's ability to question individual readers.

Not all of Pittsburgh's branches had the range of controlling devices used at Lawrenceville. The Hazelwood, West End, and Mt. Washington branches were built without radial stacks altogether (see figs. 3.36, 3.39

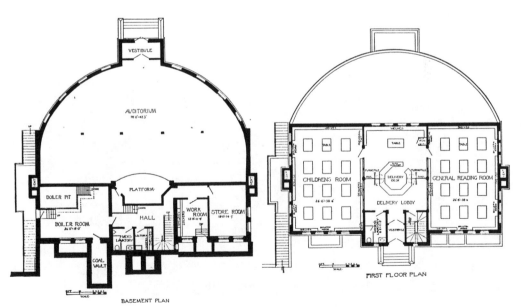

Figure 3.36 Carnegie Library of Pittsburgh, Hazelwood Branch, (*right*) first-floor and (*left*) basement plans. Koch, *Book of Carnegie Libraries* (1917).

and 3.40). Small reference rooms took their place in the center of the rear of the building, while books were stored on shelves lining the reading rooms walls. This plan type, however, is a variation motivated by economy rather than a departure from Lawrenceville's design principles. In all three cases, low room partitions and centralized circulation

Figure 3.37 Alden & Harlow, Carnegie Library of Pittsburgh, Wylie Avenue Branch, Pittsburgh, 1899. Courtesy of Carnegie Library, Pittsburgh.

Figure 3.38 Alden & Harlow, Carnegie Library of Pittsburgh, West End Branch, Pittsburgh, opened 1899. Courtesy of Carnegie Library, Pittsburgh.

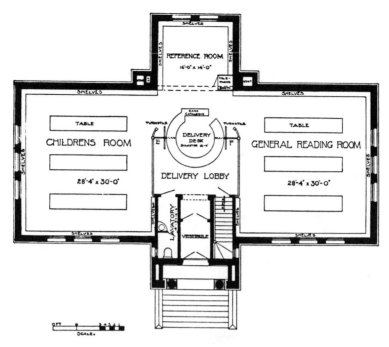

Figure 3.39 Carnegie Library of Pittsburgh, West End Branch, first-floor plan. Koch, *Book of Carnegie Libraries* (1917).

desks facilitated visual supervision, while one-way turnstiles continued to control access to all reading and book-storage areas. The radial stack continued to be the ideal; at Hazelwood, the semicircular rear wall of the basement auditorium was intended to accommodate a radial stack room in a future enlargement.

In addition to discouraging the theft of books, these early branches were also intended to encourage patterns of behavior favored by the middle class. Whether aimed at young or old, reading rooms offered readers an orderly space with tables regimented in neat rows. Period photographs depict readers in approved postures, seated with both feet on the floor, chair pulled up close to the table, and with their attention focused on the books immediately in front of them (see fig. 5.7 below). At the Mt. Washington branch, the application of middle-class values extended even beyond encouraging approved postures; there a basin in the corner of the children's reading room enabled librarians to oversee the washing of the faces and hands of their young charges.[51] In this context, the branch library was more than a place to learn to read. It also served as a training ground in middle-class behavior, preparing working-class readers to fit in at school, at work, or at church. In a sense, Carnegie's brand of reform did not serve to eradicate poverty per se, but worked on eradicating its outward appearance.

Coping with Class: The Library Board and the Branch Library

Urban library boards greeted Carnegie's evolving policies with mixed emotions. After all, their support for cultural institutions sprang from a

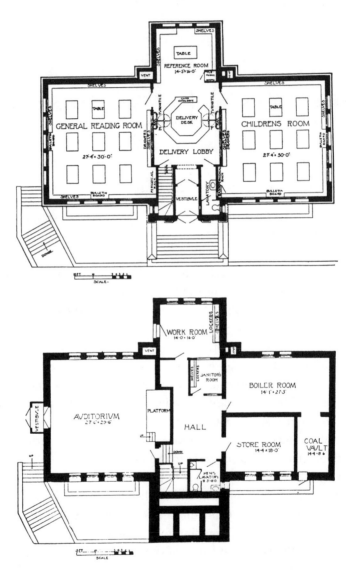

Figure 3.40 Alden & Harlow, Carnegie Library of Pittsburgh, Mt. Washington Branch, Pittsburgh, 1899–1900, (*upper*) first-floor and (*lower*) basement plans. Koch, *Book of Carnegie Libraries*, (1917).

very different source than Carnegie's. Faced with the erosion of the political power that their families had wielded in the nineteenth century, a new generation of the social elite had begun founding cultural institutions to legitimize the newly-created rift between highbrow and lowbrow forms of culture from the 1880s on. Still the dominant voice on governing boards in the early decades of the twentieth century, this social elite saw libraries and museums as settings for the demonstration of taste, which they considered to be an in-born tendency toward aesthetic and literary appreciation. Seeking to use culture to maintain class distinctions, urban library boards found themselves in direct conflict with Carnegie's goals of establishing branch libraries to facilitate upward mobility.

If library boards hoped to use Carnegie funds to finance the "serious" reading of their middle-class neighbors, the intensity with which working-class voters (like those in Detroit) expressed their displeasure at using public funds to support library endeavors was a formidable obstacle to their plans. Under these conditions, branch libraries emerged as double-pronged political tools. They could first be used to convince working-class voters of their stake in library appropriations, and in this way facilitate the process of securing a Carnegie gift; afterwards, they could be used to rationalize the middle-class focus of the central library.

To the extent that they viewed branch libraries as political expediencies, library boards devoted less than their full attention to the process of locating sites and securing architectural designs. They spent less time on these matters in their meetings, relied more heavily on the advice of their librarians, and adopted a variety of policies that allowed them to streamline their decision making. The unintended result of this relative indifference was a group of library buildings that responded positively to contemporary theories of library service and design.

The process of selecting library sites held the greatest political danger for library boards. Eager to avoid accusations of favoritism, library boards resorted to a range of selection processes that cloaked their actions in the respectable clothing of objectivity and fairness. In Detroit, for instance, the library board distributed that city's six original Carnegie-financed branches at regularly spaced intervals in a crescent that roughly paralleled the course of Grand Boulevard as it ringed the city approximately two to three miles from the downtown.

In Oakland, California, the site selection process depended more on the professional assessment of library needs. Branch libraries had first been established there in 1891, and by the time Carnegie financed the building of permanent branches in 1914, their number had grown to ten. The locations of these rented quarters were carefully calculated by the library staff. Indeed, just the year before Carnegie extended his branch offer to Oakland, the head of the city branch-library department mapped the residences of "an average number of borrowers from each branch." Finding that "one or two of the oldest branches were no longer in the center of the districts they served," she adjusted accordingly, moving one of the branches a mere two blocks to provide better service to the existing population.[52] When it came time to locate the four Carnegie-financed branches, the library board listened to public input over a two-month period, and were even swayed by the lobbying efforts of the middle-class residents of the Melrose district who were anxious to obtain a branch for themselves.[53] Nonetheless, the board was guided by the locations of existing branches, and exercised their preference for the Melrose district only when it coincided with the more objective recommendations of the library's professional staff.

The nature of the sites selected reinforced the difference in treatment between central libraries and neighborhood branches. Although branch libraries were intended for residential neighborhoods, they extended the American planning tradition of setting public buildings in the center of open lots. The Carnegie branches in Manhattan were the exceptions; there the siting of branch libraries was constrained by the relentless urban grid. Even with their generous swaths of surrounding lawn, however, branch sites in residential neighborhoods were substantially smaller, less costly, and less elaborate than the central library's City Beautiful locale. In Detroit, for instance, the six original branch sites ranged in price from $2,500 for the Conely branch to $10,500 for the Bowen branch. With a combined price of $40,880, all six branch sites cost a fraction of the $1,194,349.72 that the same board spent on the main library site.[54]

To the extent that they saw branch libraries as political necessities, library boards were less concerned with the specifics of their built forms, and further distanced themselves from the process once sites were selected. In direct contrast to their attitude toward the central library, board members felt that branch libraries simply did not merit the time and expense of an architectural competition. Rather than selecting the architect for a branch library on the basis of a design, library boards depended instead on the architect's professional reputation. In Detroit, there were six library commissioners and (initially at least) six Carnegie-financed branches, a coincidence that seems to have suggested an easy solution to the problem of selecting architects: in contrast to their procedure for the main library each commissioner simply named an architect to design one of the branches.[55]

The tendency for library boards to give branches only a fraction of the attention that they lavished on central libraries was established early in the wholesale phase of the Carnegie library program by the trustees of the New York Public Library, Astor, Lenox and Tilden Foundations. Carnegie's 1901 offer of $5,200,000 had been enthusiastically received by city officials, but confronted library trustees with the daunting task of overseeing the erection of sixty-five branch libraries while they were still in the throes of building the massive central library; indeed, they would be involved with that building for another ten years. City officials eased this burden somewhat by establishing a separate committee charged with building branches in Brooklyn and Queens, limiting the responsibility of the New York Public Library board to the branches in the boroughs of Manhattan, the Bronx, and Richmond. Still, this meant taking on the building of forty-two branches at an average cost of $80,000 each.[56]

The trustees' response was to appoint an advisory committee that consisted of three of New York's most prominent architects. Charles Follen McKim, of McKim, Mead & White, had established his reputation as a library architect with the design of the Boston Public Library in the 1880s. Likewise, John M. Carrère's firm was then at work on the central library in Manhattan. The third member of the advisory board was Walter Cook, who was not known as a library architect, but whose firm was completing Carnegie's mansion on 91st Street at Fifth Avenue.

In the fall of 1901, they made their recommendations to the trustees, emphasizing the need for uniformity in the design, materials, general character, and scale of the branches, and suggesting that the trustees could best achieve this uniformity by appointing a small number of architects to serve as an architectural board, with responsibility for coordinating the design of all forty-two buildings. The advisory board's stated rationale was that this uniformity would give the buildings a distinctive appearance, making them immediately recognizable as branch libraries. Yet, their emphasis on cooperation suggests that they also recognized other, unspecified advantages of a uniform style, including reducing design time, lowering material costs by buying in larger quantities, and cutting construction prices by letting contracts in groups. The trustees rewarded this balanced consideration of art and practicality by appointing the firms of McKim, Carrère, and Cook as the board of architects responsible for designing forty-one branch libraries.[57]

The designs for New York's branch libraries were particularly good examples of the approach that library boards took when confronted with the political necessity of constructing branch libraries. No more trusting of working-class readers than Carnegie had been, they used similar architectural mechanisms for controlling the interaction between readers and books. Yet, in contrast to Carnegie's practice in the Pittsburgh branches, they packaged their branch libraries with architectural imagery that reiterated their view that culture and class were naturally linked.

In contrast to the attempt in Pittsburgh's branches to create public library imagery, New York's branches relied consistently on the architectural vocabulary of the Renaissance palazzo (figs. 3.41–3.44). Rustication, engaged columns, stringcourses, or some combination of these elements, indicated the different floor levels, giving these buildings a more modest scale than the central library in midtown Manhattan. Domestic references in these libraries were all the more obvious to contemporary observers, who recognized immediately the formal similarities with New York's most common nineteenth-century residential form, the rowhouse. The three-story height, the three-bay facade and the side entrance were all part of a common format for elegant townhouses built for the upper middle class throughout the preceding century. The branch library even paralleled important aspects of the rowhouse's spatial organization, particularly in devoting one-third of each floor to circulation and service functions (see fig. 3.42). Located in the compact area behind the main stairs and never more than a single bay wide, the library's dumbwaiters, public toilets, and librarian's work room paralleled the regular location of backstairs, bathrooms, and hall bedrooms of the nineteenth-century rowhouse. Basement and attic levels typically contained no public facilities and were rarely illustrated in the professional press. Nonetheless, verbal descriptions make it clear that these areas also paralleled domestic usages. Indeed, the library's receiving and packing room and the domestic kitchen shared analogous positions in the rear of the basement, while the attic quarters used by domestic servants were transformed into janitor's apartments on the uppermost floors of New York's branch libraries.[58]

These domestic analogies, however, cannot be interpreted simply as an attempt on the part of library trustees to make working-class readers feel at ease in the library. Despite respecting the street-line and cornice height of their urban contexts, New York's branch libraries rarely blended into their working-class neighborhoods. In contrast to Alden & Harlow's brick libraries in Pittsburgh, a New York branch was often the only limestone facade in a neighborhood of brick and brownstone and was also typically larger in scale than the rowhouses and commercial blocks that flanked it. For the Progressive-minded professional library staff who advised the library board, the rowhouse imagery may have served a positive function; like settlement houses that sought to trans-

Figure 3.41 Babb, Cook & Willard, New York Public Library, 67th Street Branch, New York, opened 1905. *Architectural Record* 17 (March 1905): 240.

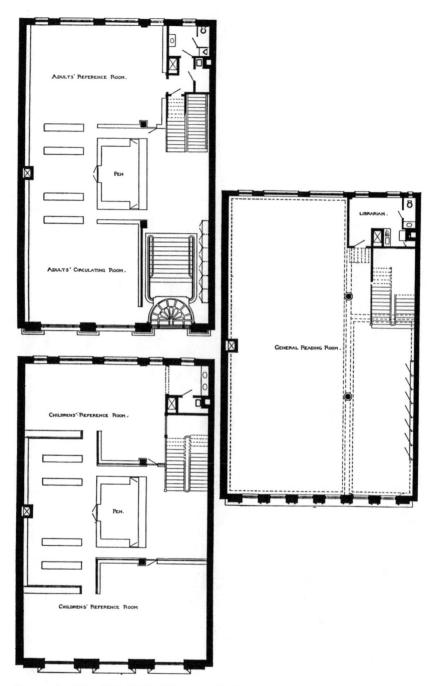

Figure 3.42 New York Public Library, 67th Street Branch, (*upper left*) first-, (*lower left*) second-, and (*right*) third-floor plans. *Architectural Record* 17 (March 1905): 238–39.

form working-class life by establishing outposts of education and culture in the slums, branch libraries were intended to stand out from their surroundings, the better to serve as object lessons in middle-class values and behaviors. In contrast, the library trustees made it clear that they did not trust the ability of working-class residents to interpret the architectural messages of these library facades. Instead, they instructed their board of architects to advertise the function of branch libraries in other less symbolic ways as well, insisting on reading rooms located near enough to the sidewalk to allow passers-by "to look as it were into a

Figure 3.43 McKim, Mead & White, New York Public Library, 125th Street Branch, New York, opened 1904. *Architectural Record* 17 (March 1905): 242.

Figure 3.44 Carrère & Hastings, New York Public Library, Riverside Branch, New York, opened 1905. *Architectural Record* 17 (March 1905): 243.

shop window and see the readers"[59] From their point of view, then, the appeal of the format proposed by the board of architects had less to do with attracting prospective readers than with announcing the library's continuing role as a locus of elite culture. For them, the sharp contrast between the architectural forms of the library and its neighbors was intentional and necessary, for it allowed library facilities to exist in working-class neighborhoods without acknowledging that cultural pursuits were a natural part of that stratum of the urban environment.

Manhattan's long, narrow sites required the use of multiple stories in these branches, and heightened the perceived need for spatial and visual control. In an adaptation of the row house prototype, the solid wall that defined the boundary between the relatively public areas of the domestic hallway and the more private parlors and bedrooms was replaced in the library by a row of columns that provided a visually penetrable line. In these libraries where reading facilities were distributed over a number of floors, the need for spatial control became even more acute. Large rectangular circulation desks were full-fledged enclosures with work stations for two or more librarians (fig. 3.45). Called "pens" on contemporary plans, they served double duty. In conjunction with glass-topped partitions, they created narrow passages that allowed librarians to enforce a one-way traffic pattern for readers moving in and out of reading rooms where books were stored. They also marked the boundary between the work space of middle-class librarians and the reference and reading spaces of working-class patrons.

If the specific form of Manhattan's branches was unique to New York's urban environment, the ambivalent attitude toward working-class library users was common in the early years of the twentieth century. Indeed, the planning innovations introduced in Pittsburgh in the mid-

Figure 3.45 Illustration from a Library Bureau catalogue, showing the charging desk, or pen, in a branch library in Manhattan. Library Bureau, *Charging Desks* (n.d.), 7.

1890s were commonly used to maintain visual and spatial control over readers in the first decade of the century. Opened in 1907, St. Louis's Cabanne branch allowed readers to enter the adult and children's reading rooms directly from the circulation area (fig. 3.46). Nonetheless, the radial arrangement of the stack room emphasized intense surveillance of the entire area, while the position of the circulation desk established a one-way traffic pattern in and out of the stacks, and allowed the librarian to scrutinize each reader individually.

In some cases, library boards seemed to have assumed a criminal intent on the part of all readers, and commissioned buildings that treated them accordingly. Brooklyn's Carnegie-financed Pacific branch, for instance, expanded on the idea of Pittsburgh's radial stack rooms, collecting books, reading tables, and circulation desk into a single hemispherical space (figs. 3.47 and 3.48). What is more, these elements were deployed in a way that mimicked the planning devices of prison architecture, particularly those of Jeremy Bentham's Panopticon. Radial stacks subdivided and supported two levels of reading alcoves (reminiscent of prisoners' cells in Bentham's scheme), while the delivery desk served the function of the inspector's lodge. Dramatic back-lighting provided by the large floor-to-ceiling windows made the Panopticon analogy almost exact. Although an extreme example, the Pacific branch was motivated by the same interest in scrutinizing each and every reader that lay behind the more common radial stack design.[60]

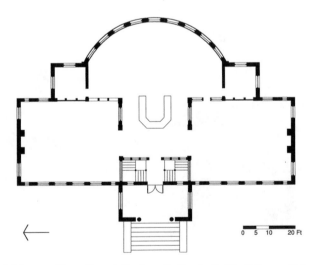

Figure 3.46 Mauran, Russell, and Garden, St. Louis Public Library, Cabanne Branch, St. Louis, opened 1907, first-floor plan. Author.

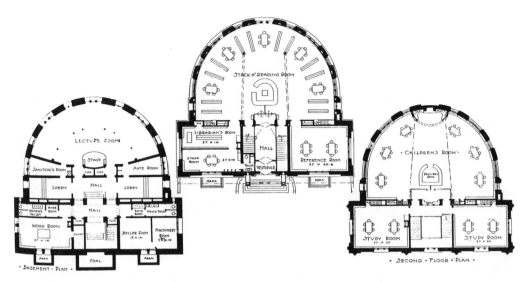

Figure 3.47 Raymond F. Almirall, Brooklyn Public Library, Pacific Branch, Brooklyn, c. 1907, (*left*) basement, (*center*) first- and (*right*) second-floor plans. *Brickbuilder* 16 (May 1907): plate 78.

Reaching the Reader: Librarians and the Open Plan

In these same years, however, professional librarians began to temper this general distrust of the reading public. Indeed, in order to defend the library's social usefulness (as well as their own), they needed to maintain their faith that working-class readers were redeemable, susceptible to the library's power to uplift. It is true that many leaders in the field, men like Arthur Bostwick of St. Louis, continued to complain about the tendency of newspaper rooms to attract "the tramp element— rough and often dirty persons who come to lounge or rest, perhaps to sleep, rarely to read."[61] Yet, in identifying "tramps" as the problem group, librarians had made a subtle shift in their thinking. Untrustworthy library users certainly still existed, but they were now defined as the exception, rather than the rule. What is more, in equating library malfeasance with other sorts of visible antisocial behavior, librarians were better prepared to trust working-class readers who adopted the outward trappings of middle-class respectability. As a result, large groups of readers no longer posed a threat to library administration, and the drive to isolate readers from one another in order to enhance scrutiny of the individual reader seemed less acute. Focusing on the positive aspects of a group dynamic, librarians came to celebrate the "sobering and quieting effect" of "a considerable number of other busy persons."[62]

Figure 3.48 Brooklyn Public Library, Pacific Branch, stack and reading room. *Brick-builder* 16 (May 1907): plate 79.

To the extent that librarians began to see the untrustworthy reader as an anomaly, their new attitude undermined the importance of the radial stack plan. The planning mechanisms that promoted the close scrutiny of each reader seemed largely unnecessary, and were increasingly acknowledged as counterproductive to many aspects of library administration. Indeed, the radial stack itself was expensive to build and impossible to expand. As a result, the radial stack plan fell out of use only a decade after its introduction in the mid-1890s.

In its place, urban libraries began to use the open plan, a single, large rectangular space with bookshelves lining its perimeter walls. While the centrally placed delivery desk maintained the librarian's ability to supervise the entire library, it was easy to build, easy to expand, and exposed readers to the beneficial influence of "other busy persons" and, of course, the books themselves. Early examples, like Philadelphia's Tacony branch, reveal some of the anxiety involved in giving readers this new freedom (fig. 3.49). In this building (opened in November 1906), a

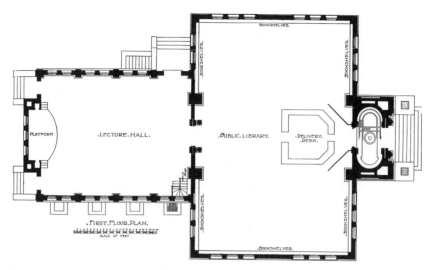

Figure 3.49 Lindley Johnson, Free Library of Philadelphia, Tacony Branch, Philadelphia, opened 1906, first-floor plan. *Brickbuilder* 15 (November 1906): plate 153.

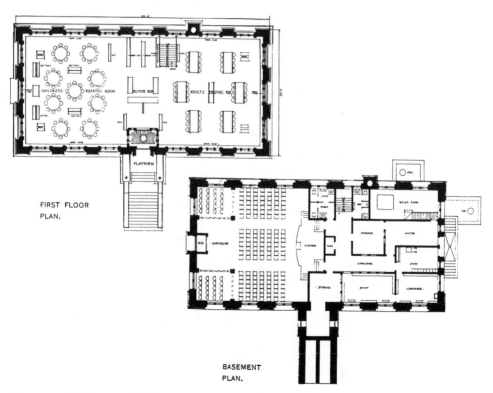

Figure 3.50 Mariner and LaBeaume, St. Louis Public Library, Divoll Branch, St. Louis, opened 1910, (*lower*) basement and (*upper*) first-floor plans. *Brickbuilder* 20 (September 1911): plate 117.

familiar arrangement of the delivery desk and partitions directly in front of the door forced readers to move in and out of the library in a single file under the watchful eye of the library staff. Such concerns, however, were short-lived. By 1910, cities like St. Louis were building branches that allowed working-class readers to move in and out of the library with much greater freedom (fig. 3.50). While the furniture arrangements shown in plans and officially-sponsored period photographs indicate that library officials still treasured a middle-class ideal of library use in which quiet users sat at tables in approved postures, the overt architectural coercion of the late nineteenth-century branch library had been abandoned.[63]

Conclusion

For larger American cities, then, a Carnegie grant affected the politics of culture in complex ways. Library trustees belonging to a social elite maintained their control over the decision-making process in library matters. Ambivalent about public access to culture, they continued the nineteenth-century practice of reserving a palatial central library building for upper-class use.

At the same time, however, Carnegie's own interest in working-class users and his policies regarding municipal involvement in library affairs ensured that established attitudes identifying culture as an upper-class concern no longer seemed normative. Instead, library trustees and the librarians they employed were forced to articulate and examine the assumptions that lay beneath library policies. Since their attitudes were similar but not identical, their dialogue on these issues resulted in subtle changes. Indeed, to the extent that professional librarians buoyed their own professional prestige by promoting their ability to reach working-class readers, they supported architectural changes that reformed the branch library type in the first decade of the twentieth century. Although this open-plan ideal was increasingly challenged by children's librarians familiar with Progressive educational theory (a development discussed in chap. 5), it formed the basis for the planning advice that Bertram received from library leaders. With the help of the Carnegie Corporation's "Notes on Erection of Library Bildings," such open-plan branch libraries remained the officially-sanctioned norm for branch libraries throughout the tenure of the Carnegie library program and into the interwar period.

TAKING
Libraries and Cultural Politics
Part II

4 THE LAST YEARS OF THE NINETEENTH century were important ones for library building in smaller American towns. After 1890 (when the federal census declared the frontier officially closed), the focus of activity in areas west of the Appalachians shifted from the establishment of new towns to the development of existing ones. Eager to recreate the amenities available to city dwellers, many towns established libraries, opera houses, fraternal lodges, city halls, commercial blocks. As provincial as these institutions may have seemed to their big-city cousins, residents of hundreds of small towns were justifiably proud of the range of governmental, commercial, and cultural institutions that lined Main Street by the turn of the century.[1]

Cultural Politics in Smaller Towns

If the library was as important to the public landscape of smaller western towns as it was in more established cities, it was often the product of a different experience of town life. In contrast to the industrialized East where a wealthy man often endowed the town library, throughout the West it was more common for middle-class women to take responsibility for establishing town libraries. Western women were so active in establishing and administering libraries for their towns that in 1933 the American Library Association credited women's clubs with initiating 75 percent of the public libraries then in existence.[2] Although largely invisible to the history of architecture, libraries established by women were the most common library type in the last decades of the nineteenth century.[3]

For the most part, Western women pursued library organizing as an outgrowth of membership in all-female study clubs. These clubs had made their appearance in the years after the Civil War, beginning with Sorosis in New York and the New England Woman's Club in Boston, both founded in 1868. By the 1880s, however, they were becoming a common feature of town life across the country. The establishment of the General Federation of Women's Clubs (GFWC) in 1890 reflected the existence of clubs in great enough numbers to warrant federation, while the GFWC's national meetings attracted new members in increasing numbers. By 1910, over one million American women had become club members.[4]

Founded as informal social groups, clubs were initially intended to provide middle-class women with the opportunity to continue the literary discussions that they may have enjoyed at school.[5] Organized around a small circle of friends, most clubs were apolitical entities with charters that strictly forbade discussion of current events. Although Union City, Indiana, had a population of only three thousand in 1903, it supported no fewer than twelve women's clubs, including the Merry Nines, Over the Teacups, the Inseperables [*sic*], and the Merry Go Rounds. Both their numbers and their names suggest the intimate size and the social nature of these clubs.[6]

At the end of the century, women's clubs nationwide began to take a more active role in the life of their communities, with the encouragement of the GFWC and its founder Jane Cunningham Croly. Supplementing their study of Shakespeare with discussions about the sanitary city, club women increasingly left the tea table to spearhead local campaigns for civic beautification; to establish playgrounds, hospitals, homes for invalids, and needlework guilds; to investigate school conditions; and to lobby for child-labor and temperance laws, and protective legislation for working women. Eventually, club women even demanded the right to vote as a means of ensuring the success of their reforms.[7]

Despite their greater activity in community affairs, club women did not set out to challenge the status quo of gender relations. In response to critics who saw the club movement as a threat to family stability, official histories of the General Federation of Women's Clubs stressed woman's proper role as man's helpmeet and insisted that club women "do not figure in the divorce court," but enjoy a "harmonious, well-ordered and happy" homelife.[8] Such pronouncements were certainly calculated to diffuse hostility, but they were more than empty rhetoric. Club women, the majority of them married, were unwilling to engage in activities that might unsex them in the eyes of their family, friends, and neighbors. Never intending to usurp power in a male sphere, they interpreted their activities as a means of extending accepted female talents into the public realm. For the married women who dominated the club movement, club-sponsored projects were just an extension of roles they played at home, a form of municipal housekeeping.[9]

Town libraries were particularly appealing to club women, who strove to maintain their femininity while taking an active role in the life of their community. Libraries were, after all, a logical extension of the club's original charter; in the years before federation, many clubs had established small private libraries to help members prepare the literary reports that were a regular part of club meetings. From there, it was a short step to opening the library to a wider audience. Likewise, if a woman's "natural" talents equipped her to exert a civilizing influence on her immediate family, who better to dispense culture to the community?[10]

If this ideal of municipal housekeeping made sense at the level of ideology, the actual built environment reveals that its practical application was more problematic. Entrusted with responsibility for dispensing culture in the public realm, women were denied access to the economic power necessary to accomplish the task. As a result, most town libraries were organized as subscription libraries, limiting borrowing privileges to members who paid a small annual membership fee.[11] Since even modest fees made library membership prohibitive for poorer families, these town libraries were rarely open to everyone. Yet, for middle-class club women who found it easier to extend their motherly influence to their community's social elite, fees were a mixed blessing.

Although politically-oriented women's groups increasingly insisted on their right to conduct cash-based fund-raising at the turn of the century, many club women adhered to established boundaries of appropriate female behavior and remained reluctant to break the taboo on engaging in commerce, no matter how high-toned the cause. Although their cash budgets were limited to funds gleaned from book fines and membership fees, club women were hesitant to ask for cash, even to ask their neighbors to buy a ticket to a family entertainment. Since even well-to-do women only controlled the household funds given them by their husbands, few club members could contribute more than their own family membership to the subscription library.[12]

Without cash on hand, women forged alternative strategies for attracting support for the library. Although the precise nature of their efforts varied from club to club and from town to town, club women adopted strategies that combined self-sacrifice with coquettish appeals to men who had the cash or power to aid their cause. Club members regularly volunteered to staff the delivery desk themselves, often keeping the library open only one or two afternoons a week. In 1901, Mrs. George J. Russler helped support the library in Hobart, Oklahoma, by organizing a peach sale at which the first peach was auctioned off for $3.50, while strawberry festivals and cookbook sales were among the annual or seasonal events designed to garner financial support. One writer facetiously counted box suppers, socials, and lyceum courses among "the devious ways of women's organizations" for supporting the library cause.[13]

Among these special events, the book social was a particular favorite of library organizers. Although cash donations were always welcome at book socials, currency was rarely a part of these events. Typically, the admission price was the donation of a used book. Once inside, visitors made the circuit of booths that housed homemade refreshments or games devised by club members. Such cash-free entertainments allowed women to trade their domestic skills for books rejected from home libraries, and could result in substantial contributions. When the GGG's of Union City, Indiana, held a book social in 1901 in the basement of the Methodist Church, they netted 350 books. Yet, book collections formed in this way were uneven at best. The Xenia, Ohio, library, for instance, opened it doors with titles like *Smoking and Chewing*, Combe's *Phrenology*, and a *Treatise on Cattle*.[14]

The prohibition on handling cash made it particularly difficult for club women to find a home for the library. When prospective recipients of Carnegie library grants returned questionnaires about existing library conditions, their answers revealed that town libraries were housed in a wide variety of architectural settings. Of a sample of eighty-two towns, eleven had no library at the time they asked for a Carnegie gift, while another eleven did not specify how their existing library was housed. Of the sixty respondents who did offer specific information about the physical setting of their library, only four had existing purpose-built library buildings. In contrast, twenty-six (or about 43 percent) housed their libraries somewhere in the city hall, sixteen used rented rooms in a commercial block, six used a room in the school building, and four used a room in the county courthouse. In four remaining towns, the libraries were located in the Soldiers Memorial Hall, the YMCA, a church basement, and on the shelves of a drugstore, respectively.

These statistics point to regional differences in library building. The East may have seen a great library building boom in the 1880s, but purpose-built library buildings were still a rarity in the West. What is more, Western women who did attempt to build libraries soon found that the gender system continued to complicate their activities. In Helena, Arkansas, for instance, the members of the Pacaha Club established a library on the upper floors of the Grand Opera House, in what was a typical first move for literary clubs. Almost immediately, however, they began their efforts to build a permanent home for their collection of over eight hundred books. Initially, club members established a savings and loan account, and succeeded in selling some shares to their husbands. When enthusiasm for the campaign waned after a few weeks with only forty shares sold, club members were forced to pursue another strategy. In return for male support of a town bond issue, the club women offered prime rental space in the proposed building to the fraternal lodges that had just lost their meeting space at a local school. This strategy was a mixed success; the building was complete in 1891, but the club women who owned the building were forced to rent out the greater portion of it in order to meet the mortgage. The building's main spaces were not used for library purposes until 1914.[15]

When club women who dominated the Western library movement did manage to build, they eschewed the Richardsonian library type that was still the model for many Eastern libraries. The Helena library built by the Pacaha Club was a large two-story cubical brick structure with a Mansard roof, completely without the exterior articulation of function that was such an important part of Richardson's library designs (fig. 4.1). Its relationship to the street, its scale, its stylistic vocabulary, all belong to conventional domestic architecture of the 1880s. Indeed, it is only the words "Public Library" above the door that suggest that this is not the substantial home of one of the town's first families.

A similar domestic imagery lay behind the library building built in Cawker City, Kansas, by the Women's Hesperian Library Club (fig. 4.2).[16] Built in 1884 of local stone, this small one-story building is more modest than Helena's Second Empire mansion. Yet, its size, central porch, machine-produced ornament, and central gable are all reminiscent of the cross-gabled cottages first popularized by A. J. Downing's *Cottage Residences* in 1842, and still reproduced in farmers' magazines in the 1880s as a potent image of progressive rural domesticity.[17] In such visible manifestations of their activities, club women used architectural form to emphasize the domestic grounding of their public roles.

Such opportunities for self-presentation, however, were uncommon for club women who established libraries in the West. As the Carnegie statistics suggest, it was more common to find a library in makeshift quarters that lacked the ordered gentility that women's clubs treasured.

In school buildings, for instance, the library was often located in a room that functioned primarily as a classroom, limiting library use to after-school hours. City halls and county courthouses offered social libraries the double advantage of official government sanction and rent-free accommodations, but were often accompanied by their own brand of inconvenience. In Hamburg, Iowa, for instance, the library was forced to share its small space, which was also used for a ladies' resting room and for various meetings.[18] Just as often, social libraries were forced to confront the more noxious aspects of town life. In Hamilton, Montana, the library was "housed in a small room back of the city fire department in the city hall, adjoining the room where the horses are kept," while in Macomb, Illinois, the library was on the same floor with the city council rooms and city prison.[19]

In theory, libraries on the upper floors of commercial blocks were more genteel. This was certainly the case in Xenia, Ohio, where Helen Hooven Santmyer recalled the social library as being

in the short street that cut off the courthouse square from the block to the east; it was on the second floor of the building just beyond the alley. The stairs that led to

Figure 4.1 Helena Library, Helena, Arkansas, opened 1891. Courtesy Ivey S. Gladin.

Figure 4.2 Cawker City Public Library, Cawker City, Kansas, 1884. Courtesy Kansas State Historical Society.

it were like those in all our half-dozen blocks: narrow, rickety, dusty wooden steps, squeezed between two buildings, or boxed in and hanging over an alley. . . . the building which had the library upstairs was a big one, with the post office on the ground floor, and a milliner's shop and the Woman's Exchange; the library was in a rear corner room just inside the stair door.[20]

In fact, the Xenia, Ohio, library organizers were lucky enough to have their room rent-free, thanks to the fact that one of their number was the spinster niece of the building's owner.[21] Although never explicitly stated as such, her reward for acting as his housekeeper throughout her adult life was the free use of the room for library purposes.

Less well-connected clubs were forced to part with their scarce cash to pay rent. A typical situation was that of Jerseyville, Illinois, where the library's two rooms were "subject to fire and exposed to noise and other annoyances of [the grocery] business below."[22] The regularity with which social libraries were located above noisy grocery stores suggests that club members sought to conserve their small bits of cash by renting the least desirable, and, therefore, least expensive rooms available in town.

In these public buildings, club women took special care not to flaunt their control over even a small part of their town's commercial and governmental precinct. Hoping even to disguise their appearance in public, female library organizers created settings completely devoid of the domestic imagery of their purpose-built buildings. Xenia's turn-of-the-century library room is a case in point. As Santmyer remembered it, the old library was

a great rectangular room; windows in the side wall looked down behind and beneath the stairs to the alley below; those at the end offered a view of a jumble of roofs, ending with the sheriff's house and the barred windows of the county jail. In the center of the floor was a railed enclosure and the librarians' desk; two rows of round posts, painted public institution brown, held up the ceiling, and bookcases—tall walnut bookcases with glass doors—stood against the wall all around the room. . . . the top shelves were not only out of reach—they were out of sight; however much you suspected that those were the best books, you could only hope that Miss McElwain put up there the ones that no one wanted.[23]

Figuring largely in Santmyer's description were floor-to-ceiling glass-fronted bookcases. Whether purchased with the club's precious cash budget or possibly donated from a lawyer's office, such bookcases were a palpable reminder to readers that these books were not their own to take off the shelf at will. In emphasizing the institutional quality of the room and its spatial barriers, Santmyer's description suggests that club women aspired to create settings that were more like the professional and commercial offices of their husbands and brothers than like the domestic settings they arranged at home.[24]

The irony of the situation for club women was that while they aspired to create nondomestic settings for their libraries, the gender system compelled them to repeat many of its elements. In most instances, the purchase of glass-fronted bookcases would have left little or no cash with which to buy other furniture. Not only did women donate cast-off goods to furnish their libraries, but they continued to play roles familiar from the domestic sphere, with men supplying the spatial container, while the women decorated and arranged its interior.

In short, these late nineteenth-century town libraries were complex products of an inconsistent social system that encouraged women to take part in shaping and administering cultural institutions in the public realm, but entrusted the community's economic base exclusively to male care. It was a system that virtually guaranteed that libraries established by club women would be insubstantial, always on the move, insecure, and essentially invisible in a landscape where buildings had become the most positive evidence of human activity.

Despite the precarious nature of these libraries, the club women who organized them took on a heightened presence in the life of their communities. In organizing a library they gained knowledge and experience that might have eluded them at home. In organizing book socials, they learned the limited monetary value of their domestic labor. In approaching public officials for help, they learned the techniques of political lobbying. In renting library rooms, they learned about the economics of urban real estate. Precisely because their access to cash was so limited, they learned its value very quickly. The obstacles in their way prompted the development of previously uncultivated skills, and convinced them that, with the right kind of support, the library could be transformed into a force for good in the community.[25]

Carnegie's Reception in Small-Town America

In hundreds of towns across the country, club women embraced the Carnegie library program as a means for negotiating the gap between an ideal of gender roles (that encouraged women to organize libraries) and its daily practice (that placed town libraries in such a precarious financial position). Indeed, a Carnegie subvention seemed to provide exactly what club women had been trying to achieve, albeit with mixed results. The economic support that it offered was immense. The typical grant of $10,000 was far beyond what club women could ever dream of raising on their own. The stipulation that all of the funds go to the building provided precisely what clubs had had so much trouble achieving—permanent quarters from which the library could never be ousted, and on which the rent could never be raised. A purpose-built building also ended the days of making do with rooms designed for other purposes, and, perhaps more important, offered the library a visibility in the town landscape. The requirement for tax support was equally welcome; not only did it ensure a steady and comparatively large annual income, it also signified official recognition of the library's value to the community.

Perhaps, best of all, the Carnegie program offered the opportunity of getting this support without requiring club women to behave in what they perceived to be an unfeminine way. Certainly, some clubs did feel compelled to shield themselves behind a sympathetic male; the GGG's of Union City, Indiana, for instance, convinced the superintendent of schools to approach Carnegie about a gift in 1903.[26] Many more clubs, however, took Carnegie's published willingness to give money for libraries to mean that they were not actually soliciting funds. Empowered by their roles in club work, library work, or simply as mothers, many women felt free to write to Carnegie directly.[27]

Soon after opening negotiations with the philanthropist, however, club women found themselves in an uncomfortable situation. Although they were free to place their case before him, Carnegie was careful to formalize every step of the negotiations with the elected officials of the local municipal government. The mayor's signature was required on the application form, the city government had to provide a library site, and the town council had to pass a resolution to dedicate city tax dollars to a library maintenance fund. Unable to hold public office, club women discovered that a Carnegie gift could mean losing control over the library they had established. Since middle-class club women, however, were often related to the civic leaders, their disenfranchisement was never automatic and rarely absolute. Nonetheless, the Carnegie system helped institutionalize existing patterns of gender relations in cultural matters, officially crediting female initiative in library matters to men, and officially recognizing female labor only when it was sanctioned by male authority.

This devaluation of female volunteerism was not an attack on women as such. Rather it was part of a general trend at the turn of century that implicitly devalued the amateur status of volunteers, while explicitly exalting professional expertise. Voluntary do-gooders of both sexes found themselves edged out of a wide variety of activities, ranging from campaigns for art and music to slum reform to early childhood education.[28] What is more, the very middle-class women who had swelled the ranks of voluntary organizations were often the biggest supporters of the culture of professionalism. Hardly passive victims of the system, women's clubs had often founded cultural institutions with the goal of ultimately turning them over to government financing or professional control.[29]

At the same time, however, women were disproportionately affected by the shift to professional expertise and government control. Barred from public office and from most professions, women had few avenues to make the shift from voluntary service to professional action. What is more, for the individuals who experienced it, this abrupt devaluation of voluntary efforts was often a painful phenomenon. Although club women rarely voiced open resentment, this forced disruption in familiar social practices did prompt them to express their views about cultural institutions and the role that those institutions should play in community life. In the process, club women articulated a complex and conflicted sense of their own role in community endeavors.

Male and Female Visions of the Library

In the correspondence that passed between Carnegie (or his representatives) and individual applicants, women continued to see library organizing as a gendered activity. Forced into a defensive posture by an increased emphasis on professionalism, Carnegie's female correspondents invoked conservative Victorian definitions of womanhood to justify their participation in public culture. Becoming adamant that their sex gave them special qualifications as the curators of their community's library, they went out of their way to emphasize their femininity. Reminding Carnegie that "it is only natural for a woman to talk when she thinks she has a sympathetic listener," Mrs. J. C. Reynolds, of Union City, Tennessee, expressed the hope that "we can keep the library going until the 'city fathers' cannot fail to see the good it is doing."[30] Her implication was clear; the inability of Union City's male elite to grasp the library's potential for social betterment was related to their sex.

Many other women called attention to library work as a natural extension of their role as mothers. In 1914, for instance, Mrs. C. D. Darnell and Mrs. Thomas McMann wrote to the Mayor of Kansas City, Kansas, to ask him to approach Carnegie for a library gift. Citing their "sentiment as mothers, not only in a personal sense but [in a] universial [*sic*] sense," they explicitly used the argument of municipal housekeeping to explain their concern for the generic "little fellow round the corner . . . who is mentally feeding on the husks with 'Nick Carter.'"[31]

Women also continued to invest municipal housekeeping in general and library organizing in particular with moral overtones. The club women of Nevada, Missouri, made this connection explicitly, emphasizing the role that the library would play in supplying "home-influence" to the young, unattached men of their town.[32] Approaching their library activities with an evangelical fervor, the ladies of Union City, Tennessee, saw themselves as Mohammed-like characters "struggling with a mountain," and compared their library to a foreign mission.[33]

Women maintained a special relationship with the library's moral function, even when men supported their cause. In many communities, the library seemed to offer a wholesome alternative to the avenues of vice, especially for unattached men and boys whose lack of "home-influence" made them seem particularly vulnerable to the lure of the saloon. In Lake City, Minnesota, for instance, a committee of three businessmen related the library's importance to the presence of a state military encampment that brought an influx of unattached males each summer.[34] Likewise, a large proportion of unmarried men working for the lumber industry year round gave an urgency to the appeals of Morris E. Thomas, of Cadillac, Michigan.[35] In envisioning the library as a surrogate home for unmarried men, these male writers revealed their faith that women would remain an integral part of the library's mission of moral uplift.[36]

In attacking the dime novel and the saloon with equal vehemence, Carnegie's female correspondents revealed the extent to which they saw themselves as outsiders, not merely standing apart from the commercial life of the town, but actively challenging its values as well. Disturbed by the idea that culture and leisure might lose their potency as antidotes to the evils of commercialism, club women offered their most active resistance to commercialized leisure in every form. As a surrogate home that extended the cultural enlightenment of the domestic sphere into the public realm, as a viable alternative to the commercialized leisure of the saloon, the library was treasured as a center of resistance to the values of commercialism.[37]

In direct contrast to Carnegie's female correspondents, most of the men who wrote to the philanthropist saw the library as an integral part of the commercial life of the town and pursued the library grant as part of a larger agenda of commercial boosterism.[38] A few followed the lead of women to paint a picture of hoards of single men aimlessly wandering the streets, but they were more likely to emphasize the rosiest aspects of their town's life, as embodied in its physical appearance. Composing their letters as they did their Chamber of Commerce brochures, they cited the number of miles of paved roads, the quality of the sewer system, or the recent installation of electric lighting.[39]

A case in point is the 1904 letter from attorney Hugo Seaburg of Raton, New Mexico. Outlining a plan under consideration by the city council to establish a park and library together, Seaburg argued that the combination "would be a splendid advertisement for our City." Since "it would be seen and favorably noticed by every traveler," the attorney was also confident that the library "would be of immense value not only to our City but as well to New Mexico."[40] What Seaburg failed to mention was that as someone who had recently moved to town to invest heavily in real estate, the library would also be of "immense value" to Seaburg himself.[41]

True, few men were as forthright as Hugo Seaburg was in stating outright their hope that the library would act as a magnet for development. Yet, the sexually-segregated clubs to which they belonged carried names like the Commercial Club or the Farmers and Merchants Club and took commercial interests as their very raison d'être. For many men, then, the library's true value could be measured in economic terms, rather than in moral ones. For them, the library did not stand apart from the commercial values of the community; it was intricately tied to the town's commercial success.

The Temple in the Park

These divergent attitudes about the library's role were not easily resolved. Indeed, Carnegie's insistence on local involvement in the specifics of library building meant that these differences could surface at any stage in the process, from securing a site to furnishing the completed building. Yet, unlike their urban counterparts, who struggled with class-based differences, the men and women who debated library issues in smaller American towns were all middle-class people with common economic interests and a similar concept of propriety. They were often linked as well by ties of blood, marriage, and neighborliness, and shared a background of cooperation and compromise. In fact, if men and women could adopt gender roles familiar from the process of home-building, the tensions of library-building evaporated. When the domestic model of teamwork was inapplicable, local politics determined which group would predominate.

Choosing a Library Locale

To the extent that men and women differed in their sense of the library's primary audience, they also found themselves at odds when selecting a library site. For women, siting was a particularly thorny issue. If the library were to act as a potent antidote to the commercial values of the town, it needed to be at some distance from the saloons themselves, both to remove single men from the tempting avenues of vice and to allow respectable citizens to use the library as well. At the same time, the library needed to be close enough to the saloons that its presence

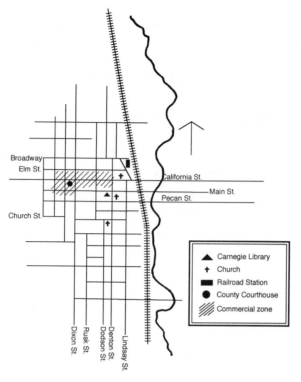

Figure 4.3 Gainesville, Texas, map. Author.

could remind single men that it existed as a wholesome alternative to commercialized leisure.

In many ways, the siting problem as perceived by women was one faced by churches of all denominations. Thus, when club women had a hand in deciding where the library would stand, they tended to follow a siting strategy similar to that practiced by churches in the late nineteenth century. In Gainesville, Texas, a successful subscription drive in 1911 raised fifteen hundred dollars and gave the women of the XLI Club unusual freedom in purchasing a library site. The lot they selected for their Carnegie building lay four blocks east of the county courthouse, at the corner of Denton Streets and Main Street, which (despite its name) ran parallel to the town's principal commercial corridor (fig. 4.3).[42] The appeal of this location was two-fold. First, it was on the edge of Gainesville's commercial zone, making the library as accessible as any other civic building. Second, oriented with its front door on Denton Street, the library stood near Queen Anne houses on Gainesville's most fashionable residential row. The Gainesville library was thus associated with a neighborhood devoted to the private pursuit of culture, and maintained its ties to late Victorian ideals of home and hearth. Located where it was, the library was also directly comparable to the church buildings in town. It stood in the same block with the Methodist Church at Denton and Pecan Streets, two blocks from the Presbyterian Church at Denton and Church Streets, and two blocks from the Episcopal Church on California Street. Like those churches, the library filled a corner lot in a predominantly residential area, with its door facing the side street. Although the exact placement of the library varied from town to town, it was usually located in an intermediary zone between the town's commercial and residential quarters.

When men's groups took the lead in library matters, however, their very different agenda for the library resulted in radically different library locations. After all, their commercial agenda was less concerned with the current residents of the town than it was with attracting future residents, an attitude that is borne out by the tendency for town boosters to print postcards picturing the Carnegie library.[43] If their wives and daughters looked to the church as a model of where to locate a library, businessmen followed the lead of the railroad station, seeking out locations that were both impressive and easily visible to strangers in town.

The Commercial Club of Raton, New Mexico, embraced an extreme version of this attitude. A division headquarters for the Atchison, Topeka, and Santa Fe Railroad, which crossed the mountains at Raton Pass, the town had first approached Carnegie through Hugo Seaburg's 1904 letters, quoted above. Although Raton did not receive its grant until 1911, Seaburg had become president of the Commercial Club in the interim, and continued to push for the park-cum-library project he had outlined seven years earlier. Raton's mayor, a former Santa Fe Railroad surgeon named J. J. Shuler, prevailed upon Santa Fe officials to deed to the city a portion of the railroad right-of-way for park purposes and to amend the deed to allow for the library when the Carnegie question came up.[44] The Commercial Club then hired Denver-based landscape architect S. R. De Boer to provide plans for the library park.

As described in the local paper and later built, the approved design was "so arranged as to show up the city's park to best effect from the direction of the main line of the Santa Fe" (fig. 4.4). Since the library was the gem of this design, the architect was particularly careful to "allow an unobstructed view of the new Carnegie library for those passing through Raton on the Santa Fe main line." To ensure that this impressive display might make a lasting impression on would-be investors, the park would include the word "Raton" in a mosaic of flowers, "in order to allow the thousands of tourists passing here an opportunity to learn to what city of the southwest this magnificent public park belongs." [45] At the same time, however, this plan forced the library to present its backside to Second Street, Raton's principal commercial thoroughfare, and to turn its back to the townspeople who were, after all, the building's intended users.

The Raton example is extreme in implementing the railroad station model so literally. A more common practice was to choose a location that would express the library's connection to the civic and commercial life of the community. As the mania for City Beautiful projects reached smaller and smaller towns in the years before the First World War, Carnegie grants were often used to subsidize at least a portion of the costs of these ambitious projects.

In Warren, Ohio, for instance, the bequest of a local philanthropist provided a site on the courthouse square, between the Central Christian Church and the Dana Institute, a music conservatory. [46] Perhaps because

Figure 4.4 I. H. Rapp and W. M. Rapp, Raton Carnegie Library, Raton, New Mexico, 1911–12 (demolished). The library stood in a public park designed by S. R. De Boer. Courtesy of Arthur Johnson Memorial Library, Raton.

Figure 4.5 Edward L. Tilton's 1904 proposal for a "group plan" for Warren. Redrawn from *Warren Daily Chronicle*, 22 December 1904, 1.

of the lot's central location, the men on the board of the Warren Library Association were enthusiastic in their support of a proposal to incorporate the library into a group plan for Warren (fig. 4.5).[47] Inspired by City Beautiful ideals, Warren's group plan offered an alternative to the expense incurred by larger American cities that rebuilt their civic centers along the planning principles of the Ecole des Beaux-Arts or in a consistent architectural vocabulary. Proposed by New York architect Edward L. Tilton, the scheme called for an architectural group "coordinated" only by contrasting architectural vocabularies. The Central Christian Church would remain in its Richardsonian Romanesque mode, the Carnegie library would have classical elements, while the Dana Institute would replace its Greek Revival building with one designed in a Dutch Renaissance revival mode.

Although never executed (possibly because the Danas balked at Tilton's offer to spend their money on a new building), Warren's group plan is nonetheless indicative of the attitudes towards the library. Praised in Warren's daily paper on the grounds that Warren's plan would be worked out "before Cleveland's much talked-of group plan [was] started," the project is a striking example of the way that a male commercial elite interpreted the library's role in bringing Warren in step with the times and allowing the town to compete with much larger cities.[48]

If a Carnegie gift had great potential for fueling heated gender-based debates about the library location, there was also the possibility of finding a site that was amenable to both men and women. In Union City, Indiana, for instance, the library had been established by the GGG's, a

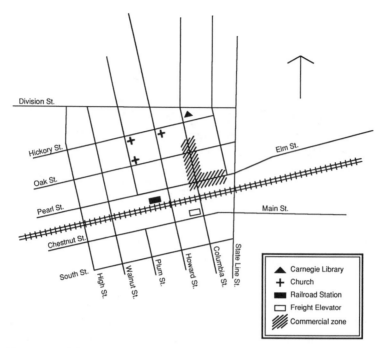

Figure 4.6 Union City, Indiana, map. Author.

society of unmarried women organized in 1887 "to cultivate the social amenities and the performance of works of benevolence."[49] They were eventually joined in their task by the other affiliates of the Local Council of Women (LCW): the Ticknor Club, the Wednesday Club, the Twentieth Century Club, the Cecillian Club, Over the Teacups, the Merry Go Rounds, etc. The identification of library matters with club work was so strong that even after Mrs. J. C. Northlane, LCW president, was appointed to the Union City Library Board in 1901, she continued to write to Carnegie on LCW letterhead.[50]

In important ways, the site met the conditions required of club women. Donated to the city in 1880, the lot was one of a number of oddly shaped blocks created by the conjunction of the rural grid to the north and the railroad grid to the south (fig. 4.6). Located on Columbia Street (the main street), the lot stood one block north of the Times Building which marked the northernmost edge of the nineteenth-century downtown. It also stood directly across the main street from the house built by W. K. Smith, son of Union City's founder. Thus, it was situated at the intersection of Union City's downtown and its best residential neighborhood.

Equally important, the site was amenable to the community's commercial and civic leaders, who had been unhappy about the use of the site for at least a decade. In the 1880s, townspeople had used the area as a cow pasture, and city officials had forced a more urban use of this site as a baseball park by erecting a high board fence breached only by two turnstiles.[51] The choice of this site for library purposes thus offered them Carnegie's financial help in their on-going struggle to eradicate rural land-use patterns from what they hoped to promote as an up-to-date town. As an added advantage, the use of land already owned by the city obviated the need for an additional cash contribution from the city.

Developing a Library Design

Once the library location was fixed, men and women found that their greatest conflicts were behind them. They tended to agree, for instance, that the library belonged in a parklike setting. Indeed, by the turn of the century, the park had become associated with a variety of institutions, even those with strongly divergent goals. In the years before the Civil War, nature had emerged in Transcendentalist thought as the ideal environment for moral, cultural, and intellectual development. Building on this tradition, town and city parks (and parklike suburbs) were established in the postwar era as affordable and accessible nature substitutes, serving as the favored settings for middle-class homes and for museums and other cultural institutions. By the turn of the century, however, the park's symbolic association with nature and culture had been augmented by other meanings. In the City Beautiful movement, the park movement, and the playground movement, the park was a symbol of progress associated with human, civic, and commercial health. As a result, whether the library was established in resistance to the forces of commercialism or as an important part of a town's commercial future, the park was perceived as an appropriate setting.[52]

When it came time to secure a library design, men and women also found it relatively easy to agree. In fact, the conventional gender roles that contributed to their conflicts over library siting actually facilitated their cooperation in building matters. Adopting their accustomed roles from the domestic realm, both men and women seemed content to allow men to direct the design and construction of the building's shell, while entrusting its interior arrangements to women.[53] This division of responsibilities worked well as long as both groups stayed within the narrow range of appropriate standards that were emerging in the early years of the twentieth century.

If convention dictated that men should make design decisions regarding the Carnegie library, it did little to prepare them for the task. Indeed, Carnegie's financial contribution complicated the project for local building committees, who considered themselves merely the middlemen between the architect and an absentee architectural patron. Equally problematic for local decision-makers was the realization that their Carnegie library was at heart an extra-local building, one among the many being built across the country. Acutely aware that they were responsible for a building that would be compared directly to its counterparts nationwide, those responsible for the Carnegie library came face-to-face with the breakdown of local autonomy that characterized the Progressive Era. The transition from "island community" to active participant in a national society could be nerve-wracking as well as exhilarating, and locals faced the process with reactions that varied from euphoria to terror.[54]

In some places, locals embraced the chance to compare themselves with their neighbors, using the Carnegie offer as an opportunity to hire an experienced architect from a larger metropolitan area to help them carry out an ambitious City Beautiful scheme. Although Calexico, California, had only been platted in 1900, the realization that the town's success depended on attracting new settlers soon prompted community leaders to pursue an aggressive civic improvement campaign. They not only hired the Los Angeles-based firm of Allison and Allison to design their high school in 1915, but they also welcomed J. E. Allison's suggestion to create a City Beautiful civic center (including the new Carnegie library, churches, the city hall, fraternal buildings, federal building, hospital, schools, and club buildings for the women's club and for the Farmers and Merchants Club) on the vacant land south of the school (fig. 4.7). Although never built as planned, the civic center scheme did get Calexico favorable coverage in the *Los Angeles Times*, and so fulfilled at least part of its advertising function.[55]

More often, however, newly-constituted library boards voiced doubt about their ability to carry out their assigned role. In Jacksonville, Illinois, for instance, the library board members themselves felt inadequate to direct an architect. L. O. Vaught, a lawyer on that board, explained their position in these terms:

I have felt that now is the chance to get something architecturally good. You know we Western people have been so hampered by stern necessity that little excepting the utilitarian side has received any attention. . . . our Library Board are just common ordinary men without the least experience or technical knowledge touching

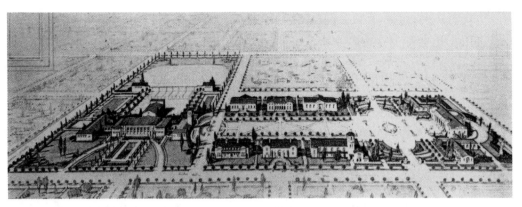

Figure 4.7 Allison and Allison's 1915 proposal for a civic center for Calexico, California. *Architect and Engineer of California* 42 (September 1912): 70.

Library Buildings. They might do exactly the right thing; but again the result may be a monstrosity. In any case the Board can not hope to equal Mr. Carnegie. The general sentiment here is a profound anxiety that he furnish us the plans.[56]

Although Vaught was certainly exaggerating when, in 1901, he invoked the excuse of frontier hardship in Illinois, his exaggeration can be taken as a measure of his "profound anxiety" at the idea of acting as an architectural client for a Carnegie library.

Other board members questioned the quality of locally available architects. In Caldwell, Kansas, the fear that local talent was not equal to the job at hand led Mrs. J. F. Robertson to write that "there is no architect near here with whose work we are well enough acquainted to trust with our building plans."[57] Others were just as uneasy about working with more experienced architects from outside the immediate area. The citizens of Ballinger, Texas, for instance, instructed their Los Angeles-based architect to design a building that could be built for $12,500. Somewhat at a loss as to how to proceed when the lowest bid came in at something over $18,000, they incurred Bertram's disdain by asking for an increase in their appropriation. Equally cowed by their East Coast patron and by their West Coast architect, they dismissed their architect immediately, without giving him the chance to revise his design and without paying his bill for work completed. While the Los Angeles architect continued to hound them for his fee, the library board turned the plans over to a local man, the pastor of the Presbyterian church, who as a young man had "learned the trade of a carpenter and had studied architecture some."[58] In short, the project was a long and difficult one.

Because of their uneasiness with many aspects of the design process, small-town recipients of Carnegie gifts pursued a number of strategies for circumventing the architect. One reaction was to ask Carnegie for ready-made plans; this was the purpose of the letters from Caldwell, Kansas, and Jacksonville, Illinois, quoted above. To be sure, some of these requests were prompted by the frustration of trying to come up with a plan that would meet Bertram's exacting standards. After failing to get approval on two sets of plans, each prepared by a different architect, the secretary of the Idaho Falls (Idaho) Public Library finally asked Bertram for the name of a town whose plans had been approved. Bertram's negative response carried with it the explanation that such information "would indirectly carry some responsibility for the cost being within the promised amount and altogether introduce an undesirable complication."[59]

Another reaction was to copy the Carnegie library in a neighboring town, resulting in a number of letters to Carnegie asking either for the names of the architects involved or for the plans themselves. Thus, McAllister, Oklahoma, hoped to copy the Carnegie library at Parsons, Kansas, while the mayor of St. George, Utah, wrote in 1913 to ask about plans for the library under construction in Cedar City, Utah.[60] It was a strategy that had a double appeal. By choosing among the Carnegie libraries they had seen in neighboring towns, they could get a finished product they liked, yet at the same time they were saved from having to enter into the process itself. To use an analogy from another sphere of activity, while Carnegie was offering them the chance to employ a tailor and choose their own cloth, many towns felt more comfortable buying off the rack.

These stated misgivings about the design process help explain the success of those architectural firms who marketed themselves as Carnegie library specialists. Even library boards who felt unqualified to assess either professional architects or their designs could use previous Carnegie commissions as an indication of professional competence. Likewise, the local desire to copy the library in a nearby town helps account for the regional concentrations of libraries designed by specialist firms.

Such apprehensions notwithstanding, the actions of local decision-makers disclosed their remarkably clear and consistent conception of the architectural product they sought. Indeed, hundreds of independent decisions resulted in exterior designs that fell within a remarkably narrow range. Particularly in the West, these smaller towns typically favored a symmetrical building, often domed, with a centrally placed entrance pavilion, detailed to emulate one of two classical forms. A sample of eighty-five Carnegie libraries (listed by the date of the grant in appendix 2, with the dollar amount of the grant and an indication of the exterior compositional type) reveals that the temple-front motif was the most popular form for the entrance pavilion. Of this sample, over 68 percent employed some type of temple-front motif, either in a monumental version with the triangular pediment set above the eave line (as at San Pedro, California; fig. 4.8), or in a more modest version, as a pedimented aedicula framing the door (as at Holdredge, Nebraska; fig. 4.9).[61] Second in popularity was the triumphal arch motif, recently popularized for the public library design by the non-Carnegie New York Public Library. Built either with an arched window above the pedimented door frame (as at San Diego, California; fig. 4.10), or without (as at Greenfield, Indiana; fig. 4.11), such buildings account for over 22 percent of the sample. Although there were a variety of design solutions that were derived from neither the temple front nor the triumphal arch, all together they account for fewer than 10 percent of the sample (graph 4.1).

The product of library innovations in the 1890s, the temple front was hardly a new form in the decade before World War I. Indeed, its popular-

Figure 4.8 San Pedro Public Library, San Pedro, California, 1906 (demolished). The design of the building has been variously attributed to H. V. Bradbeer and to the firm of Edelsvard and Saffell. Postcard from author's collection.

ity reveals conservative local expectations of what a library should look like. Yet, this conservatism should not be confused with indifference to aesthetic issues or hostility to change. Rather, this conservative ideal of library architecture should be acknowledged as a well-considered choice, consistent with its social context. Just as locals used conventional forms of social interaction (particularly in their adherence to Victorian gender roles) as a base from which to pursue new social projects (like the organization of public libraries), so they depended on conventional forms of architectural expression in order to share in an emerging national culture. Originality (although privileged by historians) would have worked against the aims of local boosters who valued the temple front precisely because so many other libraries also had temple fronts. Their conservative choice ensured that their temple-fronted library could be compared to similar institutions in neighboring towns. Moreover, like

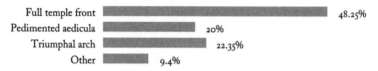

Full temple front   48.25%
Pedimented aedicula   20%
Triumphal arch   22.35%
Other   9.4%

Graph 4.1 Distribution of libraries by compositional types, 1898–1917

Figure 4.9 Carnegie Library, Holdredge, Nebraska, grant offered 1904. Postcard from author's collection.

Figure 4.10 Ackerman and Ross, Free Public Library, San Diego, California, 1901–2 (demolished). Postcard from author's collection.

Figure 4.11 Carnegie Library, Greenfield, Indiana, grant offered 1904. Postcard from author's collection.

the parklike library settings that appealed to both male boosters and reform-minded club women, the temple front was a library image that could be interpreted in a variety of ways. For the club women who founded the institution, the temple-fronted library was the cross-gabled house of the Cawker Public Library rendered in the classical language of antiquity—an appropriate way of designating the library's emergence from the shadowy realm of municipal housekeeping into the full light of official public support. For a town's male commercial elite, the classical temple front was a sign of their participation in up-to-date movements in city planning, a declaration of their faith that their own community was a City Beautiful.[62]

So important was this library imagery to small-town boosters that they clung to it tenaciously, even in the face of pointed critiques from Carnegie's representatives. Bertram campaigned aggressively against the full-blown temple front, castigating "pillars and Greek temple features, costing much money, and giving no return in effective Library accommodation."[63] When these verbal diatribes made little impact on the majority of local design decisions, he took more drastic action, providing smaller and smaller individual grants. In the sample used here, the average cost of each building dropped from over $48,000 in 1901, to under $30,000 in 1902 (table 4.1). By 1904, the average cost of each building dropped to below $15,000, and stayed there for eleven of the next thirteen years.

Bertram's policy had only limited impact on local decisions about library imagery, as library boards forged several strategies to protect the temple front from economies forced on them from above. Most sacrificed the costly dome, while many substituted pilasters for free-standing or engaged columns (graphs 4.2 and 4.3). Another common strategy was to forego the full-blown temple front in favor of the more modest (and

TABLE 4.1 AVERAGE COST PER YEAR ($)

1899	48,750.00	1909	10,000.00
1900	. . .	1910	35,735.00
1901	48,750.00	1911	11,083.33
1902	27,854.06	1912	13,500.00
1903	21,444.00	1913	10,000.00
1904	14,500.00	1914	7,833.33
1905	10,343.75	1915	12,500.00
1906	12,977.00	1916	10,000.00
1907	10,000.00	1917	20,000.00
1908	8,000.00		

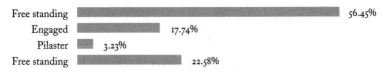

Graph 4.2 Pre-review distribution by column types, 1899–1907

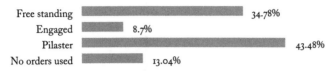

Graph 4.3 Post-review distribution by column types, 1908–1917

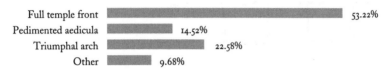

Graph 4.4 Pre-review distribution by compositional types, 1899–1907

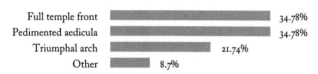

Graph 4.5 Post-review distribution by compositional types, 1908–1917

less expensive) pedimented aedicula. Indeed, the proportion of fully articulated temple fronts dropped significantly after Bertram's intervention (from 53.22 percent to 34.78 percent), while the number of library buildings with a pedimented aedicula rose (from 14.52 percent to 34.78 percent). The proportion of buildings with some version of a temple front, however, remained remarkably constant at about 68 percent throughout the duration of the library program (graphs 4.4 and 4.5).

Recipient towns were equally determined in their ideas about the interior arrangements of their libraries, manipulating the Carnegie-proposed norm to fulfill their own needs. In general, local planning deviations derived from two complimentary habits of mind inherited from the nineteenth century. The first was the desire to house a variety of cultural functions in a single building. A time-honored practice, it received renewed legitimacy at the turn of the century, notably from the tent Chautauquas which brought culture to these smaller towns, reinforcing the idea that it was more appropriate to see the interrelationship

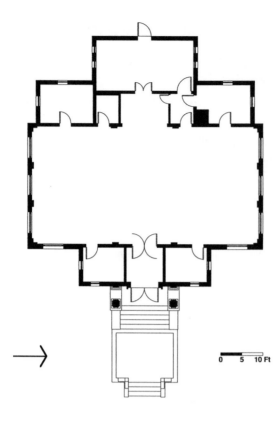

$\rightarrow$

0 5 10 Ft

Figure 4.12 William F. McCaw, Carnegie Library, Tahlequah, Oklahoma, 1905, first-floor plan. Author.

of art, science, history, and literature, than it was to emphasize their differences.[64]

While Bertram denied outright requests for multipurpose buildings, sometimes it only became apparent after the promise had been made that this is what the local library organizers had had in mind. Cambridge, Ohio, for example, submitted plans that included an upper floor about 50 feet square, more than twice the size of the small lecture room that Carnegie allowed at the basement level.[65] Likewise, the library proposed for Parkersburg, West Virginia, had a full second floor with facilities for a study room, photo room, art room, and a general purpose "special room." [66] In towns which had neither the revenue nor the population to support separate institutions of art, natural history, local history, etc., a library that could accommodate these other functions had added appeal.

The second tendency was to express this variety by isolating each function in a room of its own. For instance, the Union City, Indiana, library had two smaller rooms on the first floor, evidently intended as a reference room and a librarian's office. When first finished in 1906, the Warren, Ohio, library boasted not only a children's room, a reference room, and a librarian's room, but also a delivery room, a stack room, and alcoves.[67] Although not identified by function in contemporary records, the Tahlequah, Oklahoma, library had five rooms on the first floor separate from the main reading room (fig. 4.12). In many of these cases, the plans did not look very different from Bertram's suggestions; all the plans in his "Notes" had a separate area for the librarian, while plans B, C, and D, also had separate references areas (see figs. 1.21 and 1.22). In each case, however, the fact that these were rooms (with walls that met the ceiling) meant that in three dimensions these libraries were not arranged to allow a single librarian to supervise the entire floor from her spot at the circulation desk.

Deviations from Bertram's suggestions were even more noticeable at the basement level. Although Bertram did make one concession to non-library functions by including a lecture room in each of the five model schemes, the other room in the basement (other than those for storage, toilets, and heating plant) had to do quadruple duty as staff room, trustees room, workroom and club room. In practice, local decision-makers were more likely to separate each of these functions into its own room. In other cases, the rooms identified for club or staff uses were so big that it seems likely that they were actually intended for some other purpose not sanctioned by Carnegie. In Galesburg, Illinois, for example, Civil War veterans used the room designed as a bindery for their regular biweekly meeting and for memorial services, while the Board of Education used "a portion of the first floor" and in return paid the salary of the children's librarian and a portion of the janitor's salary.[68] Although there is no evidence to indicate that such uses were actually planned for by the people of Galesburg when the library was first built in 1901, such practices were enough to make Bertram turn a deaf ear to their requests for funds to expand the building in 1913.[69] By 1909, it seems, the limits of Bertram's gullibility had narrowed, prompting him to write to the architect of the Harriman, Tennessee, library, "There is no occasion for a club room 45 × 75, which appears about large enough to hold all the adult population of the town.[70]

If local library leaders favored plans that seemed foolish or deliberately ostentatious to Bertram, it was because library efficiency per se was not their primary concern. Particularly for club women who continued to accept responsibility for the inner workings of the library, the building was to house a complex social institution. Cash-poor libraries in smaller towns were forced to serve functions that larger cities divided between a main library and working-class branches, maintaining a sense of propriety for middle-class families, while offering a wholesome diversion for prospective saloon users. The open plans Bertram proposed could accommodate neither the variety of functions a small-town library needed to house nor the range of social classes that it was expected to serve.

In Gainesville, Texas, the library's complex role was particularly clear. Like many other towns west of the Appalachians, Gainesville had a pre-Carnegie library established by a women's literary club. In Gainesville's case, the XLI Club had established a subscription library on the second floor of a commercial block in 1903. Although the library received municipal support from 1908 on, club women continued to dominate library matters into the 1920s. Not only did the club initiate correspondence with Carnegie, but club member Lillian Gunter also continued to act as the librarian, as she had when the library was administered by the club. At the same time, the city council gave Gunter a free hand in library matters, "in order to get rid of the library, something [according to an entry in Gunter's diary] they have long suffered to please the women of the town."[71]

Whatever the reason, Gunter and the XLI Club remained closely involved in library affairs. As mentioned above, the club purchased the site for the library, and may also have been responsible for giving the design commission to William A. Tackett, an architect who had only recently purchased a practice in the neighboring town of Sherman.[72] Certainly, Gunter took a leading role in design decisions. Recalling her experience with the Carnegie library ten years later, she wrote that the building "seemed almost perfect" when it opened in 1914.[73]

Built at a time when recipients of Carnegie gifts received a copy of "Notes on the Erection of Library Bildings" as a matter of routine, the building seems to embody Bertram's ideal of "good taste in bilding." A simply massed building with a single story set on a high basement level, the library had neither a dome nor free-standing classical columns (see fig. 4.13). Instead, its paired pilasters, classical cornice, and low attic, all constructed of yellow brick, seemed to create the sort of "plain, dignified structure" that Bertram had advocated, one that did not "subordinate useful accommodation" to "architectural features."

If the building's exterior appearance conformed to Carnegie expectations, Gainesville's club women were more selective in their application of the philanthropist's planning principles, freely adjusting given models to reflect their own priorities (figs. 4.14 and 4.15). To the extent that they continued to assert woman's special relationship with the library's

Figure 4.13 William A. Tackett, Carnegie Library, Gainesville, Texas, 1913–14.
Courtesy of Cooke County Library.

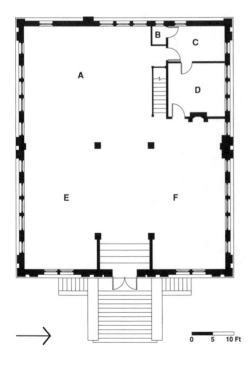

Figure 4.14 Carnegie Library,
Gainesville, first-floor plan. A =
stacks, B = toilet, C = staff room,
D = librarian's office, E = adults'
reading room, F = children's reading room. Author.

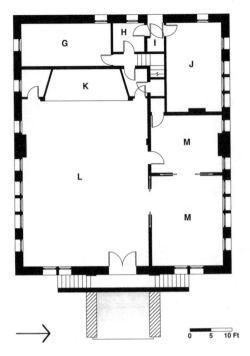

Figure 4.15 Carnegie Library, Gainesville, basement plan. G = work room, H = janitor's room, I = toilet, J = negro reading room, K = stage, L = assembly room, M = club rooms. Author.

Figure 4.16 Carnegie Library, Gainesville, interior view of first floor. Courtesy of Cooke County Library.

Figure 4.17 Carnegie Library, Gainesville, basement assembly room. Courtesy of Cooke County Library.

moral function, club women adopted the centrally-placed delivery desk that emphasized the female librarian's importance. Indeed, they even highlighted the female presence by framing the delivery desk with two square piers topped with Ionic capitals (see fig. 4.16). Yet, they abandoned the symmetry typical of Carnegie's schematic plans in order to cater to what they saw as the distinct user groups. On the south side of the building, a reading room and book stacks gave adult readers unmediated and unsupervised shelf access. In contrast, young readers were more carefully contained in their reading room which was defined by the delivery desk and the librarian's office and staff room on the north side of the building. This arrangement both limited children's access to books and also allowed close supervision of young readers. At the same time, the fireplace on the wall between the children's room and the librarian's office hinted at the librarian's role in providing home influence.

The basement floor was equally telling of the organizer's concern with accommodating Gainesville's complex social dynamic (see fig. 4.15). Below the exterior stairs was the main entrance to the basement, leading directly into the auditorium on the south side of the building (see fig. 4.17). To the north of the auditorium were two club rooms that could be used separately or together. Occupied by the XLI Club, these rooms reminded the community of the club's role in starting the library, even as the club women used them as a base for their continuing fund-raising efforts on the library's behalf.[74]

Carefully segregated from these areas devoted to officially sanctioned community functions were rooms that housed activities that Gainesville's white, middle-class library users preferred not to acknowledge. Here were the janitor's room, a second toilet, and a work room for the messier aspects of library administration. Interior stairs linked work spaces on both floors, while a basement entrance on the rear facade kept library deliveries and trash removal out of sight. Here as well was the

Figure 4.18 Carnegie Library, Gainesville, Negro reading room. At the building's opening, this basement room was designated as a reading room for Gainesville's black population, who were expected to raise money to purchase a supply of books for the room. In fact, the room was never used in this way. Instead, library service for black readers was established in a classroom in the Negro schoolhouse in 1924. Courtesy of Cooke County Library.

"negro reading room" in the northwest corner of the basement, situated to ensure that the staff and the white library patrons need never encounter Gainesville's black readers (see fig. 4.18).[75]

In short, the Gainesville Carnegie library plan did not deviate from the norm presented in Bertram's "Notes" because Gunter and Tackett were unable to read the schematic plans reproduced there. Rather, the local client and her architect rejected Bertram's suggestions for a different reason. Expressing neither the importance of the XLI Club in the town's cultural affairs nor the marginal position of the town's black inhabitants, the open plans advocated for efficiency's sake in New York could not accommodate the social realities of Gainesville.

Conclusion

In the eyes of local citizens, the library was to play a role beyond its function of distributing books. The appeal letters which Carnegie received reveal the extent to which locals felt that their towns were involved in a struggle between good and evil. Their tendency to enumerate the church buildings and saloons in town suggests that the score in this struggle was recorded in the physical landscape of the town. Equally telling was their tendency to cite the construction materials of church buildings rather than the figures for church attendance. The buildings themselves were viewed as forces for good or evil, beyond their stated purpose and apart from the human activity they were built to house. So, while Bertram could see no useful library accommodation in a dome or a temple front, for the locals these things had a very real purpose, albeit an intangible one.

Carnegie libraries, like the one in Gainesville, are by definition cultural institutions. Yet, they are also social institutions. They not only store and organize human knowledge, they mediate and shape human interaction as well. Taken as a group, Carnegie libraries demonstrate vividly that these two functions sometimes come into conflict. The Carnegie Corporation's ideal plan sought to facilitate the efficient distribution of books. At the same time, this ideal plan evened out the social experience of the library, capturing very little of the subtlety of small-town social life. A compromise between these two functions, Carnegie libraries built in small towns across the United States embody a planning variety barely hinted at by the similar classical motifs that grace their facades.

WORKING

The Feminization of Librarianship

FOR THE CARNEGIE LIBRARY PROGRAM, the librarian was a central figure, whose presence at the charging desk determined the layout of the entire building. Yet, Carnegie's ideal librarian remained an almost mythical figure, an efficient cog perfectly meshed into the smooth workings of the library machine. In reality, the actual people who staffed Carnegie libraries were quite human, amalgams of ambition, jealousy, prejudice, altruism, and other human attributes that complicated their interaction with readers and with the efficient library setting. To complicate matters further, the profession itself was in a state of flux. Beginning in the 1880s and 1890s, a new emphasis on public service, the establishment of library schools, and an influx of women into the profession transformed the character of American librarianship.[1] Although these library trends predated the wholesale phase of Carnegie's library philanthropy, the library buildings erected with Carnegie money were informed by these changes in librarianship, and in turn formed the stage upon which librarians, particularly female librarians, experimented with their new roles. In this context, Carnegie libraries took on roles and meanings that had been unanticipated by the benefactor.

Engendering American Librarianship

For those who staffed American libraries in the early twentieth century, the issue of professionalization remained an important one. As noted in chapter 2, librarians (like their middle-class counterparts in architecture) were still in the process of negotiating their claim to professional status with American society at large. Indeed, many of the changes in librarianship that began in the 1890s can be interpreted as strategies for establishing this special status. Beginning at Columbia College in 1887, schools of library science offered institutional recognition to the claim that librarianship required specialized knowledge and training. The new emphasis on public service that comprised the "modern library idea" was equally a part of this strategy, calculated to secure the good will of the general public and to convince them of the librarian's social usefulness. Likewise, the language of librarianship was reinvigorated from the 1880s on, in order to dispel the image of bookish passivity that had precluded librarianship from the ranks of the more worldly "true" professions of law and medicine.

This new language of librarianship drew its rhetorical power from the sharpness of the contrast between the old librarian and the new. Characterized almost universally as the custodian of books, the old-style librarian was presented as physically diminished, passive, and all but emasculated.[2] Typical is an article from the *Library Journal,* in which an anonymous writer explained that "the older custodian has done his work, and is everywhere retiring to private life," thus associating traditional librarianship with advanced age and physical decay. The same article cast the old-style librarian in the role of "a referee in finding the right sources of knowledge," neatly placing him on the sidelines of the active life.[3] An outspoken critic of old-style librarianship, Melvil Dewey added to the list of unflattering comparisons, likening the old type of librarian to "a crabbed and unsympathetic old fossil." Described by Dewey as "an arsenal in time of peace," the old type of library was the saddest of relics, a military installation excluded from battle.[4]

In contrast, the new librarianship was associated with vigor and action, and depended on traits that the nineteenth century attributed to masculinity. Writers emphasized the breadth of vision required of the new librarian, "the power of taking a large, impersonal view of things." Equally important, the new librarian needed to exercise authority over others, a knowledge of the world of affairs, a head for business, a willingness to court responsibility, originality, and a willingness to experiment.[5] Paralleling exactly the qualifications that the nineteenth century had required for successful businessmen, this list of traits suggests an attempt on the part of librarians to create new links between culture and commerce. Recast as an activity requiring conventionally male qualities, the new librarianship was defined to emphasize its legitimate place in the masculine sphere, and to secure its rightful place in the constellation of professions.

When describing modern librarianship, Dewey favored military analogies. In contrast to the old library's impotent arsenal, the new library was for him "an army in the field with all guns limbered."[6] By extension, he claimed that "the great librarian . . . must have a head as clear as the master in diplomacy; a hand as strong as he who quells the raging mob or leads great armies onto victory; and a heart as great as he who, to save others, will, if need be, lay down his life." Going on to explain that "most of the men who will achieve this greatness will be women," Dewey used exaggerated masculine imagery in part to highlight his support of women in the profession.[7] At the same time, this imagery belongs to a wide variety of cultural manifestations that Jackson Lears has associated with turn-of-the-century antimodernism. Dewey's military analogies parallel the martial ideal and the worship of force that developed in the late nineteenth century as an antidote to the banal routine of a rationalized culture. Likewise, his admiration for the willingness to risk one's very life in the service of others smacks of the intensity of experience favored at that time as the path to authentic selfhood. The modern library idea, then, was more than just an attempt to bring books to the people; like the glorification of the strenuous life, the emergence of organized athletics, and other attacks on the perceived feminization of American culture, the modern library idea sought to reinvest librarianship with manly vigor.[8]

In the same years that librarianship was being recast along aggressively masculine lines, women were entering the profession in increasing numbers. At the time, American library leaders wrote articles in the professional and popular press detailing the changing face of librarianship, while their British counterparts commented on this peculiarly American phenomenon; Britain's library leaders were astounded by the fact that in contrast to their own situation, large numbers of women attended ALA meetings, sometimes even outnumbering the men. Historical records bear out these contemporary impressions, showing that two-thirds of library workers in 1878 were women, while that figure had climbed to 78.5 percent by 1910.[9]

The abruptness of the shift is attributable in part to what librarianship offered to the women involved. Like the club women who founded subscription libraries in the late nineteenth century, many women were drawn to librarianship by what they perceived as their natural aptitude for disseminating culture. Indeed, many women made the transition from volunteer library work to professional librarianship within the same institution. That women would follow this path was recognized at the time; a summer course in library science at the New York State Library School in Albany, New York, was aimed specifically "for librarians . . . who desire to prepare themselves for better work in their present positions."[10] By the turn of the century, professional librarianship (with its new emphasis on public service) was increasingly attractive as a means of combatting the sense of uselessness that plagued the first generation of college-educated women. The impulse to "share the race life" that prompted Jane Addams's establishment of Hull House served to push many of her contemporaries towards careers in library work.[11]

The official reaction to this influx of women was mixed. The most active proponent of women in the field was certainly Melvil Dewey, who recognized an able and growing pool of library workers in college-educated women, excluded as they were from many other careers.[12] In an address before the Association of Collegiate Alumnae in 1886, he noted the "dearth of trained librarians," and encouraged his audience to consider librarianship as a career more pleasant than teaching and one that offered women an opportunity to be more effective than their male counterparts in the ministry.[13] Dewey also revealed that he saw little conflict in the image of the library militant with a woman leading the charge. Beginning his address with the military analogies cited above, Dewey defied logic somewhat by going on to describe librarianship as an activity closely related to domestic concerns. "The natural qualities most important in library work," Dewey assured his listeners, "are accuracy, order (or what we call the housekeeping instinct), executive ability, and above all earnestness and enthusiasm." What is more, Dewey de-emphasized the strenuousness of library work, explaining "that physically the library is less exacting than the shorter hours of the school," that "it avoids much of the nervous strain and the wear and tear of the class room," and that "there is hardly any occupation that is so free from annoying surroundings."[14] According to Dewey, then, librarianship was well suited to the conventionally-defined mental and physical abilities of women. As a recruiting talk for the new school of library science that Dewey was about to open at Columbia College in New York, the address seems to have been successful; seventeen of the twenty students in the school's inaugural class were women, a fact which infuriated Columbia's trustees and precipitated Dewey's suspension the next year, and the eventual installation of Dewey and his school at the New York State library in Albany.[15]

Few other male library leaders accepted women into their ranks so happily, as they felt the presence of women would undercut their already shaky bid for professional recognition.[16] Circumstances, however, forced reluctant male librarians to reconsider their position. The reinvigorated language of librarianship had not convinced library boards and taxpayers that librarians were entitled to remuneration comparable to that commanded by other professionals. As a result, the profession failed to attract men in sufficient numbers to meet the high demand for educated library workers created by the great increase in the number of public libraries that began independently of the Carnegie program in the 1880s.

Women offered certain advantages that their brothers did not. As one librarian so bluntly put it in 1904, they "do not cost as much as men." Indeed, while the average annual salary for a male librarian in a small library was $2,118 in 1904, his female counterpart received only $1,429 for the same work.[17] The reasons for this inequality are all too familiar. Assuming that physical frailty, emotional instability, and a preference for marriage over career would make female job performance erratic and short-lived, employers valued women workers less than their male counterparts, rationalizing the practice of unequal pay as fairness to men, who often had greater financial responsibilities.[18] Shut out from many other opportunities for respectable and useful work, women felt compelled to accept less. For libraries with tight budgets and a growing demand for books, it was an increasingly attractive partnership.

Active partners, however, were not equal partners. By the early twentieth century, library leaders had supported a highly gendered library hierarchy, in which men were to dominate executive and management positions in the field, while women were encouraged to fill less prestigious and lower-paid positions.[19] John Cotton Dana, Newark's nationally prominent librarian, was a longtime Dewey supporter and a proponent of women in library work. Yet, in a 1911 exegesis on the subject, he spelled out with unselfconcious clarity that women could aspire to be "assistants" and "subordinates" in the various departments of the library, but rarely more.

What is more, Dana listed a number of specialities within librarianship that he felt were particularly suited to female skills. He emphasized women's particular suitedness to technical work—cataloguing, classifying, index making, book repair—and work with children. In each case, intellectual ability was not a job requirement, and Dana even went to some pains to assure his readers that a woman did not need to be "distinctly bookish" to work in a library. Cataloging, for instance, he suggested for women who "have some skill with the pen, . . . write clearly, . . . are painstaking and accurate and can . . . follow exactly rules set for [their] guidance," while work at the lending desk was suited to those who "have an agreeable presence and know how to say 'no' as pleasantly as 'yes,' yet tend to be obliging rather than the opposite." Even Dana's description of reference work (arguably the most intellectually rigorous area of library work) was stripped of its intellectual content when applied to women, reduced instead to being able to "feel almost instinctively what a book, and especially an encyclopedia or any other work of reference, can tell you." [20]

Dana's description of library work for women was, of course, based upon conventional stereotypes of the ideal woman as pleasant, malleable, helpful, accurate, detail-oriented, naturally intuitive, but not too smart. By suggesting that women were innately suited for many aspects of the work, it was intended to welcome women into the field. In the context of librarianship's battle for professional recognition, it served other purposes as well. To the extent that these innate skills were defined as devoid of any intellectual spark, it helped to rationalize the lower pay offered to women in the field. Finally, by denying women the opportunity to exercise professional authority even over the reader, this definition of women in librarianship virtually guaranteed that most women would remain subordinate in the hierarchy of the library staff. For library leadership, which remained predominantly male, it was an ideal situation—a means of welcoming low-paid, but highly-skilled, workers, while reserving positions of power for themselves.

Engendering Library Design

Although Carnegie voiced no opinion on the issues that were confronting American librarianship in the early twentieth century, his library program nonetheless had an impact on the field. Most important, perhaps, his philanthropy augmented the conditions that supported the entry of women into librarianship. By funding a dramatic increase in the number of public libraries in the United States, the Carnegie program amplified the demand for qualified library staff. After 1908, the increasing emphasis on efficiency had its impact as well. An attempt on Bertram's part to reduce elaborate architectural expression on the exterior of Carnegie libraries had only mixed success (see chapter 4), but an unintended side effect was longer lasting; smaller appropriations resulted in substantially smaller annual maintenance funds. The $15,000 that was common in the years after 1904 meant that municipal governments were only required to provide the library with an annual budget of $1,500, to cover the purchase of books and fuel and the salaries of librarian, assistants, and custodial staff. Under these circumstances, library boards were more inclined to hire lower-paid females for library work.

Equally important, once Bertram espoused a specific planning ideal, he implicitly involved the Carnegie program in the on-going debate about the nature of American librarianship. Written with the advice of male library leaders, the various editions of the "Notes on the Erection of Library Bildings" can be read as the material expression of their view of librarianship (see appendix 1 for one version of the "Notes"). In this context, Bertram's inattention to large urban libraries is significant; after all, in the large staffs of these libraries the gender-based library hierarchy was relatively easy to maintain, and easy to translate into spatial terms. In contrast, the small library represented in the "Notes" was the locus of great changes in librarianship. Not only was the hierarchy more compact in a small staff, but library leaders acknowledged that the librarian of the small library was more likely to be a woman. Thus, the emphasis in the "Notes" on the planning of the small library suggests that Bertram and his professional advisors were particularly concerned about defining the scope of activity for the female librarian.

At first glance, the "Notes" themselves present a remarkably simple setting for day-to-day activities of librarianship, with only two spaces within the library designated for the librarian's use (see figs. 1.21 and 1.22). Of primary importance was the centrally-placed charging desk, around which the rest of the library was planned. Here, the librarian was expected to pass the greater part of the workday, overseeing the entire library from its central position. Also designated for the librarian's use was the multipurpose staff room, which did at least double duty, serving the staff as a rest room and providing a venue for the messier aspects of the librarian's job. Its basement location, isolated from public areas of the building, ensured that it remained of secondary importance in the librarian's workday.

This arrangement is deceptively simple, and the close relationship between librarian and charging desk communicates a great deal about the nature of librarianship as Bertram and his advisors saw it. The term "charging desk" itself is significant. In the closed stack public library of the late nineteenth century, the point of initial contact between reader and book was the delivery desk, a long, straight, uninterrupted counter designed to isolate the public from the library's treasures (see fig. 1.10). Here, readers approached to hand in their request slips, retreated while the page disappeared into the book storage area, and approached again a few minutes later to receive delivery of the books requested. Like its predecessor, the twentieth-century charging desk was also the place where readers charged out books. Yet, the charging desk was no longer perceived as a barrier between the reader and the books; indeed in the open stack library of the twentieth century, readers helped themselves to books directly from the shelf and (reversing nineteenth-century practice) presented the books to the librarian at the desk.

As the "Notes" suggest, this dramatic change in library philosophy had an impact on the form of the charging desk. Despite the fact that plans A, B, and D in the "Notes" continue to use the term "Delivery" to identify the book charging area, none of the six plans presented includes the long straight counter that had hampered public access to books in libraries built in the late nineteenth century. Instead, all the plans show the librarian's post as a smaller, compact desk, that might have slowed but never halted the movement of readers towards the book shelves. In plan B, the ends of the charging desk are canted back toward the interior of the library, actually encouraging and speeding up the encounter between the reader and the books.

Although the charging desks in the "Notes" are little more than schematic representations, their size, location, and shape (particularly in plan B) are consistent with the charging desks sold by the Library Bureau. Although the company offered charging desks as stock items at least as early as 1902, a later catalogue devoted solely to charging desks argued that the location, shape, size, and design of this crucial piece of library furniture needed to be custom fit to each library.[21] Indeed, the desks depicted varied dramatically in size and shape. A tiny U-shaped desk at the Solvay (N.Y.) public library was designed for the use of a single librarian (fig. 5.1). The V-shaped desk at the Atlantic City (N.J.) Public Library (see fig. 2.2) and the octagonal desk at one of Cincinnati's branches (fig. 5.2) could each accommodate at least two library workers. By far the largest charging desks depicted were those from Manhattan's branch libraries; these large square enclosures were the size of small rooms and could accommodate five library workers (fig. 5.3; see also fig. 3.45).

Despite the variety represented in this catalogue, Library Bureau charging desks were all designed specifically to aid in the efficient conduct of library administration. To this end, all desks were designed to respond to the spaces in which they were situated. In every case, this ensured that the desk occupied the least amount of floor space necessary to fulfill the functions of charging and discharging books. In Cincinnati, the octagonal desk further contributed to the efficient administration of the library by allowing the librarian an uninterrupted view into the radial stacks behind the desk. In New York branches, the large square enclosure, called the "pen," created narrow passages that helped librarians control the movement of readers and books; whether entering or exiting reading and book storage areas, library patrons moved in single file along a one-way passage directly adjacent to the desk (see fig. 3.42.).

The concern with maximum book-handling efficiency was equally evident in the interior details of each library Bureau charging desk (fig. 5.4; see also fig. 5.1). Indeed, according to a Library Bureau catalogue of 1902 describing a stock item,

This charging desk is so arranged that the person using it can reach all necessary material with the minimum of effort and without change of position. As shown in the illustration it is adapted particularly to the Brown charging system but it can be modified to suit other systems equally well. The center of the counter is cut

Figure 5.1 Library Bureau charging desk installed in the Solvay Public Library, Solvay, New York. Library Bureau, *Charging Desks* (n.d.), 21.

Figure 5.2 Library Bureau charging desk installed in the Walnut Hills Branch of the Cincinnati Public Library, Cincinnati, Ohio. Library Bureau, *Charging Desks* (n.d.), 13.

down to contain a tray divided into rows for charging cards. Patent adjustable blocks maintain the proper angle of the cards in any position. At either side of the center a large drawer is arranged with extension slides for borrowers' pockets. Other drawers are devoted to cash and general utility, while two contain the alphabetic register of borrowers.

Even a desk as small as that at the Solvay Public Library included a pull-out desk surface, a card catalogue on a swivel base (for the use of librarian and patrons), a charging tray (for the storage of book cards), a card-sorting drawer (divided into nine compartments), and another drawer for an alphabetic list of borrowers.[22] Date stamp, rubber bands, paper clips, every piece of equipment had its place at the charging desk. Serving to ward off dust and to hide the clutter of cards, roller covers left the desk an unencumbered surface that, at the turn of the century, was associated with efficiency.

With their emphasis on careful design to enhance library efficiency,

Figure 5.3 Library Bureau charging desk installed in a branch library in Manhattan, showing "the carefully considered interior arrangement of the desk." Library Bureau, *Charging Desks* (n.d.), 8.

such charging desks were predicated on ideals shared by Carnegie, and it is hardly surprising that the Carnegie program advocated their use. Indeed, as the centrally placed control center for library administration, the charging desk was the heart of the Carnegie library plan. Without it, the library was incomplete. With it, the library was transformed into an efficient machine for the distribution of books. Playing on this factory analogy, library literature at the time often compared the centrally placed librarian to the manager of a factory. Indeed, library leaders themselves preferred this analogy, as it seemed more closely aligned with their professional aspirations.[23]

In reality, the physical environment planned for the librarian suggested something less prestigious. Unlike the factory manager who supervised his workers from an elevated position, the librarian sat among her charges; if she could supervise their activities, they could just as easily subject her to comparable scrutiny. Indeed, the librarian in a small Carnegie library was less like a manager than she was like other pink-collar workers. Although the language of the "Notes" remains gender neutral, the charging desk was remarkably like the work stations of other jobs increasingly assigned to female workers at the turn of the century. Whether a telephone operator, a typist, or a file clerk, the middle-class working woman found herself in remarkably similar settings (figs. 5.5 and 5.6). Like other pink-collar workers, the librarian worked in a seated position, at a work station designed to minimize necessary movements; she was surrounded by technologically advanced tools that defined and structured the work into a series of repetitive tasks; and she was unable to complete the assigned tasks of the job without these specialized tools. Finally, for all these women, job success was measured quantitatively, in the number of books discharged, in the number of cards filed, in the number of calls put through, in the number of pages typed.[24]

Although such feminized tasks were often described by elevated titles like file executive or professional librarian, the physical settings in which these tasks were carried out were substantially different from the work spaces of male professionals. By the end of the nineteenth century, professional men used control over their work space as one of the sym-

This charging desk is so arranged that the person using it can reach all necessary material with the minimum of effort and without change of position. As shown in the illustration it is adapted particularly to the Brown charging system but it can be modified to suit other systems equally well. The center of the counter is cut down to contain a tray divided into rows for charging cards. Patent adjustable blocks maintain the proper angle of the cards in any position. At either side of the center a large drawer is arranged with extension slides for borrowers' pockets. Other drawers are devoted to cash and general utility, while two contain the alphabetic register of borrowers.

Figure 5.4 Library Bureau charging desk, c. 1902. *Library Catalog* (1902), 50.

bols of their authority, symbols that were carefully orchestrated to intimidate laymen, making them more receptive to expert advice. Having made an appointment to see a doctor or a lawyer, even the promptest of clients had to wait in an outer office. While waiting, the client had time to peruse the impressive framed certificates hanging on the walls or even to peer at the spines of the leather-bound textbooks on the shelf. As if these signs of erudition were not enough to inspire the client's awe, the practitioner also controlled the precise timing of the consultation, either by entering the room or by having a receptionist bring the client into him.[25] Working to gain their own professional recognition, nineteenth-century librarians had used a similar ploy. The head librarian of the Allegheny City library, for example, had a private office and spatial control that were symbols of his professionalism (see fig. 1.7).

In contrast, women in predominantly female occupations had no such control of their work spaces. Whether seated in tight rows in the typewriter operators' department of Frank Lloyd Wright's Larkin Company

Figure 5.5 Typewriter Operators' Department in Frank Lloyd Wright's Larkin Building, Buffalo, New York, photo c. 1915. Courtesy of William Clarkson.

Figure 5.6 Telephone exchange at Metropolitan Life Insurance Company, 1908.
Courtesy of MetLife Archives.

Building, or at a bank of switchboards at the local telephone exchange, their work environment was completely controlled by others, with their work equipment bolted in place, and they themselves were under constant scrutiny by a male supervisor. Instead of having offices of their own, women in female occupations often had jobs that reinforced spatial barriers that underlined and enhanced the professional prestige of the men who actually wielded authority.[26]

Transcending the Limits of the Gendered Work Station

As it developed, there was a substantial gap between the theory of female librarianship and its practice. Although women who entered librarianship at the turn of the century conscientiously worked to present a unified front with the established male leadership, their actions reveal that they did not share the official view of the female librarian as a passive contributor to the library's mission.[27] Indeed, differences between male and female views on women as library workers seem almost inevitable. Male library leaders looked at feminization in the context of the profession, assessing its implications with respect to their own professional status, while incorporating women into the social hierarchy that already existed within the library. As outsiders, women were free to consider this issue in a wider context, looking at librarianship as only a part of the social web. For reform-minded women attracted to librarianship, the question was not how women should adapt their behavior to the library profession, but how the library profession could change to contribute more actively to contemporary social reform movements.

There is a strong thread of irony woven through this episode in American library history. Dewey and others had adopted a militaristic rhetoric to imply that librarianship was an aggressive, militant occupation naturally suited to men, an occupation in which passive handmaidens played only supporting roles. The women who actually answered the call, however, did not interpret this rhetoric as gender-specific. Instead of interpreting the militaristic imagery of librarianship as a rationale for gender-based barriers to professional advancement, female librarians embraced the ethos of aggressive librarianship as their own creed. Taking up a weapon originally forged against them, female librarians used it to move the library and librarianship in new directions.

These new library directions were closely linked to the Progressive movement. Indeed, the new librarians were committed to such articles of the Progressive faith as the importance of the physical environment in causing or curing social ills, the moral good of efficiency, and the role of education in achieving social cohesion. They were also completely enmeshed in the dense network of Progressive practice: They knew and compared notes with the settlement worker, the school teacher, the county demonstrator, and other reform-minded women in newly created or recently feminized professions. They read and contributed to Progressive journals, learning their techniques of documentation and persuasion along the way. And, this new generation of librarians opened their libraries to a wide variety of Progressive activities.[28]

Especially important for the new direction of librarianship was the development of specialities within librarianship, the focus of which was determined largely by the social ideals of Progressivism. In urban systems, Progressive concerns with child-saving and with the reform of immigrant families prompted librarians to forge a specialty out of work with children, while in rural settings Progressive librarians focused on county library systems and the efficient dissemination of scientific knowledge to farm families. Although built upon conventional definitions of the female sphere, these new professional specialties actually helped women cope with the threat of professional marginality. For one thing, as new fields that served lower-class clients, these activities provided an effective arena for women who wished to remove themselves from direct competition with their male colleagues.[29] Most important, the new specialties provided a theoretical knowledge-base that was integral to winning and maintaining professional prestige; the children's librarian, for instance, had to be well versed in the theories of the emerging field of child psychology. New specialists also used this mastery of theoretical knowledge to claim higher pay and greater autonomy within the library hierarchy.[30] Thus, while the physical settings created by the new specialists tell us much about Progressive attitudes toward race and ethnicity, they also provide equally important insights into librarians' attitudes about themselves.

At Work in an Urban Branch

For those who worked at branch libraries in urban neighborhoods, librarianship was one of a number of reform-oriented occupations closely associated with the child-saving movement. Indeed, child-saving had become the watchword in urban reform from the middle of the nineteenth century on, as the number of children on city streets convinced middle-class Americans that slum families incapable of socializing their own children were the primary threat to the nation's social harmony. In the 1880s, child-saving was the excuse for drastic interference with slum families, as Charles Loring Brace and the Children's Aid Society "placed out" slum children to what they assumed were more capable farm families.[31]

By the 1890s, the concern with child-saving was still strong, but skepticism about the institutions that served as surrogate families changed the emphasis of this work. Instead of removing children from their urban homes, Progressive reformers, many of them women, focused instead on establishing channels for improving the quality of life within slum households. Tenement reform, municipal water reform, and the establishment of playgrounds all worked to improve the infrastructure necessary for a healthy homelife. Day nurseries and a program of home-visitors from the Infant Welfare Society sought to improve the home-making practices of immigrant mothers. Even more numerous were Progressive programs intended to make up for the inadequacies of the slum families, without actually removing the child from home. In day nurseries, kindergartens, kitchen gardens, public schools, and public libraries, women acted as professional mothers to slum children, giving them the nurture that they would have received in the "most refined homes." [32]

For the female librarians who worked in urban branches, the public library was primarily a child-oriented institution. Although some librarians established small collections of foreign-language books to attract adult readers from immigrant families, most of their attention was focused on the children of slum neighborhoods. The library, they argued, was an even more effective child-saving institution than the public school. Children came to the library willingly, and were therefore more receptive to its educational possibilities. Open for extended hours, and not requiring a long time commitment, the library was also more effective at reaching children who had had to leave school, either to go out to work or to stay home to care for younger brothers and sisters. Librarians even held out the hope that enthusiastic young readers might convince their parents to accompany them; thus, children were seen as the primary objects of the library's mission and as an integral part of the institution's successful expansion. [33]

Like their Progressive counterparts in other fields, children's librarians were particularly sensitive to the environment's role in reform efforts. [34] But while these new specialists were consistently interested in questions of the physical form of the children's room, their ideas changed substantially over time as they sought to master and incorporate the findings of child psychology into the library's planning, arrangement, and furnishing. Beginning in the 1890s and continuing unabated until World War I, discussions about the proper form of the children's room had a direct impact on the ideal library plans propagated by the Carnegie library program, and eventually lead children's librarians to reject some elements of that physical form.

Since the first experiments with library service to children, there had been increasing concern among librarians about physical arrangements that would best accommodate young readers. The children's corner of the 1890s, specially fitted with low tables and chairs, was replaced, in theory and in practice, by completely separate reading rooms for children by 1900. [35] At about the same time, a host of other planning and furnishing ideas were advocated by professional women specializing in children's librarianship. One such librarian was Clara W. Hunt, the superintendent of the Children's Department at the Brooklyn Public Library. In a series of articles written for the *Library Journal* between 1901 and 1903, Hunt described her ideal of a "wide, lofty, spacious" children's room, with ample natural and artificial light, with neither alcoves nor book cases to block the librarian's view, with a sound-deadening floor covering, and furnished with chairs that could not be easily overturned. For Hunt, the order and spaciousness of such a room contrasted sharply with the tenement apartment, "a cramped little flat, where one can hardly set foot down without stepping on a baby," and offered an important antidote to what she perceived as the inadequate homelife of working-class readers. Hoping to create an environment in which the child "feels free to express himself in a natural, friendly atmosphere," Hunt began to imbue the children's room with the qualities and functions of a middle-class home. Indeed, in writing of "the child's love for the room," Hunt implicitly saw the children's room as a surrogate home for young readers.[36]

The "natural, friendly atmosphere" advocated by Hunt was bounded by some firm limits. Hunt regularly encouraged librarians to impress upon young readers that the children's reading room was a place for reading and study. A child who misbehaved was to be sent out at once, a child wandering aimlessly was to be encouraged to go to the park, and even eager library users were to be taught "what a library reading room means." Indeed, Hunt's interest in the arrangement and furnishing of the children's room was predicated on the idea that the right physical environment made it easier to maintain order in the library. Spaciousness, for instance, had "a tendency to check the behavior that goes with tenement-house conditions," while covered floors encouraged readers to keep their voices low. Bent on eradicating discomfort and its attendant restlessness, Hunt was less concerned with accommodating individual readers than she was with minimizing their threat to library order.

This overriding concern with maintaining order in the library affected several urban branches built with Carnegie funds. In Brooklyn, in Pittsburgh, and in St. Louis, all branch libraries followed accepted practice and included separate reading rooms designated for children's use (see figs. 3.34, 3.36, 3.39, 3.40, 3.46, and 3.47). Yet, in each case, the children's room was practically identical to the comparable room for adults, both in size, in shape, in the orderly arrangement of tables, and in decorative treatment. Period photographs showing children seated at almost every chair, facing the table squarely, and concentrating intently on the books in front of them were almost certainly staged for the camera; nonetheless, they reveal that library officials who commissioned the photos envisioned remarkably similar patterns of room use in both adult and children's reading rooms (fig. 5.7). In other words, young readers were kept separate from adults, but were expected to behave like their older counterparts.[37]

More important for the history of Carnegie libraries, it was this turn-of-the-century image of the children's room that was codified in Bertram's "Notes" in the second decade of the twentieth century. Although Plan A is particularly close to the overall arrangement of branch libraries in Brooklyn, Pittsburgh, and St. Louis, the children's rooms in all six ideal plans share characteristics with these early examples. With their ample proportions, their simple footprints, and their rectangular tables set in neat rows, they seem designed to encourage orderly behavior. Indeed, Carnegie's insistence on open planning to allow for supervision from the centrally placed charging desk meant that adult and children's reading rooms were largely open to one another, and reinforced the need for children to behave like small adults while in the library.

By the time the "Notes" appeared in 1911, ideas about the planning

Figure 5.7 Alden & Harlow, Carnegie Library of Pittsburgh, Hazelwood Branch, Pittsburgh, 1899–1900, children's room. Courtesy of Carnegie Library, Pittsburgh.

of children's rooms had already begun to change in important ways. Instead of seeing the children's room as a means of minimizing the adverse effects of children on the library, librarians increasingly considered the children's room as an opportunity for maximizing the library's positive impact on the child. Initially, this movement ignored the library's educational role, treating it instead simply as a means of providing slum-dwellers with the light and air lacking in tenement neighborhoods. This message was brought home to the reform-minded readers of *Charities and the Commons* by a pair of photographs that contrasted the open-lot site of the Hudson Park Branch of the New York Public Library with the congested area "between the tenements back of the library" (fig. 5.8). Juxtaposing the good and the bad, the technique was borrowed from reform photographers who regularly published in the journal, and underlines the library's role as one of a number of urban institutions that Progressives used almost interchangeably in their war on urban squalor.[38]

Progressive concerns with light and air eventually lead librarians to make more drastic changes in the form of their libraries. Inspired by the popularity of a roof garden at the nearby University Settlement, librarians included an open-air reading room on the roof of Manhattan's Rivington Street branch when it was built with Carnegie funds in 1906 (see fig. 6.2 below). Tiled, enclosed with a rail, lined with flower boxes, and topped with an awning, the roof top reading room attracted a daily attendance of forty or fifty children, providing "a pleasant outdoor effect" and a respite from the sweltering heat of the crowded summer streets. Advertised as the first of its kind in the United States, Rivington Street's roof-top reading room became the model for comparable facilities in at least three other Manhattan branches.[39]

Even more important to Progressive ideas about the proper form of the children's room were the new theories developed in the late nineteenth century by psychologists like G. Stanley Hall and his better-known student, John Dewey. Envisioning child development as essentially the recapitulation of human evolution, Hall argued that childhood was a series of natural stages, each very different from the others, but each crucial to the development of the child; children could no more skip one of these phases than the human race could leap to a more advanced level of civilization. Pursuing the practical implications of this theory, Hall criticized what he dubbed the "scholiocentric" school, where the needs of the institution came first, requiring students to adjust to a uniform curriculum. In contrast, Hall's ideal was a "pedocen-

Figure 5.8 "Contrast of Library and Tenement." *Charities and the Commons* 15 (17 March 1906), 887.

tric" school, one in which the needs of the child and the scientifically-determined stages of child development determined the content and format of the lesson plan.[40]

For children's librarians, Hall's advice was a revelation. Although he did not extend his analysis beyond the school to other supporting educational institutions, his analysis confirmed the need for children's librarianship, and helped clarify the goals of this new female-dominated professional specialty. When the children's librarian distinguished herself from the generalist only by the age of the reader she served, she placed herself in a degraded professional position; when her readers were perceived as small, inadequate versions of adult readers, her claims to professional expertise suffered. However, when the children's librarian distinguished herself from the generalist by a knowledge of the scientifically-established stages of child-development, she placed her claims to professional status on a sounder footing; when her readers were perceived as passing through a crucial stage in human development, she was in a better position to garner professional recognition. In short, by redeeming the child, child psychology also helped redeem the children's librarian.[41]

Like their male counterparts of a previous generation, the women who dominated children's librarianship in the 1910s, sought to express and consolidate their professional status by claiming a particular expertise in library design, and particularly in the design of children's rooms. Advanced for the 1890s, the library designs codified in Bertram's "Notes" now seemed old-fashioned. Worse yet, in assuming that the goal of the children's room was to accommodate young readers who acted like adults, they were what Hall might call "scholiocentric" libraries; now children's librarians began to take a more active role in defining and securing the "pedocentric" library.

In Detroit, the campaign for the pedocentric library was fought early, beginning in 1910 when the city began the first of its eight Carnegie branches.[42] It is difficult to pinpoint who acted as the client for these branch buildings. The Detroit Library Commission had responsibility for the branches, but took only a supervisory role in the process. Even the procedure used for selecting an architect precluded any group discussion of library planning issues; as noted in chapter 3, each commissioner was allowed to name an architect, with site assignments made by lottery. Although the commissioners approved finished plans, they did not engage in detailed discussions of programmatic requirements for the buildings. Instead, the commissioners relied heavily on the professional advice of local librarians. While Detroit's chief librarian, Henry M. Utley, and his assistant, Adam Strohm, were the official voice of librarianship in commission meetings, Detroit's branch librarians seem to have acted as clients for the branch buildings. Having visited branch libraries in Cleveland and Pittsburgh in October of 1910, the branch department reported to the commissioners that they were "giving much time and thought to the plans," with an eye to "certain improvements that appeal to the people who will have the buildings in charge."[43]

In theory, the idea of having librarians act as client was perfectly consistent with Carnegie's ideals. After all, the "Notes," then in the final throes of preparation, were intended to codify the advice of librarians for towns that had no librarian. In reality, the Detroit branches were a far cry from the schematic plans presented in the "Notes." This is particularly true of the Herbert Bowen branch, designed by the firm of Stratton and Baldwin as the first of Detroit's Carnegie branches (figs. 5.9 and 5.10). Important figures in Detroit's Arts and Crafts Movement, the architects rejected the classical temple front used to create a formal image in so many American library buildings.[44] Adopting the practice of English contemporaries like William Lethaby and Edwin Lutyens, they turned instead to English classicism of the seventeenth century, utilizing the handcrafted treatment of English-bond brick, while the distilled classicism of the granite door frames signalled the public nature of the building. Likewise, the building's T-shaped footprint acknowledged the strict symmetry of library planning practice. Yet, its placement on the site with the stem of the T facing the street, and its off-axis entries, subverted the formality usually associated with symmetrical planning.

Inside, the plan of the Bowen branch revealed more abrupt depar-

Figure 5.9 Stratton and Baldwin, Detroit Public Library, Herbert Bowen Branch, 1910–12. Author.

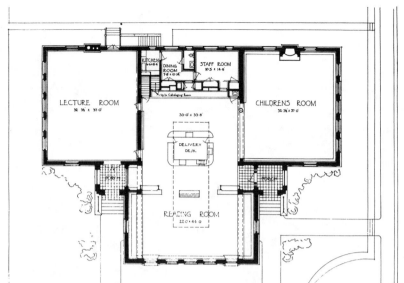

Figure 5.10 Detroit Public Library, Bowen Branch, first-floor plan. Courtesy of the Burton Historical Collection of the Detroit Public Library.

tures from planning practices that Bertram advocated (fig. 5.11). Although both adult and children's reading rooms were easily visible from a centrally-placed delivery desk, the adults reading room was set at right angles to the children's room, in the stem of the T at the front of the building. The area behind the delivery desk contained a suite of rooms devoted to the library staff (including a multipurpose staff room, a dining room, a kitchen, and a bathroom) on the first floor, with a second-floor cataloguing room above. Although this second-floor room led to a gallery overlooking the charging area and adult reading room, it was an enclosed space and assumed the presence of more than one librarian. Finally, Stratton and Baldwin located the lecture room on the first floor, echoing the children's room.

Predictably, this plan did not appeal to Bertram, who identified the lecture room's first-floor location, the position of the entrance and delivery desk, and the balcony as elements that departed too radically from general principles that were proving successful in other branch libraries. Yet, when Bertram asked William Howard Brett and Edward L. Tilton to comment on the plans, they did not provide the unequivocal support that he was expecting. Brett announced himself in favor of a main-floor auditorium, noting that it was hard enough to make a lecture room pay without the convenience and lighting offered by a street-level location. After a visit to Detroit at the expense of the library commission, Tilton

Figure 5.11 Detroit Public Library, Bowen Branch, adult reading room, from gallery. Courtesy of the Burton Historical Collection of the Detroit Public Library.

modified his initial critique, acted as Detroit's advocate in New York, and finally convinced Bertram to accept the plans with minor changes.[45]

As built, then, the Bowen branch is testimony to the changes in professional opinion that were taking place in both architecture and librarianship regarding library planning, and particularly to changes in attitudes toward library work with children. At heart, the Bowen branch rejects the idea of giving children library facilities identical to those for their adult counterparts. The L-shaped configuration of reading rooms continued to allow visual supervision of both reading rooms from the delivery desk, but it provided greater visual separation between the children's room and both the entrance and the adult's reading room. Children were literally around the corner in a realm of their own.

In the Bowen branch, this special realm was further distinguished by furniture and fittings, that together created a home-like setting for young readers (fig. 5.12). Furniture in the children's room was distinguished by its smaller scale, a regular practice in children's rooms since the 1890s.[46] Here, however, even the form of the furniture was different. In the adult reading room, the classical detailing of the furniture signalled the public nature of the space, while the rectangular tables allowed adult readers to sit in isolation from one another. In the children's room, the Arts and Crafts aesthetic of the middle-class bungalow prevailed, while young readers faced one another around circular tables in imitation of the family circle gathered around the parlor table. A tile-fronted fireplace—the only one in the building—served as the focal point of the room. Above the mantle, in the room's most important position, hung a framed image of a woman holding a child. Substantially larger than the small reproduction of Gilbert Stewart's unfinished portrait of George Washington by the door, this image completed the domestic imagery of the room.[47]

Despite great formal differences, branch libraries built in Detroit and elsewhere after 1910 distinguished their children's room from the adult reading areas in a similar fashion. While the rigid order of rectangular

Figure 5.12 Detroit Public Library, Bowen Branch, children's reading room. Courtesy of the Burton Historical Collection of the Detroit Public Library.

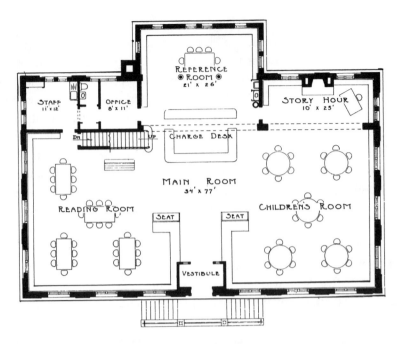

Figure 5.13 H. B. Clement, Detroit Public Library, Edwin F. Conely Branch, 1911–13, first-floor plan. Courtesy of the Burton Historical Collection of the Detroit Public Library.

tables remained the practice in adult reading rooms, informality was the rule in furnishings for children. At another Detroit branch named for library commissioner Edwin F. Conely, architect Hugh Clement specified round tables for young readers, (fig. 5.13) while at Toledo's Eliza Kent branch, architect L. G. Welker omitted furniture layout from the "juvenile" room altogether, indicating the freedom of movement intended for younger readers (fig. 5.14). Here in 1917 was the physical equivalent of the ideal that librarian Mary Emogene Hazeltine had expressed in 1904, a children's room where "the child has come into his own, where he can 'tumble about' almost at will." [48]

Progressive educational theories also led increasingly to including other areas within the children's rooms reserved for specific activities or age groups. In Toledo's Anna C. Mott branch of 1918, an area at the far end of the children's room designated for "little children" suggested a sensitivity to Hall's idea of "natural" education, providing different experiences for children of different ages (fig. 5.15). Indeed, Hall's 1901 emphasis on storytelling as the best way to fire the imagination of children under the age of thirteen seems largely responsible for the renewed popularity of the reading alcove as a regular feature of children's rooms and its designation specifically for story hour use. In three of Detroit's Carnegie-financed branches, separate story hour rooms were adjacent to the children's room (fig. 5.16; see also fig. 5.13).

Fireplaces also enjoyed renewed popularity in the years before World War I, becoming almost ubiquitous in children's rooms; they appeared in all eight of Detroit's Carnegie-financed branches, for instance. In three of these cases, the fireplace was located within a small story-hour alcove, creating what by 1914 was becoming an almost story-book image of domesticity (fig. 5.17; see also fig. 5.13).

The importance of domestic imagery in pre–World War I branch libraries is particularly evident in Toledo's David R. Locke branch (figs. 5.18 and 5.19). Opened in 1917, the building's asymmetrical massing, its bent plan, the arched door at the reentrant angle between the gabled body of the building and its lateral wing, and the banded windows of

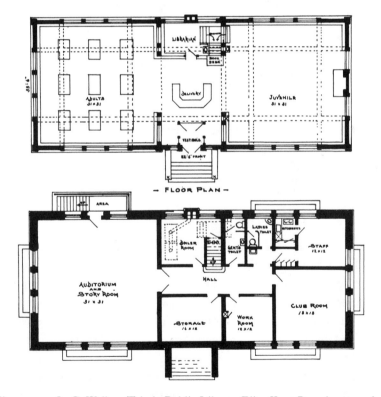

Figure 5.14 L. G. Welker, Toledo Public Library, Eliza Kent Branch, opened 1917, (*lower*) basement and (*upper*) first-floor plans. Toledo Public Library, *Branch Libraries 1918*, Toledo, 1918, 4.

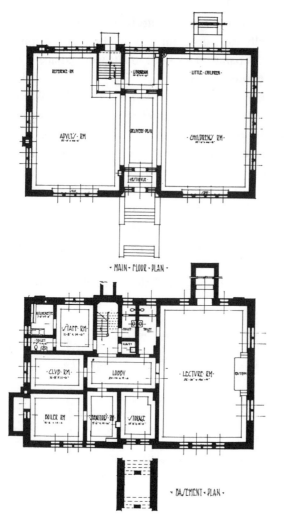

Figure 5.15 Bernhard Becker, Toledo Public Library, Anna C. Mott Branch, opened 1918, (*lower*) basement and (*upper*) first-floor plans. Toledo Public Library, *Branch Libraries 1918*, Toledo, 1918, 8.

· MAIN · FLOOR · PLAN ·

· BASEMENT · PLAN ·

this wing, all recall H. H. Richardson's town libraries of the 1870s and 1880s. Even the Tudoresque style in Toledo parallels Richardson's choice of a nonclassical historical vocabulary. Yet, the coordination of plan and elevation is gone; the banded windows do not indicate Richardson's alcoved book hall, but light the simple rectangular adult reading room. Used independently of Richardson's library plan, the Richardson facade elements serve a symbolic function, marking this building unmistakably as a library for passersby. Yet, instead of aping library symbolism blindly, architect M. M. Stophlet incorporated the story hour alcove into the gabled entrance feature, and transformed the alcove's chimney into the facade's dominant vertical element. By conflating public library im-

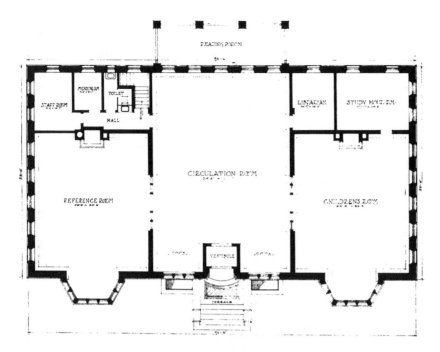

Figure 5.16 Albert Kahn, Detroit Public Library, Magnus Butzel Branch, 1911–13, first-floor plan. Courtesy of the Burton Historical Collection of the Detroit Public Library.

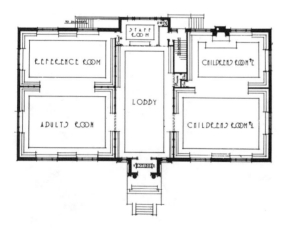

Figure 5.17 Mildner and Eisen, Detroit Public Library, Bernard Ginsburg Branch, 1915–17, first-floor plan. Courtesy of the Burton Historical Collection of the Detroit Public Library.

agery and domestic imagery in this way, Stophlet gave exterior expression to the child-centered library.

Although these changes in library design and philosophy were intended to have their most direct impact on young readers, the child-centered library was also the work environment for many female librarians employed in urban areas. From the plans of these buildings, we learn that female librarianship was not exclusively identified with the charging desk, but that it was also largely associated with the children's room. At Toledo's Locke Branch, for instance, the librarian's office opened directly into the children's room, as it did at the Frances D. Jermain Branch in the same city. In Detroit's Conely branch, a desk for the children's librarian was located next to the fireplace in the story hour alcove. Even in cases where the plan does not indicate a special relationship between the librarian and the children's room, period photographs tell a different story. Photographed soon after its completion, the children's room of Detroit's Bowen branch was arranged with a chair on either side of the fireplace, creating an arrangement akin to a fireplace inglenook (see fig. 5.12). As other period photographs reveal, the female children's librarian periodically occupied one of these adult-sized chairs in order to conduct the story hour (see fig. 6.3 below).

During the story hour, the children's librarian adopted a professional persona that had not been wholly anticipated by the male library establishment. Seated by the hearth, often within an alcove, reading to children gathered at her feet, she played mother to her young clients, and fulfilled an important part of the Progressive mission by providing immigrant children with a middle-class model of motherhood that they did

Figure 5.18 M. M. Stophlet, Toledo Public Library, David R. Locke Branch, opened 1917. Courtesy of Toledo–Lucas County Public Library.

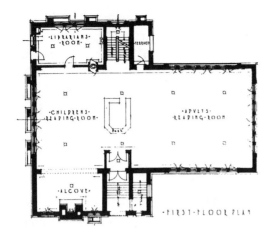

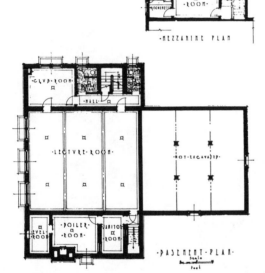

Figure 5.19 Toledo Public Library, Locke Branch, (*lower*) basement, (*center*) mezzanine, and (*upper*) first-floor plans. Toledo Public Library, *Branch Libraries 1918*, Toledo, 1918, 6.

not have at home. At the same time, however, the children's librarian stepped away from the protective shell of the charging desk, and found that contrary to the assumptions of Victorian culture, a woman could negotiate a path through an urban environment defined by ethnic and class diversity. She found as well that her professional contribution in the library was not dependent upon the charging desk or the many other laborsaving devices marketed by the Library Bureau. Instead, her effectiveness as a librarian depended on the more personal attributes of imagination, expression, voice, and gesture. In short, she found that her femininity was not something to be denied, disguised, protected; rather, it was made a positive contribution to her professional performance.

Such a revelation had an impact on the use of library space. Freed from the charging desk, librarians moved farther and farther afield. In Cleveland, librarians sat in a circle on the grass to read to children (fig. 5.20), while New York's librarians went into nearby parks to conduct story hour. In short, the library building enhanced many aspects of library work, but no longer defined the universe of library activities.

At Work in a Small-Town Library

On the surface, the Carnegie-financed libraries erected in smaller towns seem to adhere more closely to the Carnegie ideal of library planning and practice. After all, hundreds of these buildings have the symmetrical floor plan, centrally placed charging desk, and open planning recom-

Figure 5.20 Cleveland Public Library, West Side Branch, story hour. Courtesy of Cleveland Public Library Archives.

mended in the Corporation's "Notes." At the same time, surveys of librarianship conducted before World War I confirm that small-town libraries were more likely to have a female librarian in control, suggesting that for many women who entered librarianship in the first part of the century the canonical Carnegie library design defined their work environment and shaped the character of their workday.[49]

In fact, these surface appearances disguise the fact that small-town librarians rarely used their libraries strictly in the way that was intended by their donor. Archival evidence suggests that small-town librarians were no more likely than their big-city counterparts to spend their day as passive technicians at the charging desk. Having first been associated with libraries as an extension of their study-club work, many of these women had a particularly clear personal vision of the library's contribution to their community's cultural life. In small-town settings, as in large urban settings, the library was required to play a complex social role, confronting and sometimes bridging social gaps of race, class, and ethnicity. Unwilling to sacrifice that vision for an abstract standard of efficiency, these newly professionalized library workers often established patterns of library use never intended by Carnegie.

These unintended patterns of use are crucial for understanding how librarians and readers alike experienced the library. Yet, to the extent that these patterns were ephemeral and not permanently encoded in the built form, they are often difficult for the historian of material culture to reconstruct from plans alone. The period photographs and journalistic reports authored by librarians were also less common in smaller towns than they were in larger cities. In smaller towns, library boards rarely seem to have deemed photographic documentation a worthy expense, and then only to record the completed building devoid of its human inhabitants. Although small-town librarians often shared the Progressive reform fervor of their urban counterparts, the major reform periodicals kept their focus firmly on the urban scene, and may well have discouraged small-town and rural Progressives from contributing.

These limitations make it impossible to build an analysis on the common characteristics of a number of examples. Nonetheless, a diary preserved in the Texas State Archives provides the critical evidence needed to complete a detailed case-study of the actual use of the Carnegie library of Gainesville, Texas. Written by librarian Lillian Gunter, the diary spans 1921 and 1924, but reflects back on Gunter's earlier library experiences. When supplemented with other sources, this diary offers remarkable insights into a librarian's perception of the design and use of the Carnegie building in its first ten years of existence.

Lillian Gunter: A Progressive Librarian in Rural Texas. Lillian Gunter was born in 1870 outside of Gainesville, Texas, on a plantation then recently established by her father, who had settled in the Red River Valley after serving in the Confederate Army during the Civil War. Educated at the Sacred Heart Convent in St. Louis and at the Wesleyan Institute in Staunton, Virginia, Gunter assumed the management of her family's Texas plantations when her father died in 1892. In 1901, Gunter moved into town with her mother and sister, and joined the XLI Club, a genteel way for an unmarried woman of thirty-one to make female friends. As noted in chapter 4, her club membership soon involved her in library matters, first as the chairman of the club's library committee, then as librarian, and eventually as secretary of the Gainesville Public Library Association as well. She took a leading role in securing a site for the Carnegie library and in directing the local architect in the design of the building.[50]

This involvement with the Carnegie building helped clarify Gunter's role in library affairs, paralleling her personal transition from amateur club woman volunteering her time to the library, to a professional woman paid for her skilled service to the library. For Gunter, the transition was a gradual one, beginning in the spring of 1913, when the design process seems to have sparked Gunter's recognition of her own aspirations to professional status. In that summer, she traveled from Gainesville to the New York State Library School in Albany to take part in the six-week summer library training course designed specifically to give working librarians the basics of professional training. By the time the Gainesville Carnegie building was formally dedicated in the fall of 1914, the city council was prompted to recognize Gunter's new status formally by creating the office of public librarian at a monthly salary of $50.[51]

This shift to professional status involved a thoroughgoing realignment of Gunter's values. Her diary of the early 1920s gives a good sense of the extent to which Gunter had reinterpreted the relationship between gender and library work. Particularly telling is the rejection of the ethos of municipal housekeeping that emerges from her account of attempts to establish a branch library in the neighboring town of Walnut Bend. There, she "found things in bad shape": books piled in a spare room, some even lost, and the record box overturned. Worse yet, "they had never sent in a report." Gunter placed the blame squarely on "the girl who agreed to take charge, [who] eloped soon after wards."[52] At the turn of the century, this girl's actions would hardly have been cause for censure; indeed, putting family life before library work was not only an accepted practice of reform-minded library volunteers, but woman's primary identity as wife and mother was the theoretical basis on which the rationale of municipal housekeeping was built. Yet, the professional code adopted by Gunter after 1914 demanded the reversal of older priorities and precluded an easy integration of personal and professional roles. Gunter's condemnation of this Walnut Bend newlywed was in part a defense of her own unmarried status.

Gunter's professionalism also involved a more active denial of her younger self, expressed in her attitudes about club women. To be sure, she continued to rely upon women's clubs for help in library matters, particularly in her efforts to establish far-flung branch libraries; when the woman who had hosted a county branch in the nearby town of Myra moved, Gunter "left the problem of relocating the library with the woman's club." [53] Yet, her own membership in the XLI Club did not prevent her from becoming increasingly critical of club women as library workers. For a branch library in Era, she "took new books and taught two club women how to run the library," but admitted that she was "very doubtful about the experiment of having a different club woman take charge every month." [54] Strictly speaking, this was not an experiment at all; twenty years earlier the members of the XLI Club had maintained the Gainesville library itself as a subscription library with several members frequently spelling the annually elected regular librarian. [55] Since Gunter knew of this practice and had participated in it, the doubts she expressed in 1922 are a sign of the thoroughness with which she rejected her own past, adopting new standards of professional behavior with their greater emphasis on efficiency, accuracy, and accountability.

The Gainesville plan is equally telling of Gunter's new ideas about the nature of library work (see figs. 4.14 and 4.15). The volunteering club women who had originally established the library found their position within the library redefined in important ways. Two spacious and interconnected club rooms are the architectural acknowledgment of the important role that the XLI Club had played in the library's past, and express the faith that the club would continue to be an important part of the library's future. At the same time, the basement location of the rooms and their proximity to the all-purpose public auditorium suggests that the club's involvement with the library would be social in nature, supportive of—but now also peripheral to—the administration of the library proper. In contrast, the private office in the corner of the library's main floor attests to the new presence of a paid librarian, while its privacy and seclusion announce the librarian's new professional status. The building's form was crucial in educating Gainesville's library users about Gunter's new role, allowing them to experience in spatial terms the distinction between Gunter, the club volunteer, and Gunter, the public librarian.

At the same time, Gunter's professionalized vision of the library was more inclusive socially than the vision formerly pursued by the XLI Club. Facilities for black readers within the walls of the public library, for instance, were unknown in Texas. Despite the fact that its subordinate position isolated from the building's "public" spaces reflects and parallels the marginalized position of its intended audience, Gainesville's "negro reading room" is the most visible evidence of Gunter's campaign to provide library service to all. Gunter's description of the building, prepared at the time of its opening, explained that Gainesville's black community would be responsible for purchasing books for the segregated facilities, an arrangement that Gunter seems to have accepted in order to get the council's approval on the library plans.[56] As it happened, the county commissioners' decision that "it might not be a good plan to bring the children of the two races together," prevented Gunter from ever opening this room to black readers. Such a reading room was not opened until 1924, and then only in a room in the Gainesville Colored School.[57]

This campaign to provide library service to Gainesville's black community was part of the liberal sentiment that led her to celebrate the wide variety of library users, noting that "the home demonstrator, the county agent, the school teacher, . . . the oil geologist, the promoter, the book agent, the Ku Klux politician, the Catholic priest, the artist, the poet, . . . the old timer, the new comer, the Confederate veteran, the California tourist, the gilded youth, the travelling missionary, . . . the man who thinks churches hold back the worlds [sic] progress, the fundamentalist: all these frequent the library."[58] That Gunter does not reveal her own membership in any of these opposing moral camps is a sign of her commitment to the professional ethic of serving all readers.

If this professional creed had great appeal at the abstract level, its implementation could be more problematic. Consider this account of a typical afternoon, recorded in her diary in January of 1923:

The monthly report must be handed in to the new commissioner's court and it is not yet finished. The assistant librarian is at home, ill with the flue. I have a reference to look up, "Find a copy of a mock marriage." A high school history teacher, who like Joshua, expects "the sun, moon and stars to stand still for her," is looking up books with my assistance, to put on reserve. Ten children want to use the same number of the "Reader's Guide." Ten more want to find a recitation or declamation. Six or seven are hovering around the loan desk to have their books charged or discharged. A branch librarian is selecting books to take back with her. Two teachers from the country want help with their work.

After recounting a number of telephone interruptions, Gunter finished the passage with the editorial comment, "Ye Gods!" [59]

In fact, Gunter was a leader in her profession, a founding member of the Southwest Library Association, an early advocate of the county library idea, and the author of Texas county library legislation.[60] Yet, her work environment reinforced a very different perception of her. In this setting, her own work seemed unimportant, interruptible; whatever she was doing at the moment was less important than what a given reader wanted her to do. Because she was always on call, she was bombarded with a large number of simultaneous requests that made it difficult for her to complete the easiest task. Constant interruptions required mental agility, stamina, and patience; but if any of those slipped even for a moment, she risked seeming scattered, even scatterbrained.

Gunter was not a helpless pawn in this situation, and found a variety of ways to express her growing dissatisfaction with her work space. One way was by participating in regional library associations which gave Western librarians a professional forum for challenging the universal applicability of East Coast library practices. By early in 1924, the Southwest Library Association had established a Committee for Plans for Small Library Buildings for the Southwest, with Gunter as one of its most active members.[61] Focusing her attention on climatic conditions, she rightly blamed the Carnegie Corporation's requirements for "the high windows which prevent us from feeling any breeze whatever, and make the library so hot that it is impossible to live through the summer without the electric fan in continous operation." [62] Having already suffered through nine Texas summers in a Carnegie building, she advised other Southwestern towns to build one-story buildings with patio or roof-garden reading rooms.

Soon, however, Gunter began to envision a more dramatic departure from the classically detailed library type that so many cities had built with their Carnegie grants. In Santa Fe in the fall of 1924, for the first regular meeting of the Southwestern Library Association, she came to see the ideal library for the Southwest as a blue-eyed adobe hut, with a beamed and stick ceiling just like St. Francis hall in the state museum, its interior a blue, orange and grey symphony . . . whitewash tempered with a little yellow ochre on the outside, blue doors and window sash, red barn paint for the roof, and inside a neutral color on the walls with all the furniture painted a lovely soft blue. Orange cotton crepe windows shades and the bookcases blue on the outside and a glowing orange within.[63]

Convinced that "no such ideal can be realized . . . in our more sophisticated part of the country," she made no attempt to communicate her "ravings" to her fellow librarians; yet, within a month of her return from Santa Fe, she created "gorgeous" bookcases in the new Negro reading room with an application of orange and blue paint.[64]

Gunter's conversion experience in Santa Fe is notable at a number of levels. Given that St. Francis hall stood in a building designed only eight years before by architects born in Illinois, it suggests how successful Anglo-American newcomers to Santa Fe had been in creating an Hispanicized image of the city for tourist consumption.[65] Gunter's realization of her Santa Fe vision in the Negro reading room also reveals the complexity of race relations at the time. On one hand, Gunter recognized the rights of Gainesville's black population to library facilities; on the other, she was willing to impose her personal vision on those readers least able to voice any possible opposition, while the vision itself was predicated on a sense of racial superiority which made it seem appropriate to dress the Negro reading room in architectural garb deemed too unsophisticated for white Gainesville.

The image of the "blue-eyed adobe hut" is also significant as evidence of how much Gunter's ideal of library architecture deviated from the ten-year-old Carnegie building over which she still presided. Her experience in the building itself had suggested that good library design was more than the application of abstract principles of efficiency. It was no longer enough to suggest small refinements in individual details of the Carnegie model; what was required was a wholesale reformulation of the building type. In choosing as her model what she thought of as a regionally-specific vernacular building, she rejected the assumption of universal applicability, and ultimately challenged the authority of the Eastern library leadership.

More important for understanding Gunter's reassessment of her work space in the Carnegie library was the fact that she increasingly disassociated her ideas of library service from any architectural container. This is particularly true of her interest in establishing a county library system with small branches located closer to rural readers. On one hand, she envisioned the Carnegie building as the center of Cooke County's library system; indeed, she translated this vision of the library into graphic form for an American Library Association meeting in 1921, pasting "a Kodak" of the Carnegie building over Gainesville on a postal map of the county and connecting it with red lines to the locations of branch libraries, similarly marked with images of the houses pressed into library service. On the other hand, Gunter tended to see this as a centrifugal constellation; the red lines represented the flow of library activity out of the Carnegie building and into the surrounding area. In practice, she resented rural readers who were drawn to the Carnegie library as the magnet that held the system together. To the extent that it lured "the best readers" from outlying areas to the library in town, it siphoned patrons away from county branches, jeopardizing both the survival of the smaller libraries and their ability to attract new readers from the rural population.[66]

Particularly in its early years, the county library work gave Gunter many excuses to leave the Gainesville library altogether. Assessing rural needs, fostering community support, finding a location for each branch in a house or store, training volunteers to check books in and out—all of these activities involved site visits to remote villages, as did the ongoing task of delivering the rotating selection of books to each branch. While Gunter's diary documents a certain amount of exasperation with the methods of her volunteers, it also reflects her great enthusiasm for her work in the county. Indeed, Gunter entitled her diary, "Adventures of a County Librarian."

Gunter was not the only woman to embrace county library work so enthusiastically. Although James Louis Gillis is recognized as the conceptual force behind California's much admired county library network, the success of the scheme depended on the sustained efforts of an army of women. Harriet G. Eddy, for instance, served as California's first county library organizer, coordinating the efforts of regional organizers and county librarians like May Dexter Henshall, Bertha Kumli (municipal library organizer in the Gold Country), Mabel Prentiss (who worked in central California), and Ann Hadden (Monterey County librarian).[67] These women, in turn, depended upon the hard work of rural women who often volunteered to maintain branch libraries in their homes. Throughout the country, county library organizing and traveling library work quickly became a subfield that was dominated by women.[68] Just like their urban counterparts in the children's room, Gunter and her rural colleagues were remarkably successful at forging a satisfying work role that also gave them ample opportunity to break their connection with the charging desk.

Conclusion

There is much that can be learned from reintroducing human inhabitants into the buildings that we seek to understand, both about the nature of librarianship and about the nature of the Carnegie program. Male library leaders struggling with questions of professional identity during the early part of the twentieth century sought to consolidate their professional gains by reinvigorating the field with the aggressive language and military images of an exaggerated masculinity. Confronted with an unwelcome influx of women, these same librarians sought to marginalize female library workers, often in the name of efficiency. For efficiency's sake, for instance, male library leaders convinced Bertram that the small library should be designed with the librarian sitting at a centrally-placed charging desk. Tethered to the charging desk and its technical equipment, the female librarian who typically headed the small library was surrounded by a material world intended to hem in her ambition and her achievement.

The reality of working in a Carnegie library was something different. In urban settings, reform-minded librarians specialized in work with children and lobbied for physical settings that would support these efforts. Abandoning the planning ideals espoused by the Carnegie program, they sought to create a more welcoming environment for young readers. In the process, they also abandoned the factory metaphor that had sustained the ideal Carnegie library, replacing father with mother as the organizing force in the library family. In smaller towns, concerns with rural access lead librarians to see their Carnegie library as only one small part of a county library system. In both cases, female librarians ignored architectural and material attempts to marginalize them, and forged work strategies that interpreted the library building itself as of only secondary importance.

Without this sort of background, it is hard to understand Gunter's diminishing appreciation for the Gainesville Carnegie library in which she worked. With it, we can see that Gunter's reaction is in keeping with the changes occurring in librarianship during her time. Structured to express the professional ethos of 1900, the Carnegie library ideal had already begun to seem obsolete to Progressive librarians by the time Bertram codified it in 1911.

READING
The Experiences of Children as Library Users

TO THE EXTENT THAT THEY TRANSLATED "the modern library idea" into architectural form, Carnegie libraries affected the interaction between readers and books in important ways. In contrast to their nineteenth-century counterparts, Carnegie libraries catered specially to the needs of readers, giving them free access to most parts of the building and providing low shelves that encouraged them to handle books directly. If an open plan made it possible for the library staff to supervise readers, it also made it easier for readers to find their way into airy rooms where windows were arranged to provide ample light for sturdy reading tables. In theory at least, readers' needs came first in these service-oriented library buildings.

In practice, the Carnegie library experience was rarely so straightforward. Previous knowledge of public institutions, attitudes about reading, access to other urban amenities—all of these factors influenced how readers understood their own rights and responsibilities at the public library. For some former members of subscription libraries, the public nature of the Carnegie library was problematic; the liberalization of lending policies, for instance, undermined the sense of privilege often enjoyed by a community's cultured elite. For newly enfranchised readers, the library was both a strange and wonderful corner of the public sphere, "free to all," but also governed by idiosyncratic and sometimes inscrutable rules of behavior, unlike those of the street, the market, the park, or the department store. As librarians and the trustees who employed them learned, opening a cultural institution to the public did not guarantee that the public would use the institution as planned.

For young readers, the library experiences provided by the Carnegie program were particularly noteworthy. To the extent that Carnegie's philanthropy coincided with the rise of the children's room, Carnegie libraries provided the first library experience for perhaps tens of thousands of young readers in the first two decades of the twentieth century. To the extent that Carnegie libraries established a model of library design prevalent until the post–World War II era, they provided a common library experience for children in hundreds of American communities for at least half a century.

Is it possible to reconstruct that library experience and recapture a sense of what the Carnegie library meant to America's newest library users? The answer is a qualified yes, since the documentary sources are slim. After all, most young readers did not write down their reactions to the library in words that have been preserved. Librarians did publish accounts of their interaction with young library patrons, confirming that children, and particularly immigrant children, were avid library users. Yet, these reports are somewhat problematic. Inevitably, librarians who reported the behavior of juvenile readers looked at their charges through a lens colored by class and cultural differences, while librarians with a specific agenda were often prone to considerable distortions. Indeed, as David Nasaw has pointed out, "reformers—to elicit action from public and politicians—painted their picture of urban youth in most dismal tones."[1]

Recent developments in immigrant history and urban studies would seem to offer these readers an opportunity to speak for themselves. Certainly, several excellent studies have documented the social dynamics of working-class environments like the saloon, the dance hall, the amusement park, and the movie theater, as well as immigrant reactions to reform-oriented institutions like the settlement house and the public school.[2] In comparison, there has been an almost complete silence on the immigrant library experience, perhaps because the library defies easy categorization in this history. On one hand, the relatively limited compass of the library's reform efforts has made it seem less central than the settlement house to the Progressive project of acculturation. On the other, the library's role in such Americanization schemes seems to have fueled an assumption that the library stood apart from the "authentic" immigrant experience. As a result, few studies have acknowledged the library as a locus of working-class culture or grappled adequately with the ample evidence that immigrant children were regular and eager library users.

Memoirs of men and women who were among the first generation of children to use Carnegie libraries are numerous, but surprisingly disappointing.[3] Many childhood memoirs dealing with the early twentieth century appeared in the years just before and after World War II. Yet, these accounts of middle-class life in small-town America tend to be either humorous accounts of minor domestic dramas or coming-of-age tales that chart the protagonist's exploration of the public street, the railroad station, the saloon, and other undomesticated portions of the public realm. The public library is not an essential component of either narrative. Even when these memoir writers recalled their early love of books, they wrote almost exclusively of the books themselves, rather than the library that provided them.[4] By the 1980s, when the library experience itself became a more regular part of childhood memoirs, the passage of time had limited the number of writers who had used a Carnegie library early in the century.[5]

Despite their limitations, librarians' reports and later memoirs provide valuable information about the interaction of buildings and readers. Used together, they reveal common patterns that should not be ignored. When embedded in their physical and social contexts, these sources offer important glimpses into the children's room, and into the terrors and delights it held for the first generation of American children to enter its precincts.

Coming of Age in the Small-Town Library

During the past fifteen years, Carnegie libraries have begun to appear as a regular feature in reminiscences of small-town childhood. Eudora Welty included vivid memories of the Carnegie library in Jackson, Mississippi, in her 1984 autobiographical book, *One Writer's Beginnings*. In *Ohio Town* (first published in 1963, but reprinted for a mass market in 1985), Helen Hooven Santmyer devoted a full chapter to the Carnegie library in Xenia, Ohio. From a younger generation, Susan Allen Toth also recalled her long relationship with the Carnegie building in Ames, Iowa, in *Blooming: A Small-Town Girlhood* (first published in 1978, and reprinted in 1981). The common themes that emerge from all three books may be due to the fact that each was written by a woman who loved reading as a child and who went on to a successful literary career; Welty, Santmyer, and Toth may have experienced the library in a particular way because they shared a particular set of interests and concerns. Yet, given their geographical and temporal range—from Mississippi to Iowa, from the 1900s to the 1950s—these memoirs may reflect the Carnegie library experiences of native-born, small-town children more generally.[6]

Of the many children who used Carnegie libraries in the first two decades of the twentieth century, Santmyer has probably provided the most extended literary description of the experience. Indeed, she seems uniquely qualified for the task. Born in 1897 in Xenia, Ohio, Santmyer had initially borrowed books from the subscription library established by a women's study club in the 1880s, an uneven collection of books housed at the turn of the century on the second floor of the post office building. When Xenia built its Carnegie library in 1907 (fig. 6.1), she was still a child of ten, and able to compare the two libraries directly. As an adult, Santmyer pursued a writing career that often drew on her knowledge of Xenia as the basis for both fiction and nonfiction works. The building of a Carnegie library is a central element both in her 1982 novel, ". . . *And Ladies of the Club*," and in *Ohio Town*, a partly researched and partly remembered portrait of life in Xenia in the early twentieth century.

In *Ohio Town*, Santmyer begins her discussion of the Carnegie library with the observation that

all Carnegie libraries are so alike that one's memories hardly seem associated with an individual set of yellow-brick walls, white stone trim, and granite steps. One might have sat on any one of a hundred parapets to strap on a pair of roller skates: whatever town one drives through, past whatever library, at the sight of an un-

Figure 6.1 Carnegie Library, Xenia, Ohio, 1907. Courtesy of Greene County Room, Greene County Public Library, Xenia, Ohio.

known anonymous child bent over a skate buckle, one remembers rough stone through a summer dress, the sun on one's back, the pull of skates on shoe soles, and accepts as identical one's own and all others' experiences.[7]

Like most reminiscences, the passage is informed both by her childhood memories and by knowledge accumulated in the intervening years. In this case, the mention of roller skates refers directly to a child's lived experience in a specific place, while the awareness of the Carnegie phenomenon—the prevalence of the building type in the Midwest, their striking formal similarities—is clearly a product of Santmyer's adult life. Likewise, by deploying the library as a symbol of a commonly shared American experience, Santmyer constructs a utopian image of small-town America that has as much to do with the upheavals of midcentury as it does with the years before World War I.

If Santmyer incorporates the insights of both childhood and adulthood into her description, she conveys these insights in distinct ways. The adult narrator is largely dependent upon sight and speech, seeing the library, naming its materials, assessing its aesthetic merits. In contrast, Santmyer's younger self recalls the library through tactile sensations—the roughness of the stone step, the warmth of the sun, the lightness of a summer dress, the weight of roller-skates. Likewise, while the adult viewer tends to see the library as part of a larger social or physical context, the child's experience of the library is presented in a fragmented way, focusing on one small element at a time. Instead of seeing the building's classical portico as a single unit, the younger narrator mentions only "the pillar by the door" and recalls it not as a complete architectural element, but as something she "left a pair of skates behind." Instead of seeing the door as a whole, she recalls its components parts, "the handle of the summertime screen and the big brass knob of winter's oak door."[8]

By means of these fragmentary sensations, Santmyer conveys her early sense of a library comprising two distinct realms that seemed only tangentially related to one another. On the exterior, the library was not associated with books and reading at all, triggering instead a flood of details about the longer walk to the new library and roller skating on its steps. Unlike the old subscription library whose downtown locale was largely out of bounds for children, the new library was situated outside of the commercial zone, in an area that had been the edge of town just a few years earlier. Although only three blocks separated the old accommodation from the new, the new location redefined the townscape for young readers. As Santmyer admitted, "until you got used to it, the walk for your books seemed very long. Perhaps that was because you made it oftenest in the hot summertime . . . and when you had gone to the woods that way, you had never counted what lay on the town side of the pastures as part of your walk."⁹ As the young readers like Santmyer found, the location of the new library changed their sense of distances within their town, and expanded the territory that children could claim as part of their daily domain. At the same time, the Carnegie library's open lot provided public space that was neither privately owned nor controlled by civic or religious institutions where children were an anomaly. Evidently recognizing at the library a public space similar in character to the school yard, Santmyer took for granted her use of the area as an ad hoc playground.

This unscholarly use of the library notwithstanding, the young Santmyer was also an experienced library user, who had vivid recollections of the old subscription library, and particularly of the physical barriers that it maintained between readers and books. Her description of that library (quoted at length in chap. 4) emphasized the railed enclosure around the librarians' desk and the locked, glass-fronted bookcases—barriers that affected library users young and old. Such barriers, however, were disproportionately difficult for children to overcome; browsing through the topmost shelves of juvenile literature was not just awkward, it was impossible.

With this knowledge of other library systems, the young Santmyer appreciated the physical and temporal advantages that the new Carnegie library offered to young readers. In the new building, she noted, "there was a separate room for children: all the way around its walls, beneath the windows, were open shelves, none so high as to be above eye level." Equally important, "there were chairs and tables" for reading in the library, facilities that were not available in the rented rooms of a subscription library. When teamed up with extended hours, these facilities transformed the library experience from a place where you were "restricted to choosing your book and going off with it," to a place where "you could stay until suppertime if you liked." A place associated with "lovely, long, quiet afternoons," the library was increasingly becoming a welcome alternative to an afternoon at home.¹⁰

If young readers like Santmyer found unwonted freedom in such library environments, they also encountered firm limitations on their enjoyment of the library. In Xenia, these limitations were due largely to the attitude of the librarian, Miss McElwain. Like Lillian Gunter, of Gainesville, Texas, and many other women who staffed small-town Carnegie libraries in the early years of the twentieth century, Miss McElwain had started her career in the old subscription library when it was administered by the women's study club, and stayed on to work many years behind the charging desk in the Carnegie building. Something of a transitional figure, Miss McElwain was not completely comfortable with all aspects of "the modern library idea," least of all the sort of work-saving library equipment marketed by the Library Bureau. "Flustered to the end of her days by a pencil with a rubber stamp on its end," she was equally disturbed by newer trends in library service to children. As Santmyer recalled, "she regarded children as the natural enemies of books; she was quick-tempered and sharp-tongued, and too often the provoker of tears. Every child who came in was on probation." In this case, at least, the benefits that a Carnegie building offered young readers were overshadowed by the librarian herself, who stocked the library with "the best books . . . and then by her acerbity, . . . discouraged you from reading them."[11]

In the end, Santmyer's childhood experiences in the Carnegie library were complicated by the fact that the amenities promised in the building's design were neither automatically granted nor easily attained. Persistence was required of young readers as they approached the desk to look up into "sharp, hostile eyes behind flashing spectacles," and, often as not, they found themselves moved to tears by the encounter. With time, however, young Santmyer also discovered other facets of Miss McElwain's character, including a sense of humor, a passion for bird-watching, and most importantly, an "unflagging zeal" for feeding the intellectual curiosity of her readers. Eager to win the librarian's respect, she learned to follow the rules of the library—"to approach the desk with clean hands, to take your skates off outside, and to shut the door on the dog"—and in the process found that she had also outgrown much of her "old starting fear of Miss McElwain."[12]

In many ways, Santmyer's library recollections constitute a coming-of-age story, linking the process of becoming a happy library user to the process of growing up. If the fit between the child and the library was not as seamless as children's librarians hoped it would be, if the child's introduction to the library was not altogether painless, the misfit was not a cause for alarm. Indeed, as she watched her young nieces crumble in the face of Miss McElwain's familiar sharpness, the adult author came to see the confrontation between the strict librarian and younger readers as inevitable, part of a natural process of maturing that each generation of children must face.

Santmyer may have overestimated the universality of her library experience in Xenia, but a survey of other childhood memoirs reveals several common themes. Most native-born writers share Santmyer's sense that the library was a special realm, placing particular emphasis on the act of entering the library. Joan Lowery Nixon, for instance, recalled the physical challenge of entering her branch library in Los Angeles in the 1930s, through "its large oak doors—so heavy a small child had to struggle to open them."[13] Likewise, Susan Toth recalled an extensive entry sequence, that had both physical and psychological components. As she explained,

Entering the Ames Public Library I could feel its compelling power immediately. Inside the front doors a split staircase climbed elaborately to the main entrance on the second floor, and trudging up the marble steps I was enveloped by the cavernous space. A chilly breeze always seemed to be blowing up my back. The library, and the [World War I Memorial] Union Hall, seemed to be places where things lay precariously at rest, just below the surface, waiting to be summoned up again.[14]

This elision of the actual spaces of the library with the imagery of romantic adventure stories (including cavernous spaces, steep climbs, and sleeping heroes) underlines the library's role as a gateway to the realm of imagination. It also suggests that the act of reading colored the impressions that some young readers formed of the library building itself, overlaying library architecture with associative meanings unintended by the adults who provided the library facilities.

Like most epic journeys featured in late Victorian children's literature, the entry into the mythical realm of the library also required young readers to confront a formidable gatekeeper—namely, the librarian. In Ames, young Toth came to imagine that young readers and books were somewhat interchangeable in the mind of the staff. In addition to checking all books in and out, the librarian on duty at the delivery desk "glanced up and mentally checked you in as well." In Jackson, Mississippi, Eudora Welty found the librarian's gaze a substantial obstacle. "As you came in from the bright outside," she remembered, "if you were a girl, [the librarian] sent her strong eyes down the stairway to test you; if she could see through your skirt, she sent you straight back home; you could just put on another petticoat if you wanted a book that badly from the public library."[15] If the physical layout of the library did not require a close examination of young readers, it certainly facilitated it.

Inside the library, librarians continued to play a major role in shaping the childhood library experience of small-town memoir writers. To a certain extent, this was simply a continuation of the most common theme in memoirs of nineteenth-century library use. Indeed, when Newton Marshall Hall recalled using the public library as a child in the 1870s, his memories were dominated by "the awful presence" of the librarian and the various mechanisms that this "stern potentate behind the high desk" had used to hamper readers' access to books.[16] While many childhood memories of Carnegie libraries begin by painting the librarian as a daunting figure, most also document a transformation in the librarian-reader relationship, as young readers learned to value the librarian's advice. Although Jackson's Miss Calloway remained unredeemable in Welty's eyes, this was the exception rather than the rule. More common was Nixon's experience in Los Angeles, where the children's librarian developed from "a soft, shadowy figure with a large and powerful inkpad and stamp," to "[her] friend, helping [her] to find other mysteries even more exciting than the first."[17]

Toth experienced a similar transformation. Initially, she was intimidated by the librarian whom she described as "a white-haired high priestess, whose initiates, also women, found themselves sworn to whispers and lifelong devotion."[18] Indeed, the physical arrangements of the library seemed to reinforce the figurative distance between staff and readers. Whether standing in "a circular enclosure, only entered by librarians, who flipped up a small wooden shelf," or at work behind "the curtained door of Miss Jepson's office," the library staff seemed at first to inhabit a distinct physical realm off limits to mere readers.[19] Yet, by the time she began junior high school, Toth came to interpret those physical arrangements in a new light, seeing them as symbols of Miss Jepson's power, something "not many women in Ames visibly wielded."[20] Increasingly convinced that librarians had "access to all important knowledge," she briefly contemplated a career in librarianship and always treasured Miss Jepson's respect.[21]

If small-town Carnegie libraries succeeded in reaching young readers, such memoirs suggest that they often did so through the selective application of Progressive child-study techniques. All of the memoirs cited here, for instance, maintained children's rooms and children's book collections separate from their adult counterparts. In Ames, the library even maintained a junior room distinct from the children's room. Yet, in direct contrast to Progressive child-study theory, young readers rarely perceived the library as an environment where they could "tumble about." Welty's experience with the Jackson Library's petticoat policy was a somewhat extreme version of this phenomenon, but most library memoirs mention that library use required some constraint on the child's normal behavior. Welty herself drew attention to the contrast between "SILENCE in big black letters ... on signs tacked up everywhere" and the librarian's habit of speaking "in her normally commanding voice." [22] Likewise, Nixon remembered her children's room as "that cocoon of whispery hush" with "an atmosphere of reverent silence," while Toth came to treasure her public library "increasingly as a place of quiet more than as a source of knowledge." [23] Whether or not young readers found such rules easy to obey, they were acutely aware of the need to bend themselves to the rules of the library in order to be able to take advantage of its benefits.

As these memoirs reveal, small-town children experienced the library in ways that were unanticipated by library leaders who treasured library efficiency, by civic boosters who saw the library as a symbol of progress, or by club women or children's librarians who envisioned the library as a homelike space. For these young readers, the decision to enter the library was an emotional one in which a desire for reading material had to overcome fear—fear of the businesslike librarian, fear of violating one of the institution's sometimes unfathomable policies. Even children who became confident library users rarely became nonchalant library users.

Claiming New Space in Urban Branches

If young native-born readers in smaller towns could find the library experience nerve-wracking, what about their urban counterparts, many of whom were the children of the immigrant poor? Attempts to recreate their library experience is more difficult than might be expected. Progressive-era reformers were prolific chroniclers of their own activities, and efforts to extend library service to the children of recent immigrants were remarkably well publicized in *Charities and the Commons, The Work of the World,* and in a host of other journals that sprang up in the late nineteenth century to document the full spectrum of reform efforts. Despite the amount of material produced, however, the reactions of young readers are cloaked by the tendency of librarians to discuss the benefits of children's librarianship at a theoretical level, with only occasional references to their actual encounters with real children. This lacuna itself is telling; anecdotal stories of the urban library might have been more common if librarians had been more successful at predicting the response of young readers.

In library theory, the children of foreign-born parents had to be lured into the library. In practice, immigrant children were enthusiastic library users, a fact confirmed by librarians' reports and by the few immigrant narratives that mention library use. When Melech Epstein immigrated from Byelorussia to New York in 1913, he counted himself among the "serious young immigrants [who] . . . crowded the libraries, eager to learn English and to read American books."[24] Similarly, Ida Rothman Feely, the American-born daughter of Jewish immigrants from Rumania, remembered that "children of immigrants . . . were anxious to learn from the people who were Americanized and who had acquired a degree of success since their arrival," and mentioned pursuing her own education on New York's East Side in the public library, the settlement house, and the reading room in the Educational Alliance.[25]

At times, the enthusiasm of immigrant children threatened the ordered gentility that librarians had worked so hard to design into the built environment. At the Hudson Park Branch of the New York Public Library, for instance, the librarian used metaphors from both natural and man-made disasters to describe the after-school rush. At three o'clock, she explained, "the storm broke. There was what might be called a 'preliminary warning.' It was the sound of many feet pressing swiftly on from every direction and growing each instant nearer, then the big double doors swung open and an army of children marched in." Far removed from the pleasant atmosphere described in the library recruitment literature of the day, such an experience transformed the charging desk in the librarian's eyes. No longer a command post where the librarian reigned with the calm composure of a modern manager who knows that her equipment will work with smooth efficiency, the charging desk was now a defensive fortress protecting the librarian in a losing battle against hostile attack. Unable to maintain authority in ways anticipated by philanthropist and architect, the hapless staff of the Hudson Park Branch enlisted police aid; an officer stationed at the door all afternoon "kept the children in a sort of doubled-up line and only admitted one when we sent one out."[26]

While there is no doubt that young library patrons were hungry for books, other incidents suggest that the warmth of their response was also fueled by the fact that the library offered an attractive alternative to the crowded tenement apartment and to the busy streets and sidewalks of an urban neighborhood. The Hudson Park librarian, for instance, also reported that a ten-year-old girl had "stood for a moment in the dazzling sunlight from one of the big windows; then stretched out her arms as a bird might its wings—and on the tips of her toes flew from window to window, pausing at each in the sunshine." Other children showed their appreciation more prosaically, making regular trips to New York's rooftop reading rooms, especially when they had younger siblings in tow, while small children frequently brought in their toys with them (fig. 6.2).[27]

Such episodes reveal the complex nature of the relationship between urban children and child-saving reformers. Certainly, children did not submit passively to reformers' efforts to remove them from the streets.[28] Indeed, the city street was the special realm of children, who savored the freedom from adult supervision that they found there. Children not only laid claim to urban space through play, but also created and maintained invisible boundaries that reserved different parts of the streetscape for groups that varied according to gender, age group, and neighborhood affiliation. Stoops and sidewalks, for instance, were reserved for girls, who looked after babies and toddlers, while the center of the street

Figure 6.2 McKim, Mead & White, New York Public Library, Rivington Street Branch, New York, opened 1905, roof garden. Courtesy of the Photography Collection, Miriam and Ira D. Wallach Division of Art, Prints, and Photographs, The New York Public Library, Astor, Lenox and Tilden Foundations.

belonged to older boys, who patrolled their "turf" and guarded against incursions by boys from other neighborhoods.[29]

Yet, urban children did not draw an impenetrable line between the street and child-saving institutions like the library. In contrast to reformers who saw the library as an antidote to the street's moral and physical dangers, many urban children seem to have interpreted the library as an extension of the street, and behaved accordingly. They not only moved willingly and regularly off the street and into the library, they also brought noise and playfulness with them. Although librarians were appalled by what they interpreted as a violation of library rules, boisterousness was one of the methods that children used to stake their claim to public space. Used initially on the street, it was equally effective in the library.

Having claimed the library as part of their domain, young urban readers used the library with a well-developed sense of entitlement. As the librarians at the Hudson Park Branch reported "each child was bent upon having a book. No matter to them that they had not registered, that their parents objected to their taking books, that their references refused to sign for them—such trifling details did not even interest them; a book they must and would have!"[30] So strong was this sense of entitlement that many young readers remained indifferent to the influence of librarians. Despite staff attempts to take on a motherly role during story hour, urban library users rarely saw them in this light (fig. 6.3). Indeed, city kids were less likely than their small-town counterparts to think of the librarian as an individual whose respect they valued. When urban branch librarians reported verbatim conversations, they revealed that young readers often addressed them generically as "Teacher."[31] Similarly, anonymous librarians play only minor roles in immigrant narratives. In Feely's memoirs, for instance, the librarian is a featureless figure, whose only role was to send noisy children out of the library.[32]

If immigrant children failed to use the library in precisely the way that the child-savers anticipated, their actions also suggest that they appreciated at least some components of the Progressive-era urban reform agenda. To the extent that observed behavior offers a clue to what readers were thinking, librarians' reports suggest that immigrant children appreciated a chance to spend an afternoon in a warm, clean, safe, sunlit environment where they could breath fresh air. Indeed, first-person memoirs confirm this impression. Feely remembers doing her homework in the library not because it was quiet (she admits that it was not),

Figure 6.3 Detroit Public Library, Bowen Branch, children's reading room during story hour. Courtesy of Bowen Branch, Detroit Public Library.

but because "the library was heated in the fall and winter."[33] In the 1930s, Marilyn Sachs remembered the Morrisania Branch of the New York Public Library in the South Bronx as "a refuge and a sanctuary," a place to go "when things got tough or when somebody was after me— which was often."[34] In an urban situation in which children successfully subdivided the streets into neighborhood turfs, the library was a welcome neutral zone.

By the same token, the published reports of these episodes are remarkable for demonstrating how upsetting these behaviors were to librarians who observed them. Given Progressive-era concerns with breaking the connection with the street, reform-minded librarians might be expected to delight in their success at getting children out of the tenement apartment and off the street, even temporarily. Yet, librarians who reported these incidents were anything but thrilled. In most cases, the reactions of young readers befuddled the professional women who prided themselves on their knowledge of child psychology. Indeed, their reports in reform journals condemned children for using rooftop reading rooms like "the recreation pier," and asked rhetorically, "Can you take an entirely sympathetic attitude toward the little girl who has brought with her the only toy she owns, a box of beads, and is yelling at the top of her lungs because it is upset and the rest of the children are grabbing the beads or stamping on them, according to which they consider most fun?"[35] Throughout their reports, librarians display a concern for order and quiet that belies their dedication to the ideal of the children's room as a place for youngsters to "tumble about." What is more, librarians were utterly exasperated with children who refused to adopt a genteel demeanor to match their surroundings, some so much that they revived strategies from Victorian child-rearing manuals, and advocated the practice of sending away children who would use the library, even quietly, for anything other than study purposes.[36]

If librarians assumed deliberate misbehavior on the part of their young readers, the material culture of the library tells another story. As noted in chapter 5, the messages of the children's room were communicated largely through analogies with other social settings, particularly with the middle-class home. The official view of librarianship assumed that the normal home was a quiet, genteel setting, segregated from the world of work, run according to standards outlined in the prescriptive literature of Victorian homelife, and that a sad look from mother would trigger internalized guilt and restore quiet and order. It accepted as universal truths values that were culturally specific to the Anglo-American middle class of the late nineteenth century, and depended on the library users to know what was expected of them before they entered the library. As these few incidents demonstrate, the theory simply broke down when confronted with readers who did not share this cultural outlook.

Conclusion

No matter what their class or cultural background, the young generation of library patrons who came of age in the era of Carnegie were unusually well placed to understand the complex meaning of the simple phrase, "free to all." For the children of the many working-class families that could ill afford the cost of an annual subscription, a library that lent books free of charge was a clear and undeniable boon. Even the offspring of more comfortable families welcomed a cultural institution built to support more liberal policies of book retrieval and use.

Yet, children from a range of backgrounds also found that the new library demanded its own kind of payment—not in cash, of course, but in demeanor. The ideals of Progressive educational theory notwithstanding, the new library welcomed children who adhered to a narrowly-defined norm of respectable behavior. In fact, for many library supporters (including Carnegie, library trustees, and librarians), the great value of the public library lay in its potential for transforming the behavior of readers. The classical portals that graced so many Carnegie libraries were not simply symbols of public welcome; they also marked, it was hoped, the gateway to a common American culture grounded on self-improvement, individual achievement, and the principles of Protestant liberalism. Like their Modernist contemporaries, Carnegie libraries were self-consciously designed to encourage a process of social and cultural transformation.

The experiences of young readers, however, reveal that architecture's transformative powers were limited by the fact that its signals are socially and culturally coded. If many working-class and immigrant children remained untouched by the library's message, it was because the library attempted to communicate in a language that these young readers did not understand. By overestimating architecture's universality, Progressive-era library supporters inadvertently undercut their own attempts to bridge the cultural divide that separated them from their young patrons.

Postscript

No new Carnegie library grants were issued after 1917. On the surface, this decision was a response to escalating building costs caused by wartime shortages of material and labor, factors which—according to the Corporation's form letters—made it impossible to continue the library program along established lines. Yet, Carnegie trustees had already begun to reconsider the mission of the corporation as early as 1915, when they hired economist Alvin S. Johnson to assess the effectiveness of the library building program. After an extended study tour, Johnson presented a report that emphasized the primary importance of professional staffing in any successful library endeavor. Good library facilities were helpful, of course, but superior library service was ultimately a function of personnel, not architecture. Although Johnson did not recommend the discontinuation of the building program, his report clearly pointed in that direction. To the extent that it questioned the transformative power of the built environment, Johnson's report undermined the fundamental article of faith on which Carnegie's library program had been established. Using war conditions to spare Carnegie's feelings, the trustees began the process of reappraisal and planning that lasted until well after Carnegie's death in 1919. In about 1925, the Carnegie Corporation launched a new program of library support, extending grants to the American Library Association and comparable professional organizations in other English-speaking countries, to library training schools, and to academic libraries.[1]

Yet, the impact of the Carnegie library program extended far beyond 1917 and beyond the 1,679 American public library buildings constructed with Carnegie funds. Carnegie's example and his published statements explaining the rationale behind his actions encouraged other American philanthropists to support libraries, usually at a local scale. Far from viewing this as an intrusion into his area of philanthropic expertise, Carnegie welcomed their involvement.[2] Indeed, part of the attraction of philanthropy for Carnegie had been the opportunity to demonstrate how the field as a whole might be made more systematic and more efficient. As with his business ventures in railroading and steel manufacturing, Carnegie seems to have derived great satisfaction from having others imitate his innovations, seeing this not as a challenge to his achievements but as an acknowledgment of the superiority of his methods.

The influence of the Carnegie program was even more intensely felt in the area of American library planning. Indeed, "Notes on the Erection of Library Bildings" was remarkably effective until World War II in promoting the open-plan library, with its centrally located charging desk and flanking reading rooms, as the ideal for small public libraries. In the prosperous 1920s, many communities were prompted to finance their own library buildings, often hiring architects whose plans revealed their previous experience designing Carnegie libraries. In the lean years of the 1930s, the Public Works Administration (PWA) filled the financial void left by the demise of the Carnegie library program, funding small, symmetrical, classically detailed libraries with open plans (figs. P.1 and

Figure P.1. Public Works Administration, Public Library, Allenstown, New Hampshire, 1934. Courtesy of National Archives.

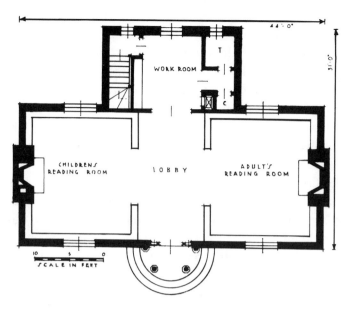

Figure P.2. Public Library, Allenstown, first-floor plan. C. W. Short and R. Stanley-Brown, eds., *Public Buildings: Architecture under the Public Works Administration 1933–1939*, Washington, D.C., 1939; reprint, New York, 1986, 110.

P.2).[3] Even as late as 1941, librarian Joseph L. Wheeler and architect Alfred Morton Githens devoted a full chapter of their book on library planning to an analysis of what they dubbed "the Carnegie rectangle," affirming the faith of their respective professions in the "sound common sense" of the "Notes."[4]

Finally, the Carnegie program helped perpetuate and reinforce a relatively narrow definition of the public library's function in American society. Under the banner of library efficiency, Carnegie abandoned the nineteenth-century model of the library as a multipurpose cultural institution, an idea that was only "rediscovered" in the art center concept of the late 1960s. More important, by defining library efficiency as the quick delivery of books into the hands of individual readers, the Carnegie program supported larger cultural trends that encouraged libraries to ignore the issue of how readers used the materials that they did borrow. In contrast to nineteenth-century social libraries which were established specifically to facilitate an active sharing of ideas (albeit among the members of an elite group), the efficiency-driven public library of the twentieth century defined reading as a solitary activity. In the process, the library lost its potential to serve as a site—literally and figuratively— for public discussion and debate.[5]

This change is worth noting, since we are still grappling with its implications. Indeed, the concern with the swift, smooth delivery of information may have started with the Library Bureau delivery desk, but it is also the motivating principle behind the much-vaunted information superhighway and its promise to deliver the written word instantaneously to each individual computer screen. What is more, as these technological advances continue to improve the efficiency of information distribution, we will be forced to question the need for the library as a physical space at all.

In short, Carnegie libraries are more than they seem from the sidewalk. At one level, they take us on welcome journeys into the past. They are familiar, conventional, and appealing buildings that have inspired several ambitious preservation projects aimed at renewing their original architectural character.[6] Yet, at another level, they open unexpected vistas into the future. Rather than simply meeting our expectations, they also challenge us—to redefine the role of reading in our culture, to reinvigorate social interaction in public spaces, to reinvent the public library as an American institution.

Appendix 1

Notes on the Erection of Library Bildings
[Version 3, c. 1915]

This memorandum is sent to anticipate frequent requests for such information, and should be taken as a guide, especially when the proposed architect has not had much library bilding experience. It should be noted that many of the bildings erected years ago, from plans tacitly permitted at the time, would not be allowd now.

Library committees, especially in small towns, ar frequently composed of busy men who, having lackt time or opportunity to obtain a knowledge of library planning, ar led to select a design which, if bilt, would yield an inadequate return of useful accommodation for the money invested, and would unwarrantably increas the expense of carrying on the library.

Some architects ar liable, unconsciously, no dout, to aim at architectural features and to subordinate useful accommodation. Some ar also apt, on account of a lack of practical knowledge of the administration of a library, to plan interiors which ar entirely unsuited for the purposes of a free public library. Small libraries should be pland so that one librarian can oversee the entire library from a central position.

The amount allowd by the Carnegie Corporation of New York to cover the cost of a library bilding is according to a standard based on (a) the population which is to pay the tax for carrying on the library, and (b) a specified minimum revenue from such tax. The donation is sufficient only to provide needed accommodation and there wil be either a shortage of accommodation or of money if this primary purpose is not kept in view, viz.: TO OBTAIN FOR THE MONEY THE UTMOST AMOUNT OF EFFECTIV ACCOMMODATION, CONSISTENT WITH GOOD TASTE IN BILDING.

The amount allowd is intended to cover cost of the bilding, complete and redy for use with indispensible furniture and fixtures, and including architect's fees.

In looking over hundreds of plans for small and medium-sized bildings, costing about $10,000, more or less, we hav noted some features leading to a wasting of space, especially in connection with the entrance feature, which, when not wisely pland, leads also to waste in halls, delivery room, etc.

The economical layout of the bilding is sacrificed or subordinated at times to minor accessories, such as too much or too valuable space allotted to cloak rooms, toilets and stairs.

The bilding should be devoted exclusively to: (main floor) housing of books and their issue for home use; comfortable accommodation for reading them by adults and children; (basement) lecture room; necessary accommodation for heating plant; also all conveniences for the library patrons and staff.

Experience seems to sho that the best results for a small general library ar obtained by adopting the one-story and basement rectangular type of bilding, with a small vestibule entering into one large room subdivided as required by means of bookcases. In cases where it is necessary, to secure quiet, glass partitions may be put above the bookcases. By a one-story and basement bilding is meant a bilding with the basement about four feet below the natural grade, the basement being from say 9 to 10 feet and the main floor from say 12 to 15 feet high in the clear. Plans hav at times been submitted for "one-story and basement" bildings, which differd from two-story bildings only by having the stair to the upper floor outside instead of inside!

The rear and side windows may be kept about six feet from the floor, to giv continuous wall space for shelving. A rear wing can be added for stack-room (when future need demands it) at a minimum expense, and without seriously interfering with the library servis during its construction. The site chosen should be such as to admit lite on all sides, and be large enuf to allow extension, if ever such should become necessary.

The accompanying diagrams [see figs. 1.21 and 1.22] ar offerd as suggestions in planning the smaller library bildings most commonly required, and wil be found to include a maximum of effectiv accommodation relativ to total area.

While these diagrams ar suggestiv rather than mandatory, nevertheless, since they ar the result of experience, those responsible for bilding projects should paus before aiming at radical departures, and see whether their alternativ is to provide as much effectiv accommodation and hav as little waste space.

An important caus of alleged inadequacy of accommodation in bildings erected years ago, when less supervision was exercised, has frequently been found to be uneconomical plan with bad layout. When applications (based on growth of population) hav been receivd for aid in extending such bildings, it has often been impossible to entertain the idea of making a grant, owing to the prohibitiv cost of demolition and re-erection relativ to net gain of superficial area.

It may not be desirable to hav library bildings pland from redy-made patterns, and yet a certain standardization of the main requirements of accommodation is as necessary for library bildings as for school bildings, which hav been advantageously subjected to strict regulations both in plan and construction. Where architecture is best appreciated there ar recognized types establisht for the various bildings of a public or semi-public character.

It wil be noted that no elevations ar given or suggestions made about the exteriors. These ar features in which the community and architect may express their individuality, keeping to a plain, dignified structure and not aiming at such exterior effects as may make impossible an effectiv and economical layout of the interior.

These notes ar of course ritten with the smaller bildings in mind; larger bildings require larger and more varied treatment, but no modification of the primary purpose.

Note: For an explanation of the Simplified Spelling used throughout this Appendix, see note 69 to chapter 1.

Appendix 2

Carnegie Libraries Sampled in Table 4.1 and Graphs 4.1–4.5
(n = 85)

1899		
1. San Diego, Calif.	60,000	A
2. Dallas, Tex.	76,000 (2)	A
3. Alameda, Calif.	35,000	B
4. Fort Worth, Tex.	50,000	B
5. Oakland, Calif.	50,000	D

1900

(A random sampling of images assembled by the author included no libraries built with grants promised in 1900.)

1901		
6. Paducah, Ken.	35,000	A
7. Canton, Ohio	60,000	A
8. St. Cloud, Minn.	25,000	A
9. Catskill, N.Y.	20,000	A
10. Columbus, Ohio	200,000	A
11. Elkhart, Ind.	35,000	B
12. Lima, Ohio	34,000	B
13. Beloit, Wis.	25,000	B
14. Aurora, Ill.	50,000	B
15. Easton, Pa.	57,500	B
16. Joplin, Mo.	60,000	B
17. Eureka, Calif.	20,000	B
18. Guthrie, Okla.	26,000	B
19. Muncie, Ind.	55,000	B
20. Huntington, Ind.	25,000	C
21. Riverside, Calif.	52,500	D

1902		
22. Bedford, Ind.	20,000	A
23. Taunton, Mass.	70,000	A
24. Chippewa Falls, Wis.	20,000	A
25. Hartford, City, Ind.	16,000	A
26. Waco, Tex.	30,000	B
27. Jacksonville, Fla.	55,000	B
28. El Paso, Tex.	37,500	B

29. Greencastle, Ind.	20,165	B
30. Traverse City, Mich.	20,000	B
31. Hastings, Nebr.	15,000	B
32. Union City, Ind.	11,000	B
33. Anderson, Ind.	50,000	B
34. Galion, Ohio	15,000	B
35. Mattoon, Ill.	25,000	C
36. Lorain, Ohio	30,000	C
37. McCook, Neb.	11,000	C

1903		
38. Council Bluffs, Iowa	70,000	A
39. Hudson, Mich.	10,000	A
40. Warren, Ohio	28,384	B
41. Parkersburg, W.Va.	34,000	B
42. Petaluma, Calif.	12,500	B
43. Cleburne, Tex.	20,000	B
44. Belton, Tex.	10,000	B
45. Greenville, Ohio	11,000	B
46. Trinidad, Colo.	15,000	B
47. Richland Center, Wis.	10,000	C
48. Ludington, Mich.	15,000	C

1904		
49. Greenfield, Ind.	10,000	A
50. Holdrege, Nebr.	8,500	C
51. San Rafael, Calif.	25,000	D

1905		
52. San Pedro, Calif.	10,375	B
53. Tahlequah, Okla.	10,000	B
54. Galena, Ill.	12,500	B
55. Dodge City, Kans.	8,500	D

1906		
56. Gilroy, Calif.	10,000	B
57. Paso Robles, Calif.	10,000	B

58.	Winchester, Ind.	12,000	B	73.	Dixon, Calif.	10,000	C
59.	Leominster, Mass.	27,500	C	74.	Sturgeon Bay, Wis.	12,500	D
60.	St. Helena, Calif.	8,362	D				
61.	Pacific Grove, Calif.	10,000	D				

1912

75.	Gainesville, Tex.	15,000	A
76.	Perry, N.Y.	12,000	B

1907

62.	Ligonier, Ind.	10,000	C

1913

77.	Price, Utah	10,000	A

1908

63.	Ferndale, Calif.	8,000	B

1914

78.	Ephraim, Utah	10,000	A
79.	Exeter, Calif.	5,000	C
80.	Unionville, Conn.	8,500	C

1909

64.	Healdsburg, Calif.	10,000	B
65.	Imperial, Calif.	10,000	B
66.	Livermore, Calif.	10,000	B

1915

81.	Grass Valley, Calif.	15,000	A
82.	Calexico, Calif.	10,000	C

1910

67.	Muskogee, Okla.	60,000	A
68.	Manti, Utah	11,470	B

1916

83.	Mt. Pleasant, Utah	10,000	D

1911

1917

69.	Wagoner, Okla.	10,000	B
70.	Sonoma, Calif.	6,000	B
71.	Raton, N.Mex.	20,000	C
72.	Ukiah, Calif.	8,000	C

84.	Lackawanna, N.Y.	30,000	C
85.	Paw Paw, Mich.	10,000	C

Note: A = Triumphal Arch, B = Full Temple Front, C = Pedimented Aedicula, D = Other.

Notes

NOTE: All citations with a date included will be found in the Primary Sources section of the Bibliography. The remainder will be located in the Secondary Sources section.

INTRODUCTION

1. For a particularly well-written example of this latter tendency, see Helen Hooven Santmyer's treatment of the Carnegie library in Xenia, Ohio, in *Ohio Town*, 187–8. Even John Jackle's more scholarly investigation of the small-town landscape treats Carnegie libraries as the product of cultural consensus, and ignores the heated debates that often accompanied the siting and construction of this building type (Jackle, *American Small Town*, 108–9).

2. For a good overview of the range of methodologies used in interpreting vernacular architecture, see Upton and Vlach, *Common Places.*

3. Recent attempts to fill the gap between high-style and vernacular architecture studies include Larson, *Spirit of H. H. Richardson;* Longstreth, *Buildings of Main Street;* Longstreth, "Compositional Types," 12–23; Lebovich, *America's City Halls;* and Gulliford, *America's Country Schools.*

4. For a discussion of the relationship between architectural history and the architectural profession, see Upton, "Architectural History," 195–6.

5. Upton, "Pattern Books," 128–36.

6. Ochsner and Hubka, "H. H. Richardson," 144–5; Scully, *Architecture of the American Summer,* 5; Lancaster, "American Bungalow," in Upton and Vlach, *Common Places,* 79–106.

7. For another exploration of the methodological implications of a landscape approach to architectural history, see Upton, "Architectural History," 196–8.

8. This approach parallels recent developments in literary theory, particularly reception theory and the examination of the reader's role in creating the meaning of a text (see Terry Eagleton, *Literary Theory,* 74–90).

9. The best interpretations of prescriptive literature include: McMurry, *Families and Farmhouses;* Ames, "Meaning in Artifacts," 240–60; and Wright, *Moralism and the Model Home.*

10. For the role of taste in architectural history, see Upton, "Architectural History," 195.

11. Other studies of Carnegie library architecture have limited their focus to a single state or province: Beckman, Langmead, and Black, *Best Gift;* Bial and Bial, *Carnegie Library in Illinois;* Culp, "Carnegie Libraries of Texas: The Past Still Present," 81–96; Culp, "Carnegie Libraries of Texas: The Past No Longer Present," 132–144; Kortum, California's Carnegie libraries; MacLeod, *Carnegie Libraries in Wisconsin;* McCroskey, "'A Mighty Influence,'" 15–23; Pepper, "Postcards from Parnas-

sus," 36–41; Perry, "Andrew Carnegie," 23–7; Randolph, "Carnegie Libraries of Connecticut," 1, 7–9; Richards, "Carnegie Library Architecture for South Dakota and Montana," 69–78; Ring, "Carnegie Libraries," 1–19.

CHAPTER ONE

1. The story of this development is told in detail in Breisch, Small public libraries.

2. For middle-class philanthropy in the post–Civil War era, see Bremner, *Public Good*, chap. 8; Bremner, *American Philanthropy* chap. 6; Katz, *Shadow of the Poorhouse*, chap. 3; Boyer, *Urban Masses*, chaps. 7, 9, and 10.

3. For post–Civil War cultural philanthropy in general, see McCarthy, *Noblesse Oblige*, and Horowitz, *Culture and the City;* for Peabody's philanthropic career, see Parker, *George Peabody;* for Newberry, see Horowitz, *Culture and the City,* 35–36; for Winn, see Gilkerson, Public Libraries, 71–72.

4. The Winn Memorial Library in Woburn, Massachusetts, was dedicated to Winn's father, Jonathan Bowers Winn. Gilkerson, Public libraries, 71.

5. Quoted in Parker, *George Peabody,* 59.

6. *Proceedings at the Reception and Dinner in Honor of George Peabody* (1856), 32.

7. Ibid., 33.

8. They are Winn of Woburn, Oliver Ames, Jr., of North Easton, Albert Crane of Quincy, and Elisha Slade Converse of Malden. Gilkerson, Public libraries, 18, 71, 98, 134. For Richardson's contributions to the building type, see Breisch, Small public libraries, 202–63.

9. Poole, "Library Buildings" (1879), 293. See also Breisch, "William Frederick Poole," 52–72.

10. Breisch, Small public libraries, 147.

11. Poole, "Library Buildings" (1879), 293.

12. Poole, "Progress" (1882), 132. For more about the Library of Congress controversy, see Cole, "Smithmeyer and Pelz," 282–307.

13. Romanesque examples of the type include the Richmond Memorial Library in Batavia, New York, by J. C. Cutler (1887–89), the Acton Memorial Library in Acton, Massachusetts, by Hartwell and Richardson (1888–89), and the Ansonia Public Library, Ansonia, Connecticut, by George Keller (1891); the Easthampton (Massachusetts) Public Library by Peabody and Stearns (1880–81), and the Greenwich (Connecticut) Public Library by Lamb and Rich (1895–96) are Queen Anne and classical versions, respectively. Breisch, Small public libraries, 267–8, 285–8.

14. Poole, "Small Library Buildings" (1885), 250.

15. Carnegie, *Autobiography of Andrew Carnegie* (1920), 46–7.

16. Morgan's comments are quoted in Livesay, *Carnegie and Big Business,* 188.

17. For Carnegie's biography, see Wall, *Andrew Carnegie.* For a brief introduction to Carnegie's business practices, see Livesay, *Carnegie and Big Business.*

18. Carnegie's notes to himself are quoted in Livesay, *Carnegie and Big Business,* 72.

19. Carnegie, "Wealth" (1889), 653–64; Carnegie, "Best Fields for Philanthropy" (1889), 682–98.

20. Carnegie, "Wealth" (1889), 663.

21. Quoted in Koch, *Book of Carnegie Libraries* (1917), 7–8. For a discussion of Carnegie's ideas about the library's role in social reform, see Ditzion, *Arsenals of a Democratic Culture,* 149–60.

22. For a discussion of Carnegie's relationship to earlier philanthropists, see Bremner, *American Philanthropy*, 106–9.

23. The exception is Fairfield, Iowa, which received a relatively small grant of $30,000 in 1892. Bobinski, *Carnegie Libraries*, 13.

24. Although it did not receive its Carnegie grant until 1901, Duquesne, Pennsylvania, was the site of another Carnegie-owned steel plant and was treated just as Braddock and Homestead had been a decade earlier. Bobinski, *Carnegie Libraries*, 77. For the relationship between Carnegie's employment practices and his library grants to steel manufacturing towns, see Krause, "Patronage and Philanthropy," 127–45, and Miner, "'Deserted Parthenon,'" 107–35.

25. They were C. L. Eidlitz and George B. Post, both of New York; Shepley, Rutan and Coolidge of Brookline, Mass.; J. W. McLaughlin of Cincinnati; E. E. Myers and Son of Detroit; William Halsey Wood of Newark; and Smithmeyer and Pelz of Washington, D.C. *Souvenir—Opening of Carnegie Free Library* (1890), 15.

26. Given the history of conflict between the library and architectural professions, it seems ironic that architects raised the question of book storage. Yet Poole's pointed critique of the Library of Congress may have prompted Smithmeyer and Pelz and their fellow competitors to pay particularly close attention to this aspect of the program.

27. *Souvenir* (1890), 17.

28. Ibid. W. S. Fraser's unsuccessful competition entry was reproduced and discussed at length in the *American Architect and Building News* 21 (12 February 1887): 75, 79–81, and plates.

29. "Carnegie Free Library, Allegheny, Pa.," (1893), 288–90.

30. Poole, "Small Library Buildings" (1885), 250–6.

31. In Poole's plan, the reading room is identified as the periodical and newspaper room; this reflects a common practice in the late nineteenth century, when libraries provided reading areas for those who could not afford to have the daily paper delivered to their homes.

32. Poole even advocated separate windows at the delivery desk, one for ladies, the other for gents. Poole, "Small Library Buildings" (1885), 255.

33. *Souvenir* (1890), 21.

34. "Andrew Carnegie's Gift," *Bulletin*, c. February 1890, preserved in the Carnegie Corporation Archives (CCA).

35. Ibid.

36. Ibid.

37. Ibid.

38. Gladden, "Tainted Money" (1895), 886–7.

39. Bremner, *American Philanthropy*, 112.

40. Scudder, "Ill-Gotten Gifts to Colleges" (1900), 675–9.

41. Taylor quoted in "Shall the Dollar's Pedigree Defeat Its Destiny?" (1905), 471–2.

42. Scudder, "Ill-Gotten Gifts to Colleges" (1900), 675.

43. Quoted in Dain, *New York Public Library*, 219.

44. Using his opposition to the Carnegie gift to ingratiate himself with organized labor, alderman Louis B. Tossy argued that Carnegie's money was "soiled with the blood of workingmen." Woodford, *Parnassus on Main Street*, 186.

45. "Detroit Spurns Carnegie's Gold," *Detroit Evening News*, 2 March 1904, clipping preserved in the Carnegie Corporation Archives.

46. Carnegie, *Gospel of Wealth* (1901).

47. Carnegie, *Gospel of Wealth* (1901), 15.

48. Carnegie defended private property, for instance, with a quote from I Kings 3:12 ("every man under his vine and under his fig tree"). Carnegie, *Gospel of Wealth* (1901), 6.

49. The expansion of the Carnegie library program was not limited to the United States. An additional 828 libraries were built in many parts of the English-speaking world, including England, Scotland, Canada, Australia, New Zealand, South Africa, and the West Indies. Anderson, *Carnegie Corporation Library Program*, 4–5.

50. Bobinski, *Carnegie Libraries*, 40, 43–5.

51. James Bertram (1872–1934) was born near Edinburgh and had worked for railroad and mining interests in Scotland and South Africa before becoming Carnegie's confidential secretary in 1897. Bertram remained in that post until Carnegie's death in 1919, and continued to serve as secretary of the Carnegie Corporation until his own death fifteen years later. Hill, *James Bertram*, 15–21.

52. Three versions of this questionnaire are reprinted in Bobinski, *Carnegie Libraries*, 203–5.

53. Ibid., 205–6.

54. Bostwick, *American Public Library* (1910), 8–9.

55. Long, *Library Service to Children*, 80–94. See also Lopez, "Children's Libraries," 316–42.

56. Bostwick, *American Public Library* (1910), 9.

57. Long, *Library Service to Children*, 80–94.

58. "Reading Rooms for Children" (1897), 125–31.

59. Bostwick, *American Public Library* (1910), 13.

60. Ibid., 10.

61. Dana, "The Public and Its Library" (1897), 244–5.

62. Ibid., 247.

63. Ibid., 249–50.

64. Soule, "Modern Library Buildings" (1902), 1–60.

65. Dana, "The Public and Its Library" (1897), 249; Wheeler and Githens, *American Library Building* (1941), 5; Montgomery, "Blueprints," 4078. Dana's assessment that the World's Columbian Exposition "delayed our [i.e., America's] architectural emancipation by many a long day" antedates Louis Sullivan's similarly dire pronouncements by twenty-seven years.

66. For the development of the T-plan, see Breisch, Small public libraries, 134–9, 271–80.

67. Academic and other private libraries were not subject to the same debates. More trusting of their limited constituencies, they often allowed readers access to books, even in alcoves.

68. The large proportion of Carnegie libraries in this sample is not surprising, given the fact that Carnegie had offered to fund the building of 316 public library buildings in the three precedings years.

69. Bertram, Letter to L. K. Johnson, 8 February 1916, CCA. What at first appear to be misspellings are the result of a simplified spelling scheme which librarian Melvil Dewey convinced Carnegie to support and use. Thus, in some original sources quoted in this text, "building" is rendered as "bilding," "money" as "mony," "effective" as "effectiv," "built" as "bilt," "are" as "ar," "have" as "hav," and "doubt" as "dout." For a discussion of Dewey's scheme, see Garrison, *Apostles of Culture*, 113.

70. The 1904 date is suggested by Bertram's correspondence with Cambridge, Ohio, on 30 January 1904, and with Taylorville, Illinois, on 5 November 1904, CCA.

71. Bobinski, *Carnegie Libraries*, 57.

72. [James Bertram], "Notes on the Erection of Library Bildings," [version 2, c. 1913], CCA. See note 74 below.

73. Mrs. Percival Sneed, Letter to Frank Harris, Editor, *Ocala Banner*, 11 May 1915, CCA.

74. Three versions of the "Notes" are preserved in the Carnegie Corporation Archives, but none are dated. The last version is presented, with original spelling, in appendix 1.

75. Tilton's contribution to the "Notes" remains unclear. Bertram certainly respected his library designs and in early 1911 (while working on the "Notes") mentioned him to grant recipients as an architect who had "successfully designed many Carnegie libraries recently." Tilton, however, was not alone in this honor; as we shall see in chapter 2, Carnegie's brother-in-law, Henry D. Whitfield, and the Chicago firm of Patton & Miller also received Bertram's unofficial endorsement in 1911. Tilton's own article on "Scientific Library Planning," published in the *Library Journal* in 1912, does not advocate the sort of open planning presented in the "Notes," focusing instead on formulas for calculating square footage of library facilities, stack size, and electrical and heating requirements. Tilton's input is not mentioned in contemporary library literature, architectural periodicals, Carnegie Corporation correspondence, or in the pamphlet itself.

The first mention of Tilton's name in connection with the "Notes" dates from 1941, when Wheeler and Githens credit Tilton with drafting the plan arrangements for the "Notes" (*American Library Building* [1941], 218). As Tilton's former partner, Githens was ostensibly a reliable source, and several subsequent authors have linked Tilton's name with the "Notes." Yet, since his partnership with Tilton did not begin until 1920, Githens lacked firsthand knowledge of these events. By the time Githens linked Tilton's name with the "Notes," those who could have verified the facts (including Bertram, Carnegie, and Tilton himself) were already dead.

76. Bobinski, *Carnegie Libraries*, 58.

77. [Bertram], "Notes," version 3.

78. Ibid.

79. Ibid.

80. Neither the Carnegie Corporation nor the more loosely organized body that preceded its incorporation in 1911 ever sent ready-made plans for library buildings. As a result, none of the elevations that grace Carnegie libraries across the country originated with the Carnegie Corporation, while their plans conform more or less to the schematic diagrams contained in Bertram's pamphlet. Far from attempting to force a certain mode of building upon hapless towns (a common misconception about the Carnegie library program that still persists), Bertram turned down frequent requests for ready-made plans. J. Bertram, Letter to Mrs. N. C. Ensign, of Madison, Ohio, 24 November 1916, CCA.

81. Soule, "Points of Agreement" (1891), 17.

82. [Bertram], "Notes" version 3.

83. James Bertram, Letter to Hon B. Smith, of Macon, Georgia, 22 November 1915, CCA.

84. That these later libraries were intended to be shrineless is borne out by subsequent events. In 1935, a later generation of Corporation officials marked the hundredth anniversary of Carnegie's birth by sending each library a portrait of its donor. Although these portraits still hang in many Carnegie libraries, library officials have had difficulty finding appropriate places for them in the reformed library.

CHAPTER TWO

1. Gwendolyn Wright is one of the few architectural historians to address directly the impact of the depression of the 1890s on the practice of architecture, noting that many architects turned away from small-scale house design in order to pursue "a program of grandeur" as a means of protecting their professional status. Wright, *Moralism and the Model Home*, 201–11. Regarding post–Civil War struggles for professional recognition of architecture more generally, see Grossman and Reitzes, "Caught in the Crossfire," 27–39; Saint, *Image*, 72–95; Boyle, "Architectural Practice," 309–17; Draper, "Ecole des Beaux-Arts," 209–37.

2. As Burton Bledstein notes, the struggle for control over one's work space was no small concern within emerging professions. Indeed, the creation and maintenance of professional status often involved rituals and ceremonies centered on the conspicuous display of new tools and carried out in carefully established spaces. Bledstein, *Culture of Professionalism*, 95.

3. To the dismay of men like William Poole, Melvil Dewey encouraged a younger generation of library leaders in the late nineteenth century to embrace efficiency as a measure of professional competence. Indeed, Dewey's brand of professional education helped redefine the librarian's role in relationship to quick and efficient distribution of books, while the motto he coined for the American Library Association ("The best reading for the largest number at the least cost") confirmed efficiency as one of the cornerstones of a new professional ethos. Casey, "Efficiency," 265–79; Garrison, *Apostles of Culture*, 144; Wiegand, *Politics*, 3.

In architecture, the shift toward efficiency was less abrupt, as Ecole-trained architects were somewhat reluctant to sacrifice their artistic aspirations to practical concerns. Even Daniel Burnham, who succeeded in applying modern management techniques to architectural practice, also took care to present himself as a lover of art. Nonetheless, the general trend in the early twentieth century toward large firms and the division of labor within the design process attest to the growing importance of efficiency as a component of architectural culture. Saint, *Image*, 80–7; Boyle, "Architectural Practice," 313–7.

4. Scholars of library science continue to debate Dewey's impact on professional education for librarians. Carl White has argued persuasively that Dewey emphasized technical training and practical methods of library administration, while Dee Garrison has drawn intriguing links between this technical emphasis, the feminization of librarianship, and the field's failure to win recognition as one of the "true" professions. More recently, Francis Miksa has used the shorthand notes of one of Dewey's first students to point out the "unexpected intellectual content" of the Columbia curriculum, but has not offered a substantive challenge to the technical-vocational interpretation of White and Garrison. White, *Introduction to Library Education*, 56–7 and 63–6; Garrison, "Tender Technicians," 147–51; Miksa, "Columbia School," 249–80.

5. Garrison, *Apostles of Culture*, 130–7.

6. "Twenty-seventh Annual Report" (1913), 21.

7. Bostwick, *American Public Library* (1910), 8–9.

8. Wilson, Pilgrim, and Murray, *American Renaissance*, 57–61; David De Long links this phenomenon (which he calls the Academic Reaction) more directly to the rise of professional schools of architecture. De Long, "William R. Ware," 13–14.

9. Recommended by the Committee on Education in 1897, these requirements for AIA membership went into effect in 1901. Grossman and Reitzes, "Caught in the Crossfire," 28–9.

10. California, Colorado, Florida, Idaho, Illinois, Louisiana, Michigan, New Jersey, New York, North Carolina, North Dakota, South Carolina, Utah, and Wisconsin required state registration for architects by 1918. "States Requiring Registration of Architects" (1918), 145.

11. The culture of professionalism is an important component in understanding the widespread use of the classical language of architecture in the United States at the turn of the century. First, it helps put the influence of the Ecole des Beaux-Arts into perspective. Since many American architects (Richardson among them) implemented the lessons of composition that they had learned at the Ecole without relying on the classical language, it is not enough to attribute the classicizing mania of the turn of the century to the number of Americans studying architecture in Paris. It would be more accurate to say that the culture of professionalism in the United States in the 1890s made American architects particularly sensitive to the success of French architects in increasing their professional prestige using the classical language of architecture as the theoretical knowledge base of their field. The culture of professionalism also helps to explain the importance of the World's Columbian Exposition in this same classicizing movement. As noted in many recent studies of the City Beautiful movement, the Chicago exposition of 1893 was not the beginning of the movement. Nonetheless, it remains central to the history of this movement as the most impressive demonstration of the existence of professional standards of design and of the usefulness of the classical vocabulary in implementing those standards. William Wilson, *City Beautiful Movement*, 60–4; Peterson, "City Beautiful," 415–34.

12. This redesign of the work environment was not unique to libraries, but is one aspect of a general transformation of the American workplace between 1870 and 1915. Schlereth, *Cultural History*, 145–76; Forty, *Objects of Desire* chap. 4; Lupton, *Mechanical Brides*, 43–50; Zunz, *Making America Corporate*, 103–24.

13. For a detailed history of the Library Bureau, see Flanzraich, Role of the Library Bureau.

14. "Charging Desks" [Library Bureau ad], *Public Libraries*, 11 (October 1906): 478–9.

15. Library Bureau, *Classified Illustrated Catalog* (1890), 4.

16. Library Bureau, *Library Catalog* (1902), 15–7.

17. Since no corporate records exist from this period, it is difficult to assess how frequently architects availed themselves of this service. The absence of any mention of it in other sources (such as the correspondence in the Carnegie Corporation Archive and the architects' correspondence), while not conclusive, suggests that the service was not often used.

18. Library Bureau, *Classified Illustrated Catalog* (1897), 5, 138.

19. Parker, *Library Bureau Historical Pamphlet* (1908).

20. "L.B. Training School: Enthusiastic opening of eight weeks summer course for prospective salesmen," *Salesmen's Bulletin* 40 (22 July 1903).

21. Although it has not received the scholarly attention it deserves, the Windsor chair was a favorite element in many reform environments in the late nineteenth century, as it was thought to convey honesty, simplicity, practicality, craftsmanship, and domesticity—a constellation of virtues that Americans like Wallace Nutting associated with the Puritan culture of seventeenth-century New England. The nationalism that was so strong a component of late nineteenth-century reform movements prompted William Morris to champion the Sussex chair, a closely related form derived from "an old chair of village manufacture picked up in Sussex." Kaplan, *"Art That is Life,"* 80, 177–8; Marling, *George Washington Slept Here*, 160–82; Dulaney, "Wal-

lace Nutting," 47–60. For the widespread appearance of Windsor chairs and associated forms in settings devoted to social and/or aesthetic reform, see the illustrations in Johnson, *Many Faces of Hull House*, plates 9, 41, 44, 45, 47, 49, and 57; "Inside the Past," 241–77; Handlin, *The American Home*, 447.

22. Library Bureau, *Library Catalog* (1902), 23, 43. For the popularity of classical and Arts and Crafts styles in home library furnishings, see Kruger, "Home Libraries," 94–119.

23. Library Bureau, *Library Catalog* (1902), 43.

24. Wayne Wiegand notes the impact of the Carnegie program in expanding the ranks of the small public library directors who formed Dewey's major constituency in the American Library Association, but he does not extend his analysis to the resulting material transformation of the library environment. Wiegand, "Melvil Dewey," 126.

25. James Bertram, Letter to C. N. Boyd [of Butler, Pennsylvania], 20 October 1919; Letter to Mrs. M. H. Stovall [of Ocala, Florida], 9 March 1915, CCA.

26. Upjohn and Notman were among the five architects that received the official approval of the New York Ecclesiological Society in 1852. Pierson, *American Buildings* 2: 201–5.

27. For a brief consideration of Albert Randolph Ross's career, see Oehlerts, *Books and Blueprints*, 66–7.

28. The following discussion of Tilton's career is based on information found in Fulton and Taves, *Collection Catalogue*, 4–6; Withey and Withey, *Biographical Dictionary*, 601; and Oehlerts, *Books and Blueprints*, 71–82.

29. Warren Library Board of Trustees minutes, 28 December 1903 and 1 January 1904, Warren-Trumbull County Public Library Archives.

30. Edward L. Tilton, Letter to B. J. Taylor, 22 August 1903, Warren-Trumbull County Public Library Archives.

31. In fact, Boring and Tilton maintained such a cordial relationship after the dissolution of the firm that many of their contemporaries seem to have assumed that the partnership remained intact until Boring's retirement in 1915. Relying exclusively on secondary sources, Withey and Withey's *Biographical Dictionary* uses this later date. In contrast, Fulton and Taves date the dissolution of the firm to 1904, a date based on the close examination of Boring's office records, now preserved in the archives of the Avery Architectural Library at Columbia. Fulton and Taves, *Boring Collection Catalogue*, 6.

32. Boring did indeed go on to garner many of the usual signs of professional success, including the deanship at Columbia's School of Architecture.

33. Tilton, "Architecture of the Small Library" (1911), 26–30.

34. Tilton, "Scientific Library Planning" (1912), 497–501.

35. Edward L. Tilton, Letter to James Bertram [re: Ludington, Michigan] 20 June 1905, CCA.

36. Unable to complete their building within their $20,000 allotment, Warren agreed to increase their tax levy to $3,000. Carnegie eventually raised their appropriation to $27,000. James Bertram, Letter to B. J. Taylor, 16 December 1904, CCA.

37. James Bertram, Letter to S. L. Lowry [of Tampa, Florida], 17 January 1911; Letter to Mrs. J. F. Robertson [of Caldwell, Kansas], 23 May 1911, CCA.

38. These were Boonville, Evansville, Greensburg, Martinsville, Mitchell, Mount Vernon, Newburgh, Owensville, Princeton, Rockport, Salem, Scottsburg, Seymour, Shelbyville, and Tell City.

39. Parker's Carnegie library designs include buildings in the Indiana towns of Bloomington, Brookville, Hebron, Liberty, Pendleton, Plainfield, Shoals, Spencer,

Thornton, and Williamsport. Wing and Mahurin designed Carnegie libraries in the Indiana towns of Alexandria, Elkhart, Muncie, and Wabash.

40. Kortum, California's Carnegie libraries, 39–40. See also Lewis, "William H. Weeks."

41. Wetherell was involved in the design of Carnegie libraries in the Iowa towns of Bedford, Bloomfield, Cherokee, Eldon, Montezuma, Oskaloosa, and Winterset. For Haire's library commissions, see Richards, "Carnegie Library Architecture for South Dakota and Montana," 73.

42. Kruty, "Patton & Miller," 110–22; Oehlerts, *Books and Blueprints*, 67.

43. N.S.P. [Normand S. Patton], Letter to A. M. Hewlitt [*sic*], 16 March 1906, CCA.

44. Ibid.

45. Patton & Miller's western Carnegie libraries include those in Caldwell, Kansas, and in the Texas towns of Tyler and Abilene. In addition, Patton completed drawings for the library in Palestine, Texas, although the commission was later given to another architect.

46. The nature of these discussions is somewhat obscure. Some months later, Patton recalled them as discussions about developing stock plans, and asked Bertram to inform the firm whenever a town in the Chicago area received a grant, something close to a monopoly on Carnegie commissions in Illinois. In his response, Bertram ignored the request and responded only to the other parts of Patton's letter regarding the design of the library in Early Park, Indiana. Since the timing of the interview coincides with the production of "Notes on the Erection of Library Bildings," it seems likely that Bertram had asked for Patton's advice on the schematic plans. Bertram's later reticence about the outcome of the interview suggests either that Patton had misunderstood Bertram's meaning or that the two men had in fact discussed stock plans, but that Bertram had come to regret the discussion. Patton's letter to Bertram, dated 17 May 1912, is located in the file on Earl Park, Indiana. CCA.

47. A good example is the misunderstanding that arose over the Palestine, Texas, library.

48. Henry N. Sanborn, Letter to James Bertram, 10 October 1916, CCA.

49. James Bertram, Letter to Henry N. Sanborn, 14 November 1916, CCA.

50. James Bertram, Letter to G. H. Baskette, of Nashville, 2 April 1910, CCA.

CHAPTER THREE

1. While we will see that these attitudes existed in smaller American towns, they have only been well documented in studies of larger American cities and their participation in the City Beautiful movement, with its emphasis on comprehensive city planning and stylistically unified civic and cultural centers. See Bluestone, *Constructing Chicago*, 153; Bluestone, "Detroit's City Beautiful," 254–6; William Wilson, *City Beautiful Movement*, 78–9; Trachtenberg, *Incorporation of America*, 145–7.

2. For the financial status of American cities, see Teaford, *Unheralded Triumph*, 284–5 and 293–4.

3. This is not to imply that all City Beautiful advocates participated in a "status revolt" of the sort posited by Richard Hofstadter, in which older, established groups resisted what they perceived as threats to their status, from the great wealth of giant business corporations above them and from mass immigration and organized labor from below. As William Wilson has pointed out, there was no direct relationship between class and support of City Beautiful schemes. In fact, the opponents of City Beautiful reforms resembled their adversaries in occupation, age, education, and

social background, while "the movement's fervent optimism . . . blanketed any fears of class conflict" (William Wilson, *City Beautiful Movement*, 85). As we will see, however, the old money social elites who dominated the boards of museums and libraries built in City Beautiful precincts tended to use these institutions to claim a small, but (to them) pivotal arena for the exercise of their authority. Hofstadter, *Age of Reform*, 131–72; William Wilson, *City Beautiful Movement*, 75–7, 85; Horowitz, *Culture and the City*, 12–3; Lawrence Levine, *Highbrow, Lowbrow*, 171–7.

4. The difference between Progressive reformers and the cultural elites who served on library boards is hardly absolute. After all, both groups participated in a general campaign to bring order and balance to city life. What is more, the definition of Progressivism is remarkably slippery, and remains one of the thorniest issues in American historiography. Indeed, the Progressive label has been applied to a wide spectrum of reform activities, at least some of which were motivated by conservative impulses. As we shall see, however, Progressive-minded librarians tended to embrace an ethos that could bring them into conflict with library trustees. For the links between Progressivism and City Beautiful concerns, see William Wilson, *City Beautiful Movement*, 75. For the conservative side of Progressivism, see Kolko, *Triumph of Conservatism*. For concise reviews of the historical literature on Progressivism, see Brownell, "Urban Progressive Reform," 3–23; and Finkel, "Social Class," 465–80.

5. To the extent that the first wave of feminist architectural history concentrated either on architectural expressions of domesticity or on recovering female architects, the role of nonprofessional women in shaping the public arena has not been adequately explored. Planning historians have done a better job at documenting the impact of middle-class club women on American urban reform, while social historians and scholars of library science have been most thorough in their treatment of club women's involvement with cultural institutions. Indeed, Scott's 1986 call for "a systematic analysis of the part played by women's associations in creating public libraries" ("Women and Libraries," 400) has helped encourage more intensive study of women's roles in shaping public institutions devoted to culture. For a discussion of architectural expressions of domesticity, see Wright, *Moralism and the Model Home*, and Hayden, *Domestic Revolution*. For information on female architects, see Torre, *Women in American Architecture*. For a study of club women and their involvement with urban reform, see Wortman, "Domesticating the American City," 531–71. For documentation of club women and their involvement with cultural institutions, see Musmann, Social libraries; Taylor, "Ladies of the Club," 324–7; Scott, "Women and Libraries," 400–5; Scott, *Natural Allies*; Martin, *Our Own Voices*; and Blair, *Torchbearers*.

6. Kerber, "Separate Spheres," 9–39.

7. For a discussion of late nineteenth-century campaigns to require genteel behavior in cultural institutions, see Levine, *Highbrow, Lowbrow*, 184–200. For the middle-class bias of nineteenth-century park administrators, see Cranz, *Politics of Park Design*, 7–24. For department stores as a training ground in middle-class behavior for workers and for customers, see Benson, *Counter Cultures*, 124–76; Trachtenberg, *Incorporation of America*, 130–6; Barth, *City People*, 129–33. For the role of railroad terminal and comfort stations treating personal hygiene and cleanliness as a public concern, see William Taylor, "Public Space," 287–309.

8. Even Sidney Ditzion (who saw the public library as a truly democratic institution) had to admit that the post–Civil War transition from proprietary library to public library was anything but smooth. Indeed, he noted that the ultimate goad to establishing public libraries may have had more to do with the weak economic base

of subscription libraries than with a dedication to making reading material accessible to the urban masses. In Chicago, both sorts of libraries existed simultaneously. Indeed, the privately endowed Newberry and Crerar Libraries were both open to the public, but purposefully distinguished themselves from the new Chicago Public Library by devoting themselves to developing noncirculating research collections. In New York, private libraries established by the Astor, Lenox, and Tilden Trusts combined to form the New York Public Library, but the trustees remained a private corporation with a consistently elite demographic profile until 1970. For further discussion of the shift from social to public library, see Ditzion, *Arsenals of a Democratic Culture*, 35–50; Shera, *Foundations of the Public Library;* and McMullen, "Decline of the Social Library," 207–25. For the Chicago situation, see Horowitz, *Culture and the City*, 98–9. For the New York situation, see Dain, "Public Library Governance," 219–50.

9. For elite ambivalence about the ability of culture to transform the unwashed masses, see Lawrence Levine, *Highbrow, Lowbrow*, 206–19.

10. For discussions of specific public library policies, see Lawrence Levine, *Highbrow, Lowbrow*, 159; and Horowitz, *Culture and the City*, 124. For a broadly conceived discussion of the elite nature of the public library, see Harris, "Purpose," 2509–14. See also Dain's rebuttal of Harris's conclusions, "Ambivalence and Paradox," 261–6.

11. Richard Wilson, Pilgrim, and Murray, *American Renaissance*, 101–3.

12. Jordy, *Progressive and Academic Ideals*, 314–75; Roth, *McKim, Mead & White*, 116–30; Richard Wilson, *McKim, Mead & White*, 131–45.

13. Jordy, *Progressive and Academic Ideals*, 333.

14. For the gap between McKim's original scheme and the built results, see Jordy, *Progressive and Academic Ideals*, 366–70.

15. For the Bibliothèque Ste.-Geneviève, see Neil Levine, "Architectural Legibility," 325–416; Van Zanten, *Designing Paris*, 83–98.

16. Reed, *New York Public Library*, 3–33; Drexler, *Architecture of the Ecole des Beaux-Arts*, 478–9; Dain, *New York Public Library*, 137–82; Lydenberg, *Foundations* (1923), 437–516; Van Zanten, "Architectural Composition," 111–324; Heckscher, "Hunt and the Metropolitan," 173–87.

17. "New Building" (1911), 221–8.

18. Richard Wilson, *American Renaissance*, 29.

19. For contemporary expressions of these values, see Bowerman, "Public Library" (1906), 105–10; Olcott, "Public Library" (1910), 849–61; "Social Evangelism by Children's Librarians" (1910), 828–9. For historical discussions of this trend, see Ditzion, *Arsenals of a Democratic Culture*, 174–89; Du Mont, *Reform and Reaction*, 31–49; Fain, "Books for New Citizens," 255–76; Bluestone, *Constructing Chicago*, 164–6. See also Du Mont, "Race in American Librarianship," 488–509.

20. Cremin, *American Education*, 653–4; Shavit, "Jewish Public Libraries in Tsarist Russia," 239–52; Epstein, "Pages from My Stormy Life" (1962), 138; Levine, "Letters of an Immigrant" (1981), 57.

21. To a certain extent, this promise remained unfulfilled. Although Progressive-minded librarians stood ready to supply foreign-language literature to recent immigrants, they defined their professional role as the selection of "good reading," and regularly exercised book censorship. It was not until 1939 that the American Library Association adopted the Library Bill of Rights, and librarians embraced their more recent role as guardians of intellectual freedom. Geller, *Forbidden Books*, 79–97, 172–6; Ross, "Metaphors of Reading," 145–63.

22. Although Teaford notes the success of conservative fiscal policies in the late

nineteenth century, Boyer argues that the drive for municipal improvements soon resulted in "a startling increase in municipal indebtedness." To the extent that it helped offset the cost of civic improvements, a Carnegie gift may have been particularly welcome in this situation. Teaford, *Unheralded Triumph*, 293; Christine Boyer, *Dreaming the Rational City*, 115.

23. The Detroit story has been well documented. See, for example, Bobinski, *Carnegie Libraries*, 89–94; Woodford, *Parnassus on Main Street*, 174–90.

24. James Bertram, Letter to H. P. Carlton, 20 January, 1908, CCA.

25. Bluestone, "Detroit's City Beautiful," 256–9; McCue, *Building Art in St. Louis*, 55. For San Francisco, see Oehlerts, *Books and Blueprints*, 47–8.

26. Bluestone, "Detroit's City Beautiful," 245–62.

27. Bluestone, *Constructing Chicago*, 183; Fogelsong, *Planning the Capitalist City*, 161–6; Manieri-Elia, "Toward an 'Imperial City,'" 101–6.

28. The cities that sponsored competitions include Oakland, California; San Francisco; Washington, D.C.; Atlanta; Louisville; Detroit; St. Louis; Pittsburgh; and Nashville.

29. A detailed description of this inspection trip is recorded in the Proceedings of the Detroit Library Commission, 11 October 1912, BHC.

30. Proceedings of the Detroit Library Commission, 11 October 1912, BHC. For information on Gilbert's involvement in library design, see Oehlerts, *Books and Blueprints*, 44–45.

31. Day was recommended for the post by the building committee, Proceedings of the Detroit Library Commission, 3 December 1912; his letter of acceptance was recorded in the Commission proceedings, 17 December 1912, BHC.

32. Angered that the rules put local architects at a severe disadvantage, the Michigan Chapter of the AIA asked Day to admit four stage-one competitors to stage two; the commissioners, however, were loathe to change rules that had already been advertised. Proceedings of the Detroit Library Commission, 18 March 1913, BHC.

33. "Detroit Public Library" (1921), 228; Edna Moore, "Detroit's New Main Library" (1921), 405–8.

34. A succinct overview of these conflicting opinions is available in Jordy, *Progressive and Academic Ideals*, 323–8.

35. William Brett, Letter to James Bertram, 1 July 1915, CCA.

36. Of the thirty-four cities that received Carnegie grants to build a main and branch libraries, at least nine (or over a quarter) supplemented the Carnegie grant to pay for the main building. In addition to the Detroit Public Library, these include the St. Louis Public Library, where the city's contribution was twice that of Carnegie's $500,000 grant; the Denver Public Library, which cost $50,000 more than Carnegie suggested (Bobinski, *Carnegie Libraries*, 73); the Springfield (Massachusetts) City Library, built with $200,000 from Carnegie and another $155,000 donated by 378 "public-spirited citizens" ("Springfield City Library Opening" [1912], 79–80); the central library in Savannah, where the city increased Carnegie's $75,000 grant by about $14,000 ("Savannah Public Library" [1917], 456–7); the main library in Somerville, Massachusetts, where the city received $80,000 from Carnegie, which they supplemented with $45,000 from the public coffers (Hall, "Opening" [1914], 35–8); the main branch of the Oakland, California, library, built with $50,000 of Carnegie's money, and another $43,000 from the city, and the San Francisco Public Library's main building, which cost $1,152,000, only $375,000 of which came from Carnegie (Kortum, California's Carnegie libraries). In each case, Bertram required the city to spend its own money first, a policy evidently aimed at ensuring that

Carnegie libraries would not be left unfinished by communities unable or unwilling to complete their financial contributions. The planning of central libraries may have been beyond Bertram's control, but he was unwilling to subject his employer to unwarranted criticism because of it.

37. "New Elizabeth Library" (1912), 509–10; "Springfield City Library Opening" (1912), 78–80; "Carnegie Library of Atlanta" (1900), 70; "Washington, D.C., Library Building" (1899), 676–7; Koch, *Book of Carnegie Libraries* (1917), 112–4.

38. Yust, "Louisville Free Public Library Building" (1909), 398–401.

39. "Springfield City Library Opening" (1912), 80.

40. The difference between "serious" and "casual" readers was well developed in descriptions of the New York Public Library written by the library's director when the new building was reaching completion. Billings, "New York Public Library" (1911), 233–4.

41. Adam Strohm, Letter to Cass Gilbert, 23 December 1913, Director's file 1913–18, BHC.

42. Teaford, *Unheralded Triumph*, 261–2; Olcott, "Public Library" (1910), 851. For Progressive support of decentralized urban amenities more generally, see Cranz, *Politics of Park Design*, 80–4; Davis, *Spearheads for Reform*, 74–83; Lubove, *Progressives and the Slums*, 188–93.

43. Certainly, the erection of a library building did not absolutely prevent the reallocation of resources, and there are many examples of Carnegie-financed branch libraries that have since been closed or sold. Yet library boards were less likely to abandon purpose-built library buildings than they were to close rented quarters.

44. James P. Bertram, Letter to Harry P. Carlton (of Oakland, Cal.), 20 January 1908, CCA.

45. This was the explanation that Carnegie gave in 1898 in his speech at the dedication of the Carnegie Library in Homestead. "The Dedication of the Carnegie Library," typescript in archives of the Carnegie Library of Homestead. The bloody events at Homestead constitute a turning point in Carnegie's career, but his role in those events are complex. According to some interpretations, Carnegie remained in Scotland during the strike, at least in part out of concern that he might agree to an expensive settlement. Whatever his motivations, Carnegie certainly gave Frick a free hand to deal with the strike, and soon found that he had lost his reputation as the workingman's friend (a title earned for his published condemnation of hiring scab labor). Feeling betrayed by the outcome of the Homestead debacle, Carnegie was increasingly wary of the working poor. Livesay, *Carnegie and Big Business*, 135–44.

46. For the conditions of the Pittsburgh gift, see Koch, *Carnegie Libraries* (1917), 122–6.

47. For a detailed study of the firm, see Floyd, *Architecture after Richardson*, particularly 127–32 and 190–241. Alden's relationship with Carnegie is documented in the Carnegie papers in the Library of Congress, both in letters to Alden himself and in other correspondence. In 1896, for instance, Carnegie instructed Charles Schwab to secure a design for a library in Homestead, Pennsylvania. While noting that several architects should be asked, he mentioned only Alden by name, stating that "he stands very high in my books." This comment was evidently clear enough to ensure that Alden & Harlow would design the Homestead building. Andrew Carnegie, Letter to Charles Schwab, 23 January 1896, Andrew Carnegie Papers, Library of Congress.

48. Breisch, Small public libraries, 326.

49. Olcott, "Home Libraries for Poor Children" (1904), 376.

50. "Lawrenceville Branch" (1897), 440–1.

51. Sinks were often included in children's rooms in nineteenth-century libraries to help keep books clean and to help check the spread of contagion. See Lopez, "Children's Libraries," 316–42.

52. Board of Directors of the Oakland Free Library, *Thirty-Sixth Annual Report* (1913–14), 18. Archives of Oakland Public Library, Oakland, California.

53. Minutes of the Oakland Public Library Board of Directors Meetings, 8 September, 28 October, 16 November 1914. Archives of Oakland Public Library, Oakland, California.

54. Proceedings of the Detroit Library Commission 8 June 1910, 22 June 1910, 4 October 1911, 4 December 1911, 2 July 1912, 18 June 1915, BHC; Woodford, *Parnassus on Main Street*, 217.

55. This policy was established on 8 June 1910. On 22 June 1910, the first five architects were named. They were Gustav A. Mueller, Stratton and Baldwin, Donaldson and Meier, B. C. Wetzel, and Albert Kahn. At the same meeting, the architects participated in a lottery for specific lot assignments. Proceedings of the Detroit Library Commision, BHC.

56. Regarding the separate administration of library gifts for Brooklyn and Queens, see Dain, *New York Public Library*, 223–5.

57. The report of the advisory board is summarized in an undated, unsigned document, entitled "Carnegie Library Buildings," preserved in the archives of the New York Public Library. The agreement between the trustees and the board of architects is reproduced in Koch, *Book of Carnegie Libraries* (1917), 38–42. The board of architects designed all of Manhattan's Carnegie-financed branches, except the Yorkville Branch; located on East 79th Street, this branch had been designed by James Brown Lord before the Carnegie offer was made. Stern et al., *New York 1900*, 98–9.

58. Sturgis, "Carnegie Libraries in New York" (1905), 237–46.

59. Walter Cook, quoted in Koch, *Book of Carnegie Libraries* (1917), 37.

60. [Raymond F. Almirall, architect], "Carnegie Library, Pacific Branch" (1907), plates 78–9. For Bentham's Panopticon, see Foucault, *Discipline and Punish*, 200–9.

61. Bostwick, *American Public Library* (1910), 67.

62. Eastman, "Library Buildings" (1901), 39.

63. [Lindley Johnson, architect], "Tacony Branch" (1906), plate 153; "Building Progress in St. Louis" (1908), 98–9.

CHAPTER FOUR

1. Longstreth, "Main Streets," 116–7; Martin, "Prairie City," 107–12; Hudson, "Midland Prairies," 130–2; Jackle, *American Small Town*, 22–9; Lingeman, *Small Town America*, 295–303.

2. Musmann, Social libraries, 33, citing Sophonisba P. Breckenridge, *Women in the Twentieth Century: A Study of their Political, Social, and Economic Activities* (New York: McGraw-Hill, 1933). The connection between women's clubs and library organizing was well documented at the time, in publications like Cotten, *North Carolina Women's Clubs* (1925); Granger, "Club Work in the South" (1906), 248–56; *Oklahoma Libraries* (1937); Rainey, *Women's Clubs* (1939); Sherman, "Women's Clubs" (1906), 227–47; West, "Achievements" (1935), 30–1, 47.

More recent works which document this connection include Scott, "Women and Libraries," 400–5; Scott, *Natural Allies;* Blair, *Clubwoman as Feminist;* Blair, *Torchbearers,* 31; Douglas, *Feminization of American Culture,* 103; Bocock, "Texas Libraries," 26; Bowers, "White-Gloved Feminists," 38–47; Jackson, "Life and Society in Sapulpa," 297–318; Marcum, "Rural Public Library," 91; Morain, *Prairie Grass Roots*, 91; Passet, "Reaching the Rural Reader," 102; Ring, "Carnegie Libraries," 2; Santmyer, *Ohio Town*, 191–2; David Taylor, "Ladies of the Club," 324–7; Underwood, "Civilizing Kansas," 300.

3. The invisibility of these libraries is in part a product of their ephemeral nature. Housed in temporary quarters, rarely photographed, and quickly replaced by purpose-built libraries (often paid for by Carnegie funds), these earlier town libraries are not easy environments to reconstruct. This natural invisibility, however, has been exacerbated by the prejudices of architectural history. Scholars working within the art historical tradition tend to ignore those environments that were not designed by professional architects. The biases of vernacular architecture scholarship, emphasizing building types and construction techniques, are equally inimical to the study of the library rooms housed in buildings constructed for other purposes.

4. Margaret Wilson, *American Woman in Transition*, 100. For the impact of the GFWC, see Croly, *Women's Club Movement* (1898); Wood, *General Federation* (1912); and Houde, *Reaching Out*.

5. For the importance of reading to upper-middle-class women of the late nineteenth century, see Sicherman, "Sense and Sensibility," 210–25.

6. These are some of the club names listed on the letterhead of the Local Council of Women in 1904. Mrs. J. C. Northlane, Letter to Andrew Carnegie, 1 December 1904, CCA.

7. Although Martin cites examples of club women who "turned their backs on [a changing world] and maintained their sense of self as student," Blair notes that most clubs developed a system of thematic departments to accommodate those members who were interested primarily in the arts and also those eager to move into social concerns. Theodora Martin, *Our Own Voices*, 174–6; Blair, *Torchbearers*, 36–7. For the range of projects that women's clubs pursued, see Underwood, "Civilizing Kansas," 298–304; Wortman, "Domesticating the American City," 548–51.

8. Wood, "Women's Club Movement," (1910), 63. For a discussion of the criticism leveled at women's clubs, see Martin, *Our Own Voices*, 117–24.

9. "Municipal housekeeping" was a phrase commonly used in the Progressive Era (by activist Mary Beard, by members of the Woman's City Club of Chicago, and by others). Wortman "Domesticating the American City," 531–71; Blair, *Torchbearers*, 32–3.

10. Women's involvement with shaping cultural institutions in the public realm calls into question the possibility of applying the concept of the separate spheres (common in discussions of Victorian gender ideology) directly to an analysis of the cultural landscape. For an overview of the historical literature that has used the concept of the separate spheres in a literal sense, see Kerber, "Separate Spheres," 30–9. For the association of women and culture in the nineteenth century, see Douglas, *Feminization of American Culture*, particularly chap. 3. For women's role in encouraging reading in the home, see Anne MacLeod, "Reading Together," 111–23.

11. The annual fee was often $1.00. This was the fee in Gainesville, Texas, Xenia, Ohio, and in the Oklahoma towns of McAlester and Guymon. Miss Gertha E. Lockard, Letter to Andrew Carnegie, 14 January 1909, CCA; Santmyer, *Ohio Town*, 191; *Oklahoma Libraries* (1937), 49, 61.

12. Although more women were willing to join the cash nexus in this era, the handling of cash was interpreted by the women themselves as a radical challenge to inherited gender roles. Clemens, "Organizational Repertoires," 777–80. For the loss of economic self-reliance among middle-class women in the nineteenth century, see Douglas, *Feminization of American Culture*, 48–56.

13. *Oklahoma Libraries* (1937), 28, 52.

14. Union City's 1901 book social is described in a typescript entitled, "History of the Library sent to State Librarian for use at St. Louis Exposition, January 2, 1904," preserved in a scrapbook in the Union City library. For Xenia's book collection, see Santmyer, *Ohio Town*, 196–200.

15. David Taylor, "Ladies of the Club," 324–27.

16. Underwood, "Civilizing Kansas," 294.

17. For later examples of the cross-gable house, see Beecher and Stowe, *American Woman's Home* (1869); McMurry, *Families and Farmhouses;* and Upton, "Pattern Books and Professionalism," 107–50.

18. Carnegie library questionnaire from Hamburg, Iowa, CCA.

19. Mrs. J. F. Sullivan [of Hamilton, Montana], Letter to James Bertram, 2 March 1914; Van L. Hampton [of Macomb, Illinois], Letter to James Bertram, 6 April 1903, CCA.

20. Santmyer, *Ohio Town*, 190–1.

21. Ibid., 191.

22. Carnegie library questionnaire from Jerseyville, Illinois, CCA.

23. Santmyer, *Ohio Town*, 202.

24. For late nineteenth-century commercial spaces, see Mayo, *Grocery Store*, 52–4; Leach, "Strategies of Display," 100–6; Schlereth, "Country Stores," 339–56; Lingeman, *Small Town America*, 148–51.

25. The club as a training ground for the wider world was a favorite theme of club members themselves, as noted in Theodora Martin, *Our Own Voices*, 176.

26. Linnaeus N. Hines, Letter to Andrew Carnegie, 12 May 1903, CCA.

27. For this phenomenon in Montana, see Ring, "Carnegie Libraries," 15.

28. DiMaggio, Edging women's organizations out; Lubove, *Professional Altruist;* Callahan, *Education.*

29. As Blair has noted, women's groups "invited a small but visible male participation, which rather effectively obscured women's critical role in American play-making and created the public perception that women's role was minor." Blair, *Torchbearers*, 147. Club women also revealed their faith in professional expertise in other ways as well—in their regular consultation with specialists before embarking on reforms, in their promotion and support of civil service schemes, and in their positive stance toward state intervention. Clemens, "Organizational Repertoires," 781–2; Underwood, "Civilizing Kansas," 299–300.

30. Mrs. James C. Reynolds, Letter to Andrew Carnegie, 22 February 1899, CCA.

31. Mrs. C. D. Darnell and Mrs. Thomas McMann, Letter to Mayor C. W. Green, 14 July 1914, CCA.

32. Mrs. W. W. Presvitt [?], Mrs. O. T. Vedder, Mrs. A. B. Cockerill, and Mrs. J. Sam Brown, Letter to Andrew Carnegie, 11 July 1902, CCA.

33. Mrs. James C. Reynolds, Letter to Andrew Carnegie, 22 February 1899, CCA. Statements like this one support Douglas's contention that literary-minded women adopted aspects of the ministerial role. Douglas, *Feminization of American Culture*, 105–9.

34. J. M. Underwood et al., Letter to Andrew Carnegie, 25 February 1909, CCA.

35. M. E. Thomas, Letter to Robert Franks, 13 June 1902, CCA.

36. Ring also notes the frequency with which Montana's residents cited a large number of unmarried men "without the advantages of home" in their letters to Carnegie, but he does not link this directly to his observation that women played a dominant role in initiating this correspondence. Ring, "Carnegie Libraries," 7.

37. A similar desire to provide alternatives to commercialized leisure prompted many women's clubs to take up historical pageantry in the 1910s and 1920s. Blair, *Torchbearers*, 124.

38. For a discussion of the links between library development and boosterism, see Ring, "Carnegie Libraries," 9–11, and Swetnam, "Library Arguments," 64–5.

39. Examples of such letters include: John F. Hendy and A. M. Hough (of Jefferson City, Missouri), Letter to Andrew Carnegie, 23 January 1900; J. M. Horten (of Wabash, Indiana), Letter to Andrew Carnegie, 8 November 1900; Committee of the Business Men's Association of Ballard, Washington, Letter to Andrew Carnegie, 1[?] December 1902; City of Pacific Grove, California, Letter to Andrew Carnegie, 8 May 1905; Zanesville (Ohio) Chamber of Commerce, Letter to Andrew Carnegie, 23 May 1905; Charles G. Bill, Letter to Andrew Carnegie (re: Unionville, Ct.), 29 December 1911, CCA.

40. Hugo Seaburg, Letter to Andrew Carnegie, 7 July 1904, CCA.

41. Seaburg's business endeavors are outlined in "Hugo Seaburg, Attorney, Real Estate and Land Script Dealer and Money Lender," *Raton (Daily) Range*, 22 December 1904, 5.

42. Allbritton, Cooke County public library, 13–4.

43. Pepper, "Postcards from Parnassus," 36–41.

44. Raton City Council Minutes, 8 February 1911.

45. "Park Now Ready for the Gardener," *Raton Daily Range*, 18 April 1911, 3.

46. The details of the bequest are outlined in Hon. George M. Tuttle's "Hon. Milton Sutliffe: The Giver and the Gift," address delivered 3 February 1906, TS in *History, Addresses, Reports, Collected and Assembled* ... (1939), Director's Office, Warren-Trumboll County Public Library.

47. "Group Plan for Warren," *Warren Daily Chronicle*, 22 December 1904, 1, cols. 6–7.

48. Ibid.

49. "History of Library sent to State Librarian for use at St. Louis Exposition, January 2, 1940," 3-page TS in a scrapbook of library history in the Union City, Indiana, Public Library archives.

50. Mrs. J. C. Northlane, Letters to Andrew Carnegie, 1 December, 9 December, 20 December 1904; Letter to James Bertram, 11 February 1905, CCA.

51. Mrs. Treva Mangas, "In 1880, James Moorman Donated Ground Where U.C. Public Library Stands Today," newspaper article preserved in librarian's scrapbook, with neither date nor newspaper identified. Mangas was librarian in the 1930s and 1940s.

52. For the multiple meaning of parks in the late nineteenth century see Cranz, *Politics of Park Design*, 3–99; Fein, "American City," 84–100; Fogelsong, *Planning the Capitalist City*, 89–166.

53. As in the domestic sphere, the balance of responsibilities in the public realm was open to individual negotiation. In Gainesville, Texas, for instance, the city council had little interest in taking an active role in library matters, and were happy to let their librarian, Lillian Gunter, make all design decisions. Lillian Gunter, Diary Entry, 11 January 1921, Gunter Papers, Austin.

54. Wiebe, *Search for Order*, xiii–xiv.

55. "Hustling Border Town Builds For Future," reprinted from the *Los Angeles Times* in the *Calexico Chronicle*, 1 November 1916, 2–3. The editors of the Calexico paper were insistent that the idea originated with the members of the Farmers and Merchants Club. However, both the timing of the original proposal and the fact that

architects made such suggestions in order to create a market for their services (as E. L. Tilton had done in Warren, Ohio) support the argument that the scheme originated with the Allisons.

56. L. O. Vaught, Letter to James Bertram, 6 March 1901, CCA.

57. Mrs. J. F. Robertson, Letter to James Bertram, 15 May 1911, CCA.

58. President of Ballinger, Texas, Library Board, Letter to Andrew Carnegie, 22 August 1908; James Bertram, Letter to President of Ballinger, Texas, Library Board, 9 September 1909; J. D. Leslie, Letter to Andrew Carnegie, 13 October 1909, CCA.

59. Addia B. Scott, Letter to James Bertram, 9 December 1913; James Bertram, Letter to Addia B. Scott, 15 December 1913, CCA.

60. While Bertram had no objections to the copying of buildings, it was the responsibility of the library board to locate a copy of the plans either from the board or the architect of the library building they hoped to emulate. William Busby, Letter to James Bertram, 14 April 1911; Thomas Judd, Letter to James Bertram, 19 June 1913, CCA.

61. For a list of towns included in the sample, see appendix 2.

62. Robertson's study of the bungalow suggests that the Carnegie library was not the only building type to serve two distinct and often contradictory sets of gender-based cultural social values. Robertson, "Male and Female Agendas," 123–42.

63. James Bertram, Letter to Flora Johnson, 13 February 1912, CCA.

64. Gould, *Chautauqua Movement;* Morrison, *Chautauqua.*

65. James Bertram, Letter to Fred L. Rosemond, 30 January 1904, CCA.

66. The plans of the Parkersburg library were published in the *State Journal,* 20 August 1904, a clipping of which is preserved in the archives of the Carnegie Corporation.

67. These are the functional names given the rooms in a contemporary newspaper article, "Library Will Be Beautiful," *Warren Daily Chronicle,* 1904.

68. Albert J. Perry, Letter to Andrew Carnegie, 22 March 1913, CCA.

69. James Bertram, Letter to Albert J. Perry, 27 March 1913, CCA.

70. James Bertram, Letter to Paul O. Moratz, 30 March 1909, CCA.

71. Lillian Gunter, Diary Entry, 11 January 1921, Gunter Papers, Austin. See also Allbritton, Cooke County public library, 9–15.

72. Although there is no mention of Tackett in the club minutes, he first appeared before the city council in December 1913 when he accompanied Gunter and two other club members to the opening of construction bids. Gainesville City Council Minutes, 2 December 1913.

73. Lillian Gunter, Diary Entry, 10 May 1924, Gunter Papers, Austin.

74. The XLI Club maintained a close relationship with the new Carnegie building. When it was time to open the library to the public on 10 October 1914, the club sponsored a reception, preparing and serving refreshments to over seven hundred visitors. In the years that followed, they continued to put their domestic skills to use in the service of the library. An ice cream supper in 1915 brought in $10.00. Minutes for 3 October 1914, XLI Club Papers. "New Carnegie is in Good Condition," *Gainesville Register,* October 1915, clipping preserved in the archives of the Cooke County Library.

75. As we will see in chapter 5, white inhabitants were so uneasy about allowing the town's black inhabitants into the library that this room was never used for this purpose. Library service to blacks was eventually established in 1924 in a classroom in the Negro schoolhouse. Lillian Gunter, Diary Entry, 14 May 1923, 6 January 1924, 27 June 1924, Gunter Papers, Austin.

CHAPTER FIVE

1. For a thorough treatment of the issues facing professional librarians in this period, see Garrison, *Apostles of Culture;* and Wiegand, *Politics.*

2. This stereotype seems to be the product of nineteenth-century developments that linked women with culture. Although Douglas notes that these developments threatened the professional status of American ministers, her analysis could be extended as well to other professions associated with culture, including librarianship and teaching. Douglas, *Feminization of American Culture,* 109–15.

3. "New Librarians" (1890), 338.

4. Dewey, *Librarianship as a Profession* (1886), 11.

5. "New Librarians" (1890) 338; Fairchild, "Women in American Libraries" (1904), 161.

6. Dewey, *Librarianship as a Profession* (1886), 11.

7. Dewey, "Ideal Librarian" (1899), 14.

8. Lears, *No Place of Grace,* 89–139.

9. This demographic shift has been the subject of a lively scholarly debate since 1973, when Garrison argued that library work exploited women, while the feminization of the field triggered a series of developments (such as the "dumbing-down" of library education and an emphasis on accommodating readers' wishes) which limited the professionalization of librarianship and stunted the development of the public library as a cultural institution. While no one has disputed the fact that female library workers were paid less than their male counterparts, Grotzinger, Maack, and Brand have taken issue with the characterization of women as victims, and offer methodological approaches (including biographical research, comparative studies, and attention to women's professional survival strategies) for treating women as agents in the history of the profession. Hildebrand and Wiegand refute the causal relationship posited by Garrison between feminization and librarianship's loss of professional prestige, arguing that women were encouraged to enter librarianship precisely because the field was already marginalized. Garrison, "Tender Technicians," 131–59; Grotzinger, "Biographical Research," 372–81; Grotzinger, "Women Librarians," 139–90; Maack, "Women in Librarianship," 164–85; Brand, "Female-Intensive Professions," 391–406; Hildebrand, "Revision versus Reality," 7–27; Wiegand, "Development of Librarianship," 99–109.

For early twentieth-century commentary on this shift, see Dewey, *Librarianship as a Profession* (1886); M. S. R. James, "Women Librarians" (1893), 146–8; Hayward, "Woman as Cataloguer," (1898), 121–3; Fairchild, "Women in American Libraries" (1904), 157–62; Dana, "Women in Library Work" (1911), 244–50.

10. New York State Library School, *Circular of Information* (1912), 29.

11. Davis, *Spearheads for Reform,* 36–7.

12. Garrison maintains that there was an erotic component to Dewey's "inordinate fondness for women." Garrison, "Tender Technicians," 148–51.

13. Dewey, *Librarianship as a Profession* (1886), 15, 23–4.

14. Ibid., 23.

15. Garrison, *Apostles of Culture,* 130–5.

16. The link between sex discrimination and an uncertain professional status has explicitly been made for other fields during these same years. For architecture, see Grossman and Reitzes, "Caught in the Crossfire," 27–39. This link is also implied in Glazer and Slater's comparative study of women in academia, medicine, research science, and social work. Glazer and Slater, *Unequal Colleagues,* 2–3, 235–41.

17. Fairchild, "Women in American Libraries" (1904), 161.

18. McReynolds, "Sexual Politics," 194–217.

19. For the development of gendered hierarchies in other professions, see Glazer and Slater, *Unequal Colleagues*, 213–6; Berlo, "Cambridge School," 27–32.

20. Dana, "Women in Library Work" (1911), 245–6.

21. Library Bureau, *Library Catalog* (1902), 50; Library Bureau, *Charging Desks* (n.d.).

22. Library Bureau, *Charging Desks* (n.d.), 72.

23. For example, see John Cotton Dana's comments, quoted in chapter 1.

24. For a lively gender analysis of the office environment, see Lupton, *Mechanical Brides*, 43–57. See also Davies, *Woman's Place*; Fine, *Souls of the Skyscraper*; Zunz, *Making America Corporate*.

25. This analysis of professional space builds on Bledstein's discussion of largely nonspatial rituals of professional culture. Bledstein, *Culture of Professionalism*, 94–6.

26. Or, as Lupton notes, the woman worker and her machine in the modern office environment function "as a technological conduit for male thought." Lupton, *Mechanical Brides*, 42.

27. Even in an article in which she documented systematic differences in pay between male and female library workers, Fairchild was quick to absolve her professional association of any blame, stating that "there is practically no discrimination with regard to sex in the American Library Association." Fairchild, "Women in American Libraries" (1904), 158.

28. For an overview of the interaction between librarians and other kinds of Progressive reformers, see Du Mont, *Reform and Reaction*, especially chap. 3. Although Marcum underestimates the degree to which rural librarians of the period were interested in social reform, she rightly points out that rural librarians had more in common with their urban counterparts than most studies have acknowledged. Marcum, "Rural Public Library," 87–99.

29. Glazer and Slater note this as one of the survival strategies used by women in medicine, scientific research, and social work, while Wright notes that serving as socially-conscious "architectural adjuncts" was a common coping mechanism for women interested in architecture, particularly during the Progressive Era. Glazer and Slater, *Unequal Colleagues*, 217; Wright, "On the Fringe," 296–300.

30. Hunt, "Maintaining Order" (1903), 167.

31. Paul Boyer, *Urban Masses*, 94–107.

32. Cremin, *American Education*, 294–301; Tiffin, *In Whose Best Interest?* 110–21.

33. Bostwick, *American Public Library* (1910), 51; Hazeltine, "Children's Room" (1904), 370; Bowerman, "Public Library" (1906), 105.

34. For the importance of the environment's role in Progressive reform, see Paul Boyer, *Urban Masses*, chaps. 15, 16, and 19.

35. Bostwick, *American Public Library* (1910), 11–3; "Reading Rooms for Children" (1897), 125–31.

36. Clara Hunt, "Opening a Children's Room" (1901), 83–6; Clara Hunt, "Maintaining Order" (1903), 164–7; Clara Hunt, "Work with Children" (1903), 53–7.

37. "Lawrenceville Branch" (1897), 440–1; "Building Progress in St. Louis" (1908), 98–9; Koch, *Book of Carnegie Libraries* (1917), 62–78.

38. Pretlow, "Opening of a Public Library" (1906), 887. For the production and use of photography by settlement house residents, see Hales, *Silver Cities*, 243–60.

39. "Open-Air Reading Room," (1906), 8025.

40. For Hall's ideas of pedocentric schools, see G. Hall, "Ideal School" (1901): 24–39; Cremin, *American Education*, 278–80.

41. For an example of the incorporation of Hall's theories in library literature, see Olcott, "Home Libraries for Poor Children," (1904), 376.

42. Woodford, *Parnassus on Main Street*, 191–207.

43. Proceedings of the Detroit Library Commission, 7 October 1910, BHC.

44. Holleman, "Arts and Crafts Architecture," 51–4.

45. William Howard Brett, Letter to James Bertram, 25 March 1911, CCA. George Osius, Letter to Edward L. Tilton, 13 May 1911, recorded in the Proceedings of the Detroit Library Commission, BHC.

46. Annie Moore, "Suggestions for a Children's Room" (1903), 2–6.

47. Many of these changes parallel developments in the furnishing of children's rooms in domestic settings, where there was a concern with developing "a visual code of childishness." Calvert, "Children in the House," 82–7.

48. Hazeltine, "Children's Room" (1904), 369. For the importance of play in the Progressive-era child-study movement, see Cavallo, "Social Reform," 509–22.

49. Fairchild, "Women in American Libraries" (1904), 159.

50. "In Memoriam: Lillian Gunter" (1935), 143; Rhoades, "Early Women Librarians in Texas," 48; Lillian Gunter biography, TS in Gunter Papers, Gainesville.

51. "Twenty-seventh Annual Report" (1913), 22; Gainesville City Council Minutes, 1 November 1914.

52. Lillian Gunter, Diary Entry, 5 September 1921 or 1922, Gunter Papers, Austin.

53. Lillian Gunter, Diary Entry, 11 January 1921 or 1922, Gunter Papers, Austin.

54. Lillian Gunter, Diary Entry, 5 September 1921 or 1922, Gunter Papers, Austin.

55. XLI Club Minutes, 3 October 1903, XLI Club Papers.

56. [Lillian Gunter], "Opening of the Gainesville Public Library," transcript enclosed in letter to Andrew Carnegie, 9 January 1915, CCA.

57. Lillian Gunter, Diary Entries, 14 May 1923, 27 June 1924, Gunter Papers, Austin. For the efforts of other female librarians of Gunter's generation to extend library service to black readers, see Carmichael, "Atlanta's Female Librarians," 376–99.

58. Lillian Gunter, Diary Entry, 8 February 1924, Gunter Papers, Austin.

59. Lillian Gunter, Diary Entry, 12 January 1923, Gunter Papers, Austin.

60. "In Memoriam: Lillian Gunter" (1935), 143; Rhoades, "Early Women Librarians in Texas," 48.

61. In addition to writing an article on the subject for *Public Libraries*, Gunter traveled to Chickasaw, Oklahoma, to address the Oklahoma Library Association, and advised a number of other communities on library design issues, among them Graham, Texas, Duncan, Oklahoma, and Clinton, Mississippi. Gunter, "Ideal Small Library Building" (1924), 227–9; Lillian Gunter, Diary Entries, 30 March 1924 and 16 August 1924, Gunter Papers, Austin.

62. Lillian Gunter, Diary Entry, 10 May 1924, Gunter Papers, Austin.

63. Lillian Gunter, Diary Entry, 7 September 1924, Gunter Papers, Austin.

64. Lillian Gunter, Diary Entry, 6 October 1924, Gunter Papers, Austin.

65. Shishkin, *Early History*. Van Slyck, "Mañana."

66. Lillian Gunter, Diary Entry, 11 January 1922, Gunter Papers, Austin.

67. Eddy, *County Free Library Organizing* (1955); Henshall, *County Library Organizing* ([1932] 1985); Sallee, "Reconceptualizing Women's History," 351–77.

68. Oregon, Minnesota, Wisconsin, Michigan, and New Jersey are just of the

few of the states to employ women as state traveling library commissioners. Passet, "Reaching the Rural Reader," 102–5.

CHAPTER SIX

1. Nasaw, *Children of the City*, ix.

2. These include Rosenzweig, *Eight Hours;* Peiss, *Cheap Amusements;* Ewen, *Immigrant Women;* Meyerowitz, *Women Adrift*. For studies that focus specifically on the experiences of immigrant children, see Nasaw, *Children of the City;* Berol, "Immigrant Children at School," 42–60; Brumberg, "Going to America, Going to School," 86–135.

3. As recently as 1991, Harvey Graff recommended the use of diaries, memoirs, and other forms of individual personal testimony to document "concrete *uses* of literacy's reading skills in their relationships to libraries in the historical context of shaping the lives of relatively ordinary persons." Yet, even Graff had to admit that "the far greatest number of personal accounts make absolutely no mention of reading or library usage." Graff, "Literacy, Libraries, Lives," 25–6.

4. See Porter, *Papa Was a Preacher* (1944); Marquis James, *Cherokee Strip* (1946); Scott, *Background in Tennessee* (1937).

5. Library memoirs from the early years of the twentieth century make up only a small proportion of the writings about libraries collected in Toth and Coughlan, *Reading Rooms*.

6. For an overview of children's experiences in smaller towns, see West, *Growing Up with the Country*.

7. Santmyer, *Ohio Town*, 187.

8. Ibid., 187–8.

9. Ibid., 205.

10. Ibid., 205–6.

11. Ibid., 203.

12. Ibid., 203, 207.

13. Quoted in Mellon, "Reflections," 86.

14. Toth, *Blooming*, 90.

15. Welty, *One Writer's Beginnings*, 29.

16. Newton Hall, "Child's Thoughts" (1901), 732.

17. Quoted in Mellon, "Reflections," 87.

18. Toth, *Blooming*, 89.

19. Ibid., 91.

20. Ibid., 96.

21. Ibid., 98.

22. Welty, *One Writer's Beginnings*, 29

23. Quoted in Mellon, "Reflections," 87; Toth, *Blooming*, 100.

24. Epstein, "Pages from My Stormy Life" (1962), 138.

25. Feely, "Growing Up" (1981), 91–2.

26. Pretlow, "Opening of a Public Library" (1906), 889.

27. Pretlow, "Opening" (1906), 889; "Open-Air Reading Room" (1906), 8025.

28. Nasaw, *Children of the City*, 35–6.

29. Ibid., 20–28.

30. Pretlow, "Opening" (1906), 888.

31. Ibid.

32. Feely, "Growing Up" (1981) 91.

33. Ibid.

34. Quoted in Mellon, "Reflections," 83.

35. Pretlow, "Opening" (1906), 888.

36. Clara Hunt, "Opening a Children's Room" (1901), 86.

POSTSCRIPT

1. A certain sensitivity to Carnegie's feelings may also explain why the Johnson report was not printed until 1919, the year of Carnegie's death. For the Johnson report, see Bobinski, *Carnegie Libraries*, 143–60; Alvin S. Johnson, *Report* (1919).

For the later phase of Carnegie Corporation library philanthropy, see Lagemann, *Politics of Knowledge;* Anderson, *Carnegie Corporation Library Program;* Lester, *Forty Years of Carnegie Giving;* Lester, *Review of Grants.*

2. Carnegie's desire to encourage library philanthropy generally is evident in the care he took to avoid preempting the largesse of other library donors. The initial request from St. Paul, Minnesota, for example, was denied on the grounds that local philanthropists had expressed an interest in pursuing library matters. Bobinski, *Carnegie Libraries*, 39.

3. Harrison, New Jersey, Allenstown, New Hampshire, Topsfield, Massachusetts, New Philadelphia, Ohio, and McMinnville, Oregon, all received PWA-funded library buildings based on the planning ideals codified in the "Notes." Short and Stanley-Brown, *Public Buildings* (1939; reprint, 1986), 108–39.

4. Wheeler and Githens, *American Library Building* (1941), 215–25.

5. For a discussion of reading as a social activity in the nineteenth-century, see Sicherman, "Sense and Sensibility," 210–25. For a provocative discussion of the American public library's inability to define its function, see Colson, "Form Against Function," 111–42.

6. For Carnegie renovation projects in Seattle, Washington, and elsewhere, see Bobinski, "Carnegies," 296–303.

Bibliography

I. PRIMARY SOURCES

A. *Personal, Corporate, and Club Papers*

Andrew Carnegie Papers, Manuscript Division, Library of Congress, Washington, D.C.

Carnegie Corporation Archives (CCA), Rare Book and Manuscript Library, Butler Library, Columbia University, New York, N.Y.

Melvil Dewey Papers, Rare Book and Manuscript Library, Columbia University, New York, N.Y.

E. J. Eckel Papers, Brunner and Brunner, St. Joseph, Missouri

Lillian Gunter Papers, Archives Division, Texas State Library Austin, Texas (Gunter Papers, Austin)

Lillian Gunter Papers, Cooke County Heritage Society, Morton Museum, Gainesville, Texas (Gunter Papers, Gainesville)

Paul Pelz Papers, Manuscript Division, Library of Congress, Washington, D.C.

XLI Club Papers, Cooke County Heritage Society, Morton Museum, Gainesville, Texas

B. *Library Archives*

Allegheny Regional Branch, Carnegie Library of Pittsburgh

Arthur Johnson Memorial Library, Raton, New Mexico

Burton Historical Collection (BHC), Detroit Public Library

Camarena Memorial Library, Calexico, California

Carnegie Library of Homestead, Pennsylvania

Cooke County Library, Gainesville, Texas

El Centro Public Library, El Centro, California

Free Library of Philadelphia

George W. Norris Regional Library, McCook, Nebraska

Imperial Public Library, Imperial, California

Lackawanna Public Library, Lackawanna, New York

New York Public Library, Astor, Lenox and Tilden Foundations

Oakland Public Library, Oakland, California

River Bluffs Regional Library, St. Joseph, Missouri

Sherman Public Library, Sherman, Texas

Tahlequah Public Library, Tahlequah, Oklahoma

Union City Public Library, Union City, Indiana

Warren-Trumbull County Public Library, Warren, Ohio

C. *Other Archives*

High Plains Museum, McCook, Nebraska

Pennsylvania Department, Carnegie Library of Pittsburgh

Raton Museum, Raton, New Mexico
Special Collections, Northeastern State University, Tahlequah, Oklahoma

D. City Council Minutes

Gainesville, Texas
Lackawanna, New York
Raton, New Mexico
Tahlequah, Oklahoma

E. Newspapers

Alleghenian, Allegheny City, Pennsylvania
Buffalo (New York) Courier Express
Calexico (California) Chronicle
Cherokee Advocate, Tahlequah, Oklahoma
Detroit Journal
Detroit News
McCook (Nebraska) Tribune
Oakland (California) Tribune
Raton (New Mexico) Daily Range
St. Joseph (Missouri) Daily Gazette Herald
St. Joseph (Missouri) Daily News
Tahlequah (Oklahoma) Arrow
Union City (Indiana) Times
Warren (Ohio) Daily Chronicle
Warren (Ohio) Daily Tribune

F. Books and Articles

Alger, G. W. "Generosity and Corruption." *Atlantic Monthly* 95 (June 1905): 781–4.
[Almirall, Raymond F., architect]. "Carnegie Library, Pacific Branch, Brooklyn, N.Y." *Brickbuilder* 16 (1907), plates 78–9.
American Library Annual, 1915–1916. New York: R. R. Bowker Co., 1916.
Beecher, Catharine E., and Harriet Beecher Stowe. *The American Woman's Home.* New York, 1869; reprint Watkins Glen, N.Y.: Library of Victorian Culture, 1979.
"Benches Instead of Chairs." *Public Libraries* 19 (March 1914): 111.
Billings, John W. "The New York Public Library." *Library Journal* 36 (May 1911): 233–7.
Bostwick, Arthur E. *The American Public Library.* New York: D. Appleton and Co., 1910.
Bowerman, George F. "The Public Library of the District of Columbia as an Organ of Social Advance." *Charities and the Commons* 16 (14 April 1906): 105–10.
Branch Libraries 1918. Toledo: Toledo Public Library, 1918.
Brett, William. "American Libraries." *Dial* 28 (May 1900): 346–9.
Brody, Catharine. "A New York Childhood." *American Mercury* 14 (May 1928): 57–66.
"Building Progress in St. Louis." *Public Libraries* 13 (March 1908): 98–9.
Burgoyne, F. J. *Library Construction: Architecture, Fittings, and Furniture.* London: George Allen, 1897.
Byington, Margaret F. *Homestead: The Households of a Mill Town.* New York: Russell Sage Foundation, 1910; reprint, Pittsburgh: University of Pittsburgh Press, 1974.
Caldwell, Bettie D. "Greensboro (N.C.) Public Library: Carnegie Building." *Library Journal* 31 (October 1906): 718–9.

Carnegie, Andrew. *Autobiography of Andrew Carnegie*. Boston: Houghton Mifflin Co., 1920.

———. "The Best Fields for Philanthropy." *North American Review* 149 (December 1889): 682–98; reprinted in Carnegie, *Gospel of Wealth*.

———. *The Gospel of Wealth and Other Timely Essays*. New York: Century, 1901.

———. "The Library Gift Business." *Collier's* 43 (5 June 1909): 14–5.

———. "Wealth." *North American Review* 148 (June 1889): 653–64; reprinted in Carnegie, *Gospel of Wealth*.

"The Carnegie Free Library, Allegheny, Pa." *Library Journal* 18 (August 1893): 288–90.

"The Carnegie Libraries." *The World Today* 13 (February 1905): 134–5.

"Carnegie Library of Atlanta." *Library Journal* 25 (February 1900): 70.

"The Carnegie Library of Pittsburgh." *Library Journal* 20 (November 1895): 382–5.

Carr, Henry J. "Notes by the Way." *Public Libraries* 4 (January 1899): 37.

Chautauquan, 59 (June 1910).

Cotten, Sallie Southall. *History of the North Carolina Federation of Women's Clubs, 1901–1925*. Raleigh, N.C.: Edwards and Broughton Printing Co., 1925.

Croly, Jennie June. *The History of the Women's Club Movement in America*. New York: H. G. Allen, 1898.

Crunden, Frederick M. "The Public Library and Civic Improvement." *Chautauquan* 43 (June 1906): 335–44.

Dana, John Cotton. "How a Town Can Get a Library." *Independent* 60 (31 May 1906): 1277–9.

———. "Library Building." *Public Libraries* 7 (November 1902): 406–7.

———. *A Library Primer*. Chicago: Library Bureau, 1899.

———. "The Public and Its Public Library." *Appletons' Popular Science Monthly* 51 (June 1897): 242–53.

———. "The Reading Public As I Know It—In a Large City." *Outlook* 71 (24 May 1902): 250–2.

———. "Women in Library Work." *Independent* 71 (3 August 1911): 244–50.

"Decoration of Libraries." *American Library Annual* (1916): 41–2.

DeForest, Robert W., and Lawrence Veiller, eds. *The Tenement House Problem*. New York: Macmillan, 1903; reprint, New York: Arno Press, 1970.

Dewey, Melvil. "The Ideal Librarian." *Library Journal* 24 (January 1899): 14.

———. *Librarianship as a Profession for College-Bred Women: An Address Delivered Before the Association of Collegiate Alumnae*. Boston: Library Bureau, 1886.

———. *On Libraries for Librarians*. New York: Dodd, Mead and Co., 1904.

Dunne, Finley Peter. *Dissertations by Mr. Dooley*. New York: Harper and Bros., 1906.

Eastman, Linda. "Furniture, Fixtures and Equipment." In *Manual of Library Economy*, chap. 11. Chicago: American Library Association Publishing Board, 1916.

Eastman, W. R. "Library Buildings." *Library Journal* 26 (August 1901): 38–43.

Eddy, Harriet G. *County Free Library Organizing in California, 1909–1918*. Berkeley: Committee on California Library History, Bibliography, and Archives of the California Library Association, 1955.

Epstein, Melech. "Pages from My Stormy Life—An Autobiographical Sketch." *American Jewish Archives* 14 (November 1962): 129–76.

Fairchild, Salome Cutler. "Women in American Libraries." *Library Journal* 29 (December 1904): 157–62.

Feely, Ida R. "Growing Up on the East Side." *American Jewish Archives* 33 (April 1981): 85–94.

[Fraser, W. S., architect]. "Competitive Design for the Carnegie Library, Allegheny, Pa." *American Architect and Building News* 21 (12 February 1887), 75, 79–81, and plates.

George, Henry, Jr. *The Menace of Privilege: A Study of the Danger to the Republic from the Existence of a Favored Class.* New York: Macmillan, 1905.

"A Gift of $10,000,000 for Colleges." *American Monthly Review of Reviews* 32 (August 1905): 146–8.

[Gilbert, Cass, architect]. "The Detroit Public Library." *American Architect* 120 (28 September 1921): 228, 232–3, and plates.

———. "St. Louis Public Library." *American Architect* 101 (13 March 1912): 125–8.

Gladden, Washington. "Tainted Money." *Outlook* 55 (20 November 1895): 886–7.

Granger, Mrs. A. O. "Effect of Club Work in the South." *Annals of the American Academy of Political and Social Science* 28 (September 1906): 248–56.

Gunter, Lillian. "The Ideal Small Library Building for the Southwest." *Public Libraries* 29 (May 1924): 227–9.

Hall, Drew B. "Opening of the Somerville, Mass., Public Library." *Library Journal* 39 (January 1914): 35–8.

Hall, G. Stanley. "The Ideal School as Based on Child Study." *Forum* 32 (September 1901): 24–39.

Hall, Newton Marshall. "A Child's Thoughts about Books and Libraries." *Library Journal* 26 (October 1901): 731–2.

Hayward, Celia A. "Woman as Cataloger." *Public Libraries* 3 (April 1898): 121–3.

Hazeltine, Mary Emogene. "The Children's Room in the Public Library." *Chautauquan* 39 (June 1904): 369–74.

———. "The Reading Public As I Know It—In a Small City." *Outlook* 71 (24 May 1902): 252–3.

Henry, W. E. "Discipline and Furniture." *Public Libraries* 19 (June 1914): 238–41.

Henshall, May Dexter. *County Library Organizing.* 1932; reprint Sacramento: California State Library Foundation, 1985.

Hunt, Clara W. "Maintaining Order in the Children's Room." *Library Journal* 28 (April 1903): 164–7.

———. "Opening a Children's Room." *Library Journal* 26 (August 1901): 83–6.

———. "Work with Children in the Small Library." *Library Journal* 28 (July 1903): 53–6.

Hunt, Myron. "The Work of Messrs. Allison & Allison." *Architect and Engineer of California* 42 (September 1915): 38–75.

"In Memoriam Lillian Gunter." *Handbook of Texas Libraries* 4 (1935): 143.

James, George Wharton. "The Influence of the 'Mission Style' Upon the Civic and Domestic Architecture of Modern California." *The Craftsman* 5 (February 1903): 458–69.

James, M. S. R. "Women Librarians." *Library Journal* 18 (May 1893): 146–8.

James, Marquis. *The Cherokee Strip: A Tale of an Oklahoma Boyhood.* New York: Viking Press, 1946.

Johnson, Alvin S. *A Report to Carnegie Corporation of New York on the Policy of Donations to Free Public Libraries.* New York: Carnegie Corporation of New York, 1919.

[Johnson, Lindley, architect]. "Tacony Branch, Carnegie Library, Philadelphia, Pa." *Brickbuilder* 15 (November 1906), plate 153.

Koch, Theodore W. *A Book of Carnegie Libraries.* White Plains, N.Y.: H. W. Wilson Co., 1917.

———. "Carnegie Libraries." *Chautauquan* 43 (June 1906): 345–51.

———. "Chautauqua." *South Dakota History,* 20 (June 1906): 116.

"Lawrenceville Branch of the Carnegie Library of Pittsburgh." *Library Journal* 22 (September 1897): 440–1.

Levine, Isaac Don. "Letters of an Immigrant." *American Jewish Archives* 33 (April 1981): 53–83.

"Library Buildings." *Public Libraries* 29 (April 1924): 185–6.

Library Bureau. *Charging Desks: A Description of Representative Types*. . . . Boston: Library Bureau, n.d.

———. *Classified Illustrated Catalog of the Library Bureau*. Boston: Library Bureau, 1890.

———. *Classified Illustrated Catalog of the Library Bureau*. Boston: Library Bureau, 1893.

———. *Classified Illustrated Catalog of the Library Department of the Library Bureau*. Boston: Library Bureau, 1897.

———. *Classified Illustrated Catalog of the Library Department of the Library Bureau*. Boston: Library Bureau, 1898.

———. *Classified Illustrated Catalog of the Library Department of the Library Bureau*. Boston: Library Bureau, 1899.

———. *Classified Illustrated Catalog of the Library Department of the Library Bureau*. Boston: Library Bureau, 1900.

———. *Filing as a Profession for Women*. Boston: Library Bureau, 1919.

———. *Library Catalog: A Descriptive List with Prices*. . . . [Boston]: Library Bureau, 1902.

———. *Library Catalog: A Descriptive List with Prices*. . . . Boston: Library Bureau, 1909.

Library Bureau Division of Remington Rand. *Library Furniture*. N.p.: Remington Rand, 1937.

Library Planning, Bookstacks, and Shelving. Jersey City, N.J.: Snead and Company Iron Works, 1915.

Lydenberg, Harry Miller. *History of the New York Public Library, Astor, Lenox and Tilden Foundations*. New York: New York Public Library, 1923.

Meleny, George B. "The Relation of the Library Bureau to Libraries." *Public Libraries* 1 (May 1896): 18–9.

Moore, Annie Carroll. "Suggestions for a Children's Room or a Children's Corner." *New Hampshire Public Libraries* 4 (1903): 2–6.

Moore, Edna G. "Detroit's New Main Library." *Library Journal* 46 (1 May 1921): 405–8.

"Mr. Carnegie's Library Benefactions." *Current History* 38 (February 1905): 99–100.

"The New Building of the New York Public Library." *Library Journal* 36 (May 1911): 221–8.

"The New Elizabeth Library." *Library Journal* 37 (September 1912): 509–10.

"The New Librarians." *Library Journal* 15 (November 1890): 338.

New York State Library School. *Circular of Information, 1912–13*. Albany: State of New York Education Department, 1912.

Oklahoma Libraries, 1900–1937: A History and Handbook. Oklahoma City: Oklahoma Library Commission, 1937.

Olcott, Frances Jenkins. "Home Libraries for Poor Children." *Chautauquan* 39 (June 1904): 374–80.

———. "The Public Library: A Social Force in Pittsburgh." *Survey* 23 (5 March 1910): 849–61.

"An Open-Air Reading Room." *World's Work* 12 (September 1906): 8025.

Parker, William E. *Library Bureau Historical Pamphlet*. Boston: Library Bureau, 1908.

Poole, William F. "Library Buildings." *Library Journal* 4 (July 1879): 293–4.

———. "Progress of Library Architecture." *Library Journal* 7 (July/August 1882): 130–4.

———. "Small Library Buildings." *Library Journal* 10 (September/October 1885): 250–6.

Porter, Alyene. *Papa Was a Preacher*. New York: Abingdon-Cokesbury Press, 1944.

Power, Effie L. *How the Children of a Great City Get Their Books*. St. Louis: [St. Louis Public Library], 1914.

Pretlow, Mary Denson. "The Opening of a Public Library." *Charities and the Commons* 15 (17 March 1906): 886–9.

Proceedings at the Reception and Dinner in Honor of George Peabody, Esq., of London, by the Citizens of the Old Town of Danvers, October 9, 1856. Boston: Henry W. Dutton and Son, 1856.

Rainey, Luretta. *History of the Oklahoma State Federation of Women's Clubs*. Guthrie, Okla.: Cooperative Publishing Co., 1939.

"Reading Rooms for Children." *Public Libraries* 2 (April 1897): 125–31.

[Ross, Albert Randolph, architect.] "Library at Columbus, Ohio." *Architectural Review* 15 (November 1908): plates 76–83.

———. "Public Library, Columbus, Ohio." *Architectural Review* 34 (August 1913): plates v–vi.

———. "Public Library, Needham, Mass." *American Architect and Building News* 83 (16 January 1904).

———. "Public Library, Old Town, Me." *American Architect and Building News* 83 (23 January 1904).

———. "Public Library, Pittsfield, Me." *American Architect and Building News* 83 (23 January 1904).

———. "Public Library, Taunton, Mass." *American Architect and Building News* 80 (20 June 1903).

"Savannah Public Library" *Library Journal* 42 (June 1917): 456–7.

Scott, Evelyn. *Background in Tennessee*. New York: Robert M. McBride and Co., 1937.

Scudder, Vida D. "Ill-Gotten Gifts to Colleges." *Atlantic Monthly* 86 (November 1900): 675–9.

"Shall the Dollar's Pedigree Defeat Its Destiny?" *American Monthly Review of Reviews* 32 (October 1905): 471–2.

Sherman, Mrs. John Dickinson. "Women's Clubs in the Middle Western States." *Annals of the American Academy of Political and Social Science* 28 (September 1906): 227–47.

Short, C. W., and R. Stanley-Brown, eds. *Public Buildings: Architecture under the Public Works Administration 1933–1939*. Washington, D.C.: G.P.O., 1939; reprint, New York: Da Capo, 1986.

Simkhovitch, Mary Kingsbury. "The New York Public Library Assembly Halls." *Charities and the Commons* 15 (17 March 1906): 885–6.

"Social Evangelism by Children's Librarians." *Survey* 23 (5 March 1910): 828–9.

Soule, Charles C. *How to Plan a Library Building for Library Work*. Boston: Boston Book Co., 1912.

———. "Modern Library Buildings." *Architectural Review* 9 (January 1902): 1–60.

———. "Points of Agreement among Librarians As to Library Architecture." *Library Journal* 16 (December 1891): 17–9.

Souvenir—Opening of Carnegie Free Library and Carnegie Hall Presented by Mr. Andrew Carnegie to Allegheny City. [Allegheny City, Pa.]: Leonard Wales, 1890.

"Springfield City Library Opening." *Library Journal* 37 (February 1912): 78–80.

"States Requiring Registration of Architects." *American Architect* 114 (31 July 1918): 145.

Study, Guy. "The St. Louis Public Library." *American Architect* 101 (13 March 1912): 125–8.

Sturgis, Russell. "The Carnegie Libraries in New York City." *Architectural Record* 17 (March 1905): 237–46.

Texas Library Association. *Handbook of Texas Libraries, Number Four.* Houston: Texas Library Association, 1935.

Thompson, J. A. "Ideal Small Libraries for the Southwest." *Public Libraries* 29 (June 1924): 283–4.

Tilton, Edward L. "The Architecture of the Small Public Library." *Michigan Libraries* 1 (1911): 26–30.

———. "Scientific Library Planning." *Library Journal* 37 (September 1912): 497–501.

[Tilton, Edward L., architect.] "City Library, Springfield, Mass." *American Architect* 101 (27 March 1912): 1892.

———. "Morristown Free Library, Morristown, N.J." *American Architect* 121 (15 March 1922): 223.

———. "Somerville Public Library, Somerville, Mass." *American Architect* 105 (18 March 1914): 1995.

———. "Wilmington Free Library, Wilmington, Dela." *American Architect* 121 (15 March 1922): 221.

"Twenty-seventh Annual Report of the New York State Library School." *University of the State of New York Bulletin* 556 (1 December 1913): 21.

Van Kleeck, Irene. "The Library and the Community." *Charities and the Commons* 21 (5 December 1908): 391–7.

"The Washington, D.C., Public Library Building." *Library Journal* 24 (December 1899): 676–7.

West, Decca Lamar. "Achievements of Three Decades of the Texas Federation of Woman's Clubs." *Southern Magazine* 2 (1935): 30–1, 47.

Wheeler, Joseph L., and Alfred Morton Githens. *The American Public Library Building: Its Planning and Design with Special Reference to Its Administration and Service.* New York: Charles Scribner's Sons, 1941.

Wood, Mary I. *The History of the General Federation of Women's Clubs for the First Twenty-Two Years of Its Organization.* New York: General Federation of Women's Clubs, 1912.

———. "The Women's Club Movement." *The Chautauquan* 59 (1910).

Yust, William F. "Louisville Free Public Library Building." *Library Journal* 34 (September 1909): 398–401.

II. SECONDARY SOURCES

Allbritton, Sylvia Dawn. History of the Cooke County public library, Gainesville, Texas. M.A. thesis, University of Oklahoma, 1965.

Ames, Kenneth L. "Meaning in Artifacts: Hall Furnishings in Victorian America." In Upton and Vlach, *Common Places.*

Anderson, Florence. *Carnegie Corporation Library Program, 1911–1961.* New York: Carnegie Corporation of New York, 1963.

Arts and Crafts in Detroit, 1906–1976: The Movement, the Society, the School. Detroit: Detroit Institute of Arts, 1976.

Axelrod, Alan, ed. *The Colonial Revival in America.* New York: W. W. Norton for the Henry Francis du Pont Winterthur Museum, Winterthur, Del., 1985.

Barth, Gunter. *City People: The Rise of Modern City Culture in Nineteenth-Century America.* New York: Oxford University Press, 1980.

Beckman, Margaret, Stephen Langmead, and John Black. *The Best Gift: A Record of the Carnegie Libraries in Ontario.* Toronto: Dundurn Press, 1984.

Benson, Susan Porter. *Counter Cultures: Saleswomen, Managers, and Customers in American Department Stores, 1890–1940.* Urbana: University of Illinois Press, 1986.

Berlo, Janet C. "The Cambridge School: Women in Architecture." *Feminist Art Journal* (Spring 1976): 27–32.

Berol, Selma. "Immigrant Children at School, 1880–1940: A Child's Eye View." In West and Petrik, *Small Worlds.*

Betsky, Celia. "Inside the Past: The Interior and the Colonial Revival in American Art and Literature." In Axelrod, *Colonial Revival in America.*

Bial, Raymond, and Linda LaPuma Bial. *The Carnegie Library in Illinois.* Urbana: University of Illinois Press, 1991.

Blackburn, Robert H. "Dewey and Cutter as Building Consultants." *Library Quarterly* 58 (October 1988): 377–84.

Blair, Karen J. *The Clubwoman as Feminist: True Womanhood Redefined, 1868–1914.* New York: Holmes and Meir, 1980.

———. *The History of American Women's Voluntary Organizations, 1810–1960.* Boston: G. K. Hall, 1989.

———. *The Torchbearers: Women and Their Amateur Arts Associations in America, 1890–1930.* Bloomington: Indiana University Press, 1994.

Blazek, Ronald. "The Library, the Chautauqua, and the Railroads in De Funiak Springs, Florida." *Journal of Library History* 22 (Fall 1987): 377–96.

Bledstein, Burton J. *The Culture of Professionalism: The Middle Class and the Development of Higher Education in America.* New York: Norton, 1976.

Bluestone, Daniel. *Constructing Chicago.* New Haven: Yale University Press, 1991.

———. "Detroit's City Beautiful and the Problem of Commerce." *Journal of the Society of Architectural Historians* 47 (September 1988): 245–62.

Bobinski, George S. "A Call for Preservation—of a Carnegie Library." *Libraries and Culture* 24 (Summer 1989): 367–79.

———. *Carnegie Libraries: Their History and Impact on American Public Library Development.* Chicago: American Library Association, 1969.

———. "Carnegies." *American Libraries* 21 (April 1990): 296–303.

Bocock, Louise Caldwell. "Texas Libraries and the Texas Federation of Women's Clubs." *Texas Library Journal* 62 (Spring 1986): 26.

Bowers, Ann M. "White-Gloved Feminists: An Analysis of Northwest Ohio Women's Clubs." *Hayes Historical Journal* 4 (1984): 38–47.

Boyer, Christine. *Dreaming the Rational City: The Myth of American City Planning.* Cambridge: MIT Press, 1983.

Boyer, Paul. *Urban Masses and Moral Order in America, 1820–1920.* Cambridge: Harvard University Press, 1978.

Boyle, Bernard Michael. "Architectural Practice in America, 1865–1965—Ideal and Reality." In Kostof, *Architect.*

Brand, Barbara E. "Librarianship and Other Female-Intensive Professions." *Journal of Library History* 18 (Fall 1983): 391–406.

Breed, Clara E. *Turning the Pages: San Diego Public Library History, 1882–1982.* San Diego: Friends of the San Diego Public Library, 1983.

———. "'Two Reading Rooms—One For Each Sex': San Diego Public Library Beginnings, 1880–1890." *Journal of San Diego History* 28 (Summer 1982): 162–71.

Breisch, Kenneth A. Small public libraries in America, 1850–1890: The invention and evolution of a building type. Ph.D. diss., University of Michigan, 1982.

———. "William Frederick Poole and Modern Library Architecture." In *Modern Architecture in America*, ed. Richard Guy Wilson and Sydney Robinson, 52–72. Ames: Iowa State University Press, 1991.

Bremner, Robert H. *American Philanthropy.* Chicago: University of Chicago Press, 1960.

———. *The Public Good: Philanthropy and Welfare in the Civil War Era.* New York: Alfred A. Knopf, 1980.

Bronner, Simon J., ed. *Consuming Visions: Accumulation and Display of Goods in America, 1880–1920.* New York: W. W. Norton for the Henry Francis du Pont Winterthur Museum, Winterthur, Del., 1989.

Brownell, Blaine A. "Interpretations of Twentieth-Century Urban Progressive Reform." In Colburn and Pozzetta, *Reform and Reformers*, 3–23.

Brownlee, David B. *Building the City Beautiful: The Benjamin Franklin Parkway and the Philadelphia Museum of Art.* Philadelphia: Philadelphia Museum of Art, 1989.

Brumberg, Stephan F. "Going to America, Going to School: The Immigrant-Public School Encounter in Turn-of-the-Century New York City." *American Jewish Archives* 36 (November 1984): 86–135.

Burlingame, Dwight F., ed. *The Responsibilities of Wealth.* Bloomington: Indiana University Press, 1992.

Callahan, Raymond E. *Education and the Cult of Efficiency: A Study of the Social Forces That Have Shaped the Administration of Public Schools.* Chicago: University of Chicago Press, 1962.

Calvert, Karin. "Children in the House, 1890–1930." In Foy and Schlereth, *American Home Life.*

Carmichael, James V., Jr. "Atlanta's Female Librarians, 1883–1915." *Journal of Library History* 21 (Spring 1986): 376–99.

Casey, Marion. "Efficiency, Taylorism, and Libraries in Progressive America." *Journal of Library History* 16 (Spring 1981): 265–79.

Casey, Phyllis A. "Memories of Cabanne Branch Library, 1916–1929." *Show-Me Libraries* 33 (July 1982): 37–9.

Cavallo, Dom. "From Perfection to Habit: Moral Training in the American Kindergarten, 1860–1920." *History of Education Quarterly* 16 (Summer 1976): 147–61.

———. "Kindergarten Pedagogy: A Review Essay." *History of Education Quarterly* 18 (Fall 1978): 365–6.

———. "Social Reform and the Movement to Organize Children's Play During the Progressive Era." *History of Childhood Quarterly* 3 (Spring 1976): 509–22.

Chandler, Alfred D. *The Visible Hand: The Managerial Revolution in American Business.* Cambridge, Mass.: Belknap Press, 1977.

Ciucci, Giorgio, et al., eds. *The American City: From the Civil War to the New Deal.* Cambridge: MIT Press, 1979; London: Granada, 1980.

Clemens, Elisabeth S. "Organizational Repertoires and Institutional Change: Women's Groups and the Transformation of U.S. Politics, 1890–1920." *American Journal of Sociology* 98 (January 1993): 755–98.

Cohen, Lizabeth A. "Embellishing a Life of Labor: An Interpretation of the Material Culture of American Working-Class Homes." *Journal of American Culture* 3 (Winter 1980): 40–55.

Colburn, David, and George E. Pozzetta, eds. *Reform and Reformers in the Progressive Era.* Westport, Ct.: Greenwood Press, 1984.

Cole, John Y. "Smithmeyer and Pelz: Embattled Architects of the Library of Congress." *Quarterly Journal of the Library of Congress* 29 (October 1972): 282–307.

———. "Storehouses and Workshops: American Libraries and the Uses of Knowledge." In *The Organization of Knowledge in Modern America, 1860–1920*, ed. Alexandra Oleson and John Voss, 364–85. Baltimore: Johns Hopkins University Press, 1979.

Colson, John Calvin. "Form against Function: The American Public Library and Contemporary Society." *Journal of Library History* 18 (Spring 1983): 111–42.

Cranz, Galen. *The Politics of Park Design: A History of Urban Parks in America.* Cambridge: MIT Press, 1982.

Cremin, Lawrence A. *American Education: The Metropolitan Experience, 1876–1980.* New York: Harper & Row, 1988.

Culp, Paul M., Jr. "Carnegie Libraries of Texas: The Past No Longer Present." *Texas Libraries* 43 (Fall 1981): 132–44.

———. "Carnegie Libraries of Texas: The Past Still Present." *Texas Libraries* 43 (Summer 1981): 81–96.

Dain, Phyllis. "Ambivalence and Paradox: The Social Bonds of the Public Library." *Library Journal* 100 (1 February 1975): 261–6.

———. *The New York Public Library: A History of Its Founding and Early Years.* New York: New York Public Library, Astor, Lenox and Tilden Foundations, 1972.

———. "Public Library Governance and a Changing New York City." *Libraries and Culture* 26 (Spring 1992): 219–50.

———. "Women's Studies in American Library History: Some Critical Reflections." *Journal of Library History* 18 (Fall 1983): 450–63.

Darton, Robert. "Toward A History of Reading." *Wilson Quarterly* 13 (Autumn 1989): 87–102.

Davidson, Cathy N., ed. *Reading in America: Literature and Social History.* Baltimore: Johns Hopkins University Press, 1989.

Davies, Margery W. *Woman's Place Is at the Typewriter: Office Work and Office Workers, 1870–1930.* Philadelphia: Temple University Press, 1982.

Davis, Allen F. *Spearheads for Reform: The Social Settlements and the Progressive Movement, 1890–1914.* New York: Oxford University Press, 1967; reprint, New Brunswick, N.J.: Rutgers University Press, 1984.

Deitch, Joseph. "Benevolent Builder: Appraising Andrew Carnegie." *Wilson Library Bulletin* 59 (September 1984): 16–22.

De Long, David G. "William R. Ware and the Pursuit of Suitability: 1881–1903." In *The Making of an Architect, 1881–1981*, ed. Richard Oliver, 13–21. New York: Rizzoli, 1981.

Dickson, Paul. *The Library in America: A Celebration in Words and Pictures.* New York: Facts on File Publications, 1986.

DiMaggio, Paul. Edging women's organizations out: Gender succession and organizational change in the campaigns for culture, 1900–1935. Paper prepared for submission to the American Sociological Association conference, 1991.

Ditzion, Sidney H. *Arsenals of a Democratic Culture.* Chicago: American Library Association, 1947.

Douglas, Ann. *The Feminization of American Culture.* New York: Alfred Knopf, 1977; New York: Anchor Books/Doubleday, 1988.

Draper, Joan. "The Ecole des Beaux-Arts and the Architectural Profession in the United States: The Case of John Galen Howard." In Kostof, *Architect.*

Drexler, Arthur, ed. *The Architecture of the Ecole des Beaux-Arts.* New York: Museum of Modern Art, 1977.

Dulaney, William L. "Wallace Nutting: Collector and Entrepreneur." *Winterthur Portfolio* 13 (1979): 47–60.

Du Mont, Rosemary Ruhig. "Race in American Librarianship: Attitudes of the Library Profession." *Journal of Library History* 21 (Summer 1986): 488–509.

———. *Reform and Reaction: The Big City Public Library in American Life.* Westport, Ct.: Greenwood Press, 1977.

Eagleton, Terry. *Literary Theory: An Introduction.* Minneapolis: University of Minnesota Press, 1983.

Eastman, Linda. *Portrait of a Librarian: William Howard Brett.* Chicago: American Library Association, 1940.

Edens, Ruth J. "'A Substantial and Attractive Building': The Carnegie Public Library, Sumter, South Carolina." *South Carolina Historical Magazine* 94 (January 1993): 34–50.

Eppard, Philip B. "The Rental Library in Twentieth-Century America." *Journal of Library History* 21 (Winter 1986): 240–52.

Ewen, Elizabeth. *Immigrant Women in the Land of Dollars: Life and Culture on the Lower East Side, 1890–1925.* New York: Monthly Review Press, 1985.

Fain, Elaine. "Books for New Citizens: Public Libraries and Americanization Programs, 1900–1925." In *The Quest for Social Justice: The Morris Fromkin Memorial Lecture, 1970–1980,* ed. Ralph M. Aderman, 255–76. Madison: University of Wisconsin Press, 1983.

Fein, Albert. "The American City: The Ideal and the Real." In *The Rise of an American Architecture,* ed. Edgar Kaufmann, Jr., 51–112. New York: Praeger Publishers for the Metropolitan Museum of Art, 1970.

Fine, Lisa M. *The Souls of the Skyscraper: Female Clerical Workers in Chicago, 1870–1930.* Philadelphia: Temple University Press, 1990.

Finkel, Alvin. "Social Class and the Progressive Era." *Canadian Review of American Studies* 15 (Winter 1984): 465–80.

Flanzraich, Gerri Lynn. The role of the Library Bureau and Gaylord Brothers in the development of library technology, 1876–1930. Ph.D. diss., Columbia University, 1990.

Floyd, Margaret Henderson. *Architecture after Richardson: Regionalism before Modernism—Longfellow, Alden, and Harlow in Boston and Pittsburgh.* Chicago: University of Chicago Press, 1994; Pittsburgh: Pittsburgh History and Landmarks Foundation, 1994.

Fogelsong, Richard E. *Planning the Capitalist City: The Colonial Era to the 1920s.* Princeton, N.J.: Princeton University Press, 1986.

Forty, Adrian. *Objects of Desire.* New York: Pantheon, 1986.

Foucault, Michel. *Discipline and Punish: The Birth of the Prison.* Trans. Alan Sheridan. New York: Pantheon, 1977.

Fox, Richard Wightman, and T. J. Jackson Lears, eds. *The Culture of Consumption: Critical Essays in American History, 1880–1980.* New York: Pantheon, 1983.

Foy, Jessica H., and Karal Ann Marling, eds. *The Arts and the American Home, 1890–1930.* Knoxville: University of Tennessee Press, 1994.

Foy, Jessica H., and Thomas J. Schlereth, eds. *American Home Life, 1880–1930: A Social History of Spaces and Services.* Knoxville: University of Tennessee Press, 1992.

Fulton, Gordon W., and Henry V. Taves. *The William Alciphron Boring Collection Catalogue.* New York: Columbia University, 1980.

Garrison, Dee. *Apostles of Culture: The Public Librarian and American Society, 1876–1920.* New York: Free Press, 1979.

————. "The Tender Technicians: The Feminization of Public Librarianship, 1876–1905." *Journal of Social History* 6 (Winter 1972–73): 131–59.

Geller, Evelyn. *Forbidden Books in American Public Libraries, 1876–1939: A Study in Cultural Change.* Westport, Ct.: Greenwood Press, 1984.

Gilkerson, Ann Melissa. The public libraries of H. H. Richardson. Honors thesis, Smith College, 1978.

Gilmore, William J. *Reading Becomes a Necessity of Life: Material and Cultural Life in Rural New England, 1780–1835.* Knoxville: University of Tennessee Press, 1989.

Glazer, Penina Migdal, and Miriam Slater. *Unequal Colleagues: The Entrance of Women into the Professions, 1890–1940.* New Brunswick, N.J.: Rutgers University Press, 1987.

Gould, Joseph E. *The Chautauqua Movement: An Episode in the Continuing American Revolution.* Albany: State University of New York Press, 1961.

Graff, Harvey J. "Literacy, Libraries, Lives: New Social and Cultural Histories." *Libraries and Culture* 26 (Winter 1991): 24–45.

Greenberg, Gerald S. "Books as Disease Carriers, 1880–1920." *Libraries and Culture* 23 (Summer 1988): 281–94.

Grossman, Elizabeth G., and Lisa B. Reitzes. "Caught in the Crossfire: Women and Architectural Education, 1880–1910." In *Architecture: A Place for Women*, ed. Ellen Perry Berkeley and Matilda McQuaid, 27–39. Washington, D.C.: Smithsonian Institution Press, 1989.

Grotzinger, Laurel. "Biographical Research: Recognition Denied." *Journal of Library History* 18 (Fall 1983): 372–81.

————. "Biographical Research on Women Librarians: Its Paucity, Perils, and Pleasure." In Heim, *Status of Women*.

Gulliford, Andrew. *America's Country Schools.* Washington, D.C.: Preservation Press, 1984.

Haber, Samuel. *Efficiency and Uplift: Scientific Management in the Progressive Era, 1890–1920.* Chicago: University of Chicago Press, 1964.

Hahn, Steven, and Jonathan Prude, eds. *The Countryside in the Age of Capitalist Transformation: Essays in the Social History of Rural America.* Chapel Hill: University of North Carolina Press, 1985.

Hales, Peter Bacon. *Silver Cities: The Photography of American Urbanization, 1839–1915.* Philadelphia: Temple University Press, 1984.

Handlin, David P. *The American Home: Architecture and Society, 1815–1915.* Boston: Little, Brown, 1979.

Hanson, Carl A., ed. *Librarian at Large: Selected Writings of John Cotton Dana.* Washington, D.C.: Special Libraries Association, 1990.

Harris, Michael H. "The Purpose of the American Public Library: A Revisionist Interpretation of History." *Library Journal* 98 (15 September 1973): 2509–14.

Hayden, Dolores. *The Grand Domestic Revolution: A History of Feminist Designs for American Homes, Neighborhoods, and Cities.* Cambridge: MIT Press, 1981.

Heckscher, Morrison H. "Hunt and the Metropolitan Museum of Art." In Stein, *Richard Morris Hunt.*

Heim, Kathleen M., ed. *The Status of Women in Librarianship: Historical, Sociological, and Economic Issues.* New York: Neal-Schuman Publishers, 1983.

Hendrick, Burton J. *The Life of Andrew Carnegie.* 2 vols. Garden City, N.Y.: Doubleday, 1932.

Hildebrand, Suzanne. "Revision versus Reality: Women in the History of the Public Library Movement, 1876–1917." In Heim, *Status of Women.*

Hill, Frank Pierce. *James Bertram: An Appreciation*. New York: Carnegie Corporation, 1936.

Hoagland, Alison K. "The Carnegie Library: The City Beautiful Comes to Mt. Vernon Square." *Washington History* 2 (1990–1): 74–89.

Hofstadter, Richard. *The Age of Reform*. New York: Vintage Books, 1955.

Holleman, Thomas. "Arts and Crafts Architecture in Detroit." In *Arts and Crafts in Detroit*.

Horowitz, Helen Lefkowitz. *Culture and the City: Cultural Philanthropy in Chicago from the 1880s to 1917*. Lexington: University of Kentucky Press, 1976; reprint, Chicago: University of Chicago Press, 1989.

———. "Hull House as Women's Space." *Chicago History* 12 (Winter 1983): 40–55.

Houde, Mary Jean. *Reaching Out: A Story of the General Federation of Women's Clubs*. Chicago: Mobium Press, 1989.

Hudson, John C. "The Midland Prairies: Natural Resources and Urban Settlement." In Larson, *Spirit of Richardson*.

Jackle, John A. *The American Small Town: Twentieth-Century Place Images*. Hamden, Ct.: Archon Books, 1982.

Jackson, Pauline P. "Life and Society in Sapulpa." *Chronicles of Oklahoma* 43 (Autumn 1965): 297–318.

Javersak, David T. "One Place on This Great Green Planet Where Andrew Carnegie Can't Get a Monument with His Money." *West Virginia History* 41 (Fall 1979): 7–19.

Johnson, Mary Ann, ed. *The Many Faces of Hull House: The Photographs of Wallace Kirkland*. Urbana: University of Illinois Press, 1989.

Jordy, William H. *Progressive and Academic Ideals at the Turn of the Twentieth Century*. Vol. 3 of *American Buildings and Their Architects*. New York: Doubleday, 1972; reprint, Garden City, N.Y.: Anchor Books, 1976.

Kaplan, Wendy. *"The Art That Is Life": The Arts and Crafts Movement in America, 1875–1920*. Boston: Museum of Fine Arts, 1987.

Katz, Michael B. *In the Shadow of the Poorhouse: A Social History of Welfare in America*. New York: Basic Books, 1986.

Kerber, Linda K. "Separate Spheres, Female Worlds, Woman's Place: The Rhetoric of Women's History." *Journal of American History*, 75 (June 1988): 9–39.

Kolko, Gabriel. *The Triumph of Conservatism: A Reinterpretation of American History, 1900–1916*. New York: Free Press, 1963.

Kortum, Lucy Deam. California's Carnegie libraries, 1899–1921. M.A. investigative project, Sonoma State University, 1991.

Kostof, Spiro, ed. *The Architect: Chapters in the History of the Profession*. New York: Oxford University Press, 1977.

Krause, Paul L. "Patronage and Philanthropy in Industrial America: Andrew Carnegie and the Free Public Library of Braddock, Pa." *Western Pennsylvania Historical Magazine* 71 (April 1988): 127–45.

Kruger, Linda M. "Home Libraries: Special Spaces, Reading Places." In Foy and Schlereth, *American Home Life*.

Kruty, Paul. "Patton & Miller: Designers of Carnegie Libraries," *Palimpsest* 64 (July/August 1983): 110–22.

Lagemann, Ellen Condliffe. *The Politics of Knowledge: The Carnegie Corporation, Philanthropy, and Public Policy*. Middletown, Ct.: Wesleyan University Press, 1989.

Lancaster, Clay. "The American Bungalow." In Upton and Vlach, *Common Places*.

Larson, Paul Clifford, ed. *The Spirit of H. H. Richardson on the Midland Prairies: Re-*

gional Transformations of an Architectural Style. Minneapolis: University Art Museum, University of Minnesota, 1988; Ames: Iowa State University Press, 1988.

Leach, William. "Strategies of Display and the Production of Desire." In Bronner, Consuming Visions.

Learned, William S. The American Public Library and the Diffusion of Knowledge. New York: Harcourt, Brace and Co., 1924.

Lears, T. J. Jackson. No Place of Grace: Antimodernism and the Transformation of American Culture, 1880–1920. New York: Pantheon Books, 1981.

Leatherman, Carolyn H. "Richmond Considers a Free Public Library: Andrew Carnegie's Offer of 1901." Virginia Magazine of History and Biography 96 (April 1988): 181–92.

———. Richmond rejects a library: The Carnegie public library movement in Richmond, Virginia, in the early twentieth century. Ph.D. diss., Virginia Commonwealth University, 1992.

Lebovich, William L. America's City Halls. Washington, D.C.: Preservation Press, 1984.

Lester, Robert M. "Carnegie Corporation." Wilson Library Bulletin 31 (1956): 255–59.

———. Forty Years of Carnegie Giving. New York: Charles Scribner's Sons, 1941.

———. Review of Grants for Library Interests, 1911–1935. New York: Carnegie Corporation, 1935.

Levine, Lawrence W. Highbrow, Lowbrow: The Emergence of Cultural Hierarchy in America. Cambridge: Harvard University Press, 1988.

Levine, Neil. "The Romantic Ideal of Architectural Legibility: Henri Labrouste and the Neo-Grec." In Drexler, Architecture of the Ecole des Beaux-Arts.

Lewis, Betty. "William H. Weeks: Architect of the Plain Citizen." California Historical Courier (July 1978).

Lingeman, Richard. Small Town America: A Narrative History, 1620–the present. New York: G. P. Putnam's Sons, 1980.

Livesay, Harold C. Andrew Carnegie and the Rise of Big Business. Boston: Little, Brown, 1975.

Long, Harriet. Public Library Service to Children: Foundation and Development. Metuchen, N.J.: Scarecrow Press, 1969.

Longstreth, Richard. The Buildings of Main Street: A Guide to American Commercial Architecture. Washington, D.C.: Preservation Press, 1987.

———. "Main Streets." In Maddex, Built in the U.S.A.

———. "Compositional Types in American Commercial Architecture." In Perspectives in Vernacular Architecture, 2, ed. Camille Wells, 12–23. Columbia: University of Missouri Press, 1986.

Lopez, Manuel D. "Children's Libraries: Nineteenth-Century American Origins." Journal of Library History 11 (October 1976): 316–42.

Lubove, Roy. The Professional Altruist: The Emergence of Social Work as a Career, 1880–1930. New York: Atheneum, 1969.

———. Progressives and the Slums: Tenement House Reform in New York City, 1890–1917. Pittsburgh: University of Pittsburgh Press, 1962.

Lupton, Ellen. Mechanical Brides: Women and Machines from Home to Office. New York: Cooper-Hewitt National Museum of Design and Princeton Architectural Press, 1993.

Maack, Mary Niles. "Toward a History of Women in Librarianship: A Critical Analysis with Suggestions for Future Research." Journal of Library History 17 (Spring 1982): 164–85.

MacLeod, Anne Scott. "Reading Together: Children, Adults, and Literature at the Turn of the Century." In Foy and Marling, *Arts and the Home*.

MacLeod, David L. *Carnegie Libraries in Wisconsin*. Madison: State Historical Society of Wisconsin for the Department of History, University of Wisconsin, 1968.

Maddex, Diane, ed. *Built in the U.S.A.: American Buildings from Airports to Zoos*. Washington, D.C.: Preservation Press, 1985.

Manieri-Elia, Mario. "Toward an 'Imperial City': Daniel H. Burnham and the City Beautiful Movement." In Ciucci et al., *American City*.

Marcum, Deanna B. "The Rural Public Library in America at the Turn of the Century." *Libraries and Culture* 26 (Winter 1991): 87–99.

Marling, Karal Ann. *George Washington Slept Here: Colonial Revivals and American Culture, 1876–1896*. Cambridge: Harvard University Press, 1988.

Martin, Judith A. "The Prairie City Comes of Age: Ambitions and Expectations in the Richardsonian Era." In Larson, *Spirit of H. H. Richardson*.

Martin, Robert S., ed. *Carnegie Denied: Communities Rejecting Carnegie Library Construction Grants, 1898–1925*. Westport, Ct.: Greenwood Press, 1993.

Martin, Theodora Penny. *The Sound of Our Own Voices: Women's Study Clubs, 1860–1910*. Boston: Beacon Press, 1987.

Mayo, James M. *The American Grocery Store: The Business Evolution of an Architectural Space*. Westport, Ct.: Greenwood Press, 1993.

McCarthy, Kathleen D. *Noblesse Oblige: Charity and Cultural Philanthropy in Chicago, 1849–1929*. Chicago: University of Chicago Press, 1982.

———. *Women's Culture: American Philanthropy and Art, 1830–1930*. Chicago: University of Chicago Press, 1991.

McCloskey, Robert Green. *American Conservatism in the Age of Enterprise; A Study of William Graham Sumner, Stephen J. Field, and Andrew Carnegie*. Cambridge: Harvard University Press, 1951.

McCroskey, Lauren L. "'A Mighty Influence': Library Philanthropy in North Dakota During the Carnegie Era." *North Dakota History* 57 (Spring 1990): 15–23.

McCue, George. *The Building Art in St. Louis: Two Centuries*. 3rd. ed. St. Louis: Knight Publishing Co., 1981.

McMullen, C. Haynes. "The Very Slow Decline of the American Social Library." *Library Quarterly* 55 (April 1985): 207–25.

McMurry, Sally. *Families and Farmhouses in Nineteenth-Century America: Vernacular Design and Social Change*. New York: Oxford University Press, 1988.

McReynolds, Rosalee. "A Heritage Dismissed." *Library Journal* 110 (1 November 1985): 25–31.

———. "The Sexual Politics of Illness in Turn-of-the-Century Libraries." *Libraries and Culture* 25 (Spring 1990): 194–217.

Mellon, Constance A., ed. "Reflections." *Journal of Youth Services in Libraries* 6 (Fall 1991): 79–90.

Meyerowitz, Joanne J. *Women Adrift: Independent Wage Earners in Chicago, 1880–1930*. Chicago: University of Chicago Press, 1988.

Mickelson, Peter. "American Society and Public Libraries." *Journal of Library History* 10 (1975): 117–38.

Miksa, Francis L. "The Columbia School of Library Economy, 1887–1888." *Libraries and Culture* 23 (Summer 1988): 249–80.

———. "Melvil Dewey: The Professional Educator and His Heirs." *Library Trends* 34 (Winter 1986): 359–82.

Milden, James W. "Women, Public Libraries, and Library Unions: The Formative Years." *Journal of Library History* 12 (Spring 1977): 150–65.

Miner, Curtis. "The 'Deserted Parthenon': Class, Culture and the Carnegie Library of Homestead, 1898–1937." *Pennsylvania History* 57 (April 1990): 107–35.

Montgomery, Helen Grace. "Blueprints and Books: American Library Architecture, 1860–1960." *Library Journal* 86 (1 December 1961): 4077–80.

Morain, Thomas J. *Prairie Grass Roots: An Iowa Small Town in the Early Twentieth Century*. Ames: Iowa State University, 1988.

Morrison, Theodore. *Chautauqua: A Center for Education, Religion, and the Arts in America*. Chicago: University of Chicago Press, 1974.

Musmann, Victoria Kline. Women and the founding of social libraries in California, 1859–1910. Ph.D. diss., University of Southern California, 1982.

Nasaw, David. *Children of the City: At Work and at Play*. Garden City, N.Y.: Anchor Press/Doubleday, 1985.

———. *Schooled to Order: A Social History of Public Schooling in the United States*. New York: Oxford University Press, 1979.

Newmyer, Jody. "The Image Problem of the Librarian: Femininity and Social Control." *Journal of Library History* 11 (January 1976): 44–67.

Ochsner, Jeffrey Karl, and Thomas C. Hubka. "H. H. Richardson: The Design of the William Watts Sherman House." *Journal of the Society of Architectural Historians* 51 (June 1992): 121–45.

O'Connor, Thomas F. "American Catholic Reading Circles, 1886–1909." *Libraries and Culture* 26 (Spring 1991): 334–47.

Oehlerts, Donald E. *Books and Blueprints: Building America's Public Libraries*. Westport, Ct.: Greenwood Press, 1991.

———. "Sources for the Study of American Library Architecture." *Journal of Library History* 11 (January 1976): 68–78.

O'Gorman, James F. *H. H. Richardson: Architectural Forms for an American Society*. Chicago: University of Chicago Press, 1987.

Parker, Franklin. *George Peabody: A Biography*. Nashville: Vanderbilt University Press, 1971.

Passet, Joanne E. "Bringing the Public Library Gospel to the American West." *Journal of the West* 30 (July 1991): 45–52.

———. "Reaching the Rural Reader: Traveling Libraries in America, 1892–1920." *Libraries and Culture* 26 (Winter 1991): 100–118.

Peiss, Kathy. *Cheap Amusements: Working Women and Leisure in Turn-of-the-Century New York*. Philadelphia: Temple University Press, 1986.

Pepper, Simon. "Postcards from Parnassus: The Cultural Aspirations of Small Town America Found in Local Libraries." *Architecture Minnesota* 15 (September/October 1989): 36–41.

Perry, Garland. "Andrew Carnegie: Santa Claus of Texas Public Libraries." *Texas Libraries* 46 (Spring/Summer 1985): 23–7.

Peterson, Jon A. "The City Beautiful Movement: Forgotten Origins and Lost Meanings." *Journal of Urban History* 2 (August 1976): 415–34.

Pevsner, Nikolaus. *A History of Building Types*. Princeton, N.J.: Princeton University Press, 1976.

Pierson, William H., Jr. *Technology and the Picturesque, the Corporate and the Early Gothic Styles*. Vol. 2 of *American Buildings and Their Architects*. Garden City, N.Y.: Doubleday, 1978.

Quinan, Jack. *Frank Lloyd Wright's Larkin Building: Myth and Fact*. New York: Architectural History Foundation, 1987; Cambridge: MIT Press, 1987.

Radway, Janice. *Reading the Romance: Women, Patriarchy, and Popular Literature.* Chapel Hill: University of North Carolina Press, 1984.

Randolph, Octavia Porter. "The Carnegie Libraries of Connecticut: An Architectural Perspective." *Connecticut Libraries* 27 (July/August 1985): 1, 7–9.

Rarick, Holly M. *Progressive Vision: The Planning of Downtown Cleveland, 1903–1930.* Cleveland: Cleveland Museum of Art, 1986.

Reed, Henry Hope. *The New York Public Library: Its Architecture and Decoration.* New York: W. W. Norton, 1986.

Rhoades, Alice J. "Early Women Librarians in Texas." *Texas Libraries* 47 (Summer 1986): 46–53.

Richards, Susan L. "Carnegie Library Architecture for South Dakota and Montana: A Comparative Study." *Journal of the West* 30 (July 1991): 69–78.

Ring, Daniel F. "Carnegie Libraries as Symbols for an Age: Montana as a Test Case." *Libraries and Culture* 27 (Winter 1992): 1–19.

Robertson, Cheryl. "Male and Female Agendas for Domestic Reform: The Middle-Class Bungalow in Gendered Perspective." *Winterthur Portfolio* 26 (Summer/Autumn 1991): 123–42.

Roff, Sandra. "The Accessibility of Libraries to Blacks in Nineteenth-Century Brooklyn, New York." *Afro-Americans in New York Life and History* 5 (1981): 7–12.

Rosenzweig, Roy. *Eight Hours for What We Will: Workers and Leisure in an Industrial City, 1870–1920.* Cambridge: Cambridge University Press, 1983.

Ross, Catherine Sheldrick. "Metaphors of Reading." *Journal of Library History* 22 (Spring 1987): 145–63.

Roth, Leland. *McKim, Mead & White, Architects.* New York: Harper & Row, 1983.

Saint, Andrew. *The Image of the Architect.* New Haven: Yale University Press, 1983.

Sallee, Denise. "Reconceptualizing Women's History: Anne Hadden and the California County Library System." *Libraries and Culture* 27 (Fall 1992): 351–77.

Santmyer, Helen Hooven. ". . . And Ladies of the Club." Columbus: Ohio State University Press, 1982; reprint, New York: Berkley Books, 1985.

———. *Ohio Town.* Columbus: Ohio State University Press, 1963; reprint, New York: Berkley Books, 1985.

Schlereth, Thomas. "Country Stores, County Fairs, and Mail-Order Catalogues: Consumption in Rural America." In Bronner, *Consuming Visions.*

———. *Cultural History and Material Culture: Everyday Life, Landscapes, Museums.* Ann Arbor: UMI Research Press, 1990.

Scott, Anne Firor. *Natural Allies: Women's Associations in American History.* Urbana: University of Illinois Press, 1992.

———. "On Seeing and Not Seeing—A Case of Historical Invisibility." *Journal of American History* 71 (June 1984): 7–21.

———. "Women and Libraries." *Journal of Library History* 21 (Spring 1986): 400–5.

———. "Women's Voluntary Associations: From Charity to Reform." In *Lady Bountiful Revisited: Women, Philanthropy, and Power,* ed. Kathleen D. McCarthy, 35–54. New Brunswick, N.J.: Rutgers University Press, 1990.

Scully, Vincent. *The Architecture of the American Summer: The Flowering of the Shingle Style.* New York: Rizzoli, 1989.

Shapiro, Michael Steven. *Child's Garden: The Kindergarten from Froebel to Dewey.* University Park: Pennsylvania State University Press, 1983.

Shavit, David. "The Emergence of Jewish Public Libraries in Tsarist Russia." *Journal of Library History* 20 (Fall 1985): 239–52.

Shera, Jesse H. *Foundations of the Public Library: The Origins of the Public Library Movement in New England, 1629–1855.* Chicago: University of Chicago Press, 1949.

Shishkin, J. K. *An Early History of the Museum of New Mexico Fine Arts Building.* Santa Fe: Museum of New Mexico Press, 1968.

Sicherman, Barbara. "Sense and Sensibility: A Case Study of Women's Reading in Late Victorian America." In Davidson, *Reading in America.*

Soltow, Lee, and Edward Stevens. *The Rise of Literacy and the Common School in the United States: A Socioeconomic Analysis to 1870.* Chicago: University of Chicago Press, 1982.

Stansell, Christine. *City of Women: Sex and Class in New York, 1789–1860.* New York: Alfred A. Knopf, 1986; Urbana: University of Illinois Press, 1987.

Stein, Susan R., ed. *The Architecture of Richard Morris Hunt.* Chicago: University of Chicago Press, 1986.

Stern, Robert A. M., et al. *New York 1900, Metropolitan Architecture and Urbanism, 1890–1915.* New York: Rizzoli, 1983.

Stevenson, Gordon, and Judy Kramer-Greene, eds. *Melvil Dewey: The Man and the Classification.* Albany, N.Y.: Forest Press, 1983.

Stielow, Frederick J. "Censorship in the Early Professionalization of American Libraries, 1876 to 1929." *Journal of Library History* 18 (Winter 1983): 37–54.

Swetnam, Susan H. "Pro-Carnegie Library Arguments and Contemporary Concerns in the Intermountain West." *Journal of the West* 30 (July 1991): 63–8.

Taylor, David. "Ladies of the Club: An Arkansas Story." *Wilson Library Bulletin* 59 (January 1985): 324–7.

Taylor, William R. "The Evolution of Public Space in New York City: The Commercial Showcase of America." In Bronner, *Consuming Visions.*

Teaford, Jon C. *The Unheralded Triumph: City Government in America, 1870–1900.* Baltimore: Johns Hopkins University Press, 1984.

Thompson, Donald E. "A History of Library Architecture: A Bibliographic Essay." *Journal of Library History* 4 (April 1969): 133–41.

Tiffin, Susan. *In Whose Best Interest? Child Welfare Reform in the Progressive Era.* Westport, Ct.: Greenwood Press, 1982.

Torre, Susana, ed. *Women in American Architecture: A Historical and Contemporary Perspective.* New York: Whitney Library of Design, 1977.

Toth, Susan Allen. *Blooming: A Small-Town Girlhood.* Boston: Little, Brown, [1978] 1981.

Toth, Susan Allen, and John Coughlan, eds. *Reading Rooms.* New York: Doubleday, 1991.

Trachtenberg, Alan. *The Incorporation of America: Culture and Society in the Gilded Age.* New York: Hill and Wang, 1982.

Underwood, June O. "Civilizing Kansas: Women's Organizations, 1880–1920." *Kansas History* 7 (Winter 1984–85): 291–306.

Upton, Dell. "Architectural History or Landscape History?" *Journal of Architectural Education* 44 (August 1991): 195–9.

———. "Pattern Books and Professionalism: Aspects of the Transformation of Domestic Architecture in America, 1800–1860." *Winterthur Portfolio* 19 (Summer/Autumn 1984): 107–50.

Upton, Dell, and John Michael Vlach, eds. *Common Places: Readings in American Vernacular Architecture.* Athens: University of Georgia Press, 1986.

Van Slyck, Abigail A. "Mañana, Mañana: Racial Stereotypes and the Anglo Rediscovery of the Southwest's Vernacular Architecture, 1890–1920." In *Gender, Class, and Shelter: Perspectives in Vernacular Architecture,* 5, ed. Elizabeth Collins Cromley and Carter L. Hudgins, 95–108. Knoxville: University of Tennessee Press, 1995.

―――. Free to all: Carnegie libraries and the transformation of American culture, 1886–1917. Ph.D. diss., University of California, Berkeley, 1989.

―――. "'The Utmost Amount of Effectiv [*sic*] Accommodation': Andrew Carnegie and the Reform of the American Library." *Journal of the Society of Architectural Historians* 50 (December 1991): 359–83.

Van Trump, James D. "The Romanesque Revival in Pittsburgh." *Journal of the Society of Architectural Historians* 16 (October 1957): 22–8.

Van Zanten, David. "Architectural Composition at the Ecole des Beaux-Arts from Charles Percier to Charles Garnier." In Drexler, *The Architecture of the Ecole des Beaux-Arts.*

―――. *Designing Paris: The Architecture of Duban, Labrouste, Duc, and Vandoyer.* Cambridge: MIT Press, 1987.

Vitz, Carl. "William H. Brett." In *An American Library History Reader: Contributions to Library Literature,* ed. John David Marshall, 242–56. Hamden, Ct.: Shoe String Press, 1961.

Wall, Joseph Frazier. *Andrew Carnegie.* New York: Oxford University Press, 1970; reprint, Pittsburgh: University of Pittsburgh Press, 1989.

Walkowitz, Daniel J. "The Making of the Feminine Professional Identity: Social Workers in the 1920s." *American Historical Review* 95 (October 1990): 1051–75.

Welter, Barbara. "The Cult of True Womanhood, 1820–1860." *American Quarterly* 18 (Summer 1966): 151–74.

Welty, Eudora. *One Writer's Beginnings.* Cambridge: Harvard University Press, 1984.

West, Elliott. *Growing Up with the Country: Childhood on the Far Western Frontier.* Albuquerque: University of New Mexico Press, 1989.

West, Elliott, and Paula Petrick, eds. *Small Worlds: Children and Adolescents in America, 1850–1950.* Lawrence: University Press of Kansas, 1992.

White, Carl M. *A Historical Introduction to Library Education: Problems and Progress to 1951.* Metuchen, N.J.: Scarecrow Press, 1976.

Wiebe, Robert H. *The Search for Order, 1877–1920.* New York: Hill and Wang, 1967.

Wiegand, Wayne A. "American Library Association Executive Board Members, 1876–1917: A Collective Profile." *Libri* 31 (1981): 153–66.

―――. "The Development of Librarianship in the United States." *Libraries and Culture* 24 (Winter 1989): 99–109.

―――. "Melvil Dewey and the American Library Association, 1876–1907." In Stevenson and Kramer-Greene, *Melvil Dewey.*

―――. *The Politics of an Emerging Profession: The American Library Association, 1876–1917.* Westport, Ct: Greenwood Press, 1986.

―――. "The Socialization of Library and Information Science Students: Reflections on a Century of Formal Education for Librarianship." *Library Trends* 34 (Winter 1986): 383–400.

Wilkinson, M. "Experience of a Field Worker in Platte County in the Early 1900s." *Wyoming Library Round-Up* 41 (Winter 1986): 50–3; (Spring 1986): 24–8.

Williams, Patrick. *The American Public Library and the Problem of Purpose.* Westport, Ct.: Greenwood Press, 1988.

Wilson, Margaret Gibbons. *The American Woman in Transition: The Urban Influence, 1870–1920.* Westport, Ct.: Greenwood Press, 1979.

Wilson, Richard Guy. *McKim, Mead & White, Architects.* New York: Rizzoli, 1983.

Wilson, Richard Guy, Dianne H. Pilgrim, and Richard N. Murray. *The American Renaissance, 1876–1917.* New York: Brooklyn Museum, 1979.

Wilson, William H. *The City Beautiful Movement.* Baltimore: Johns Hopkins University Press, 1989.

Wishy, Bernard. *The Child and the Republic: The Dawn of Modern American Child Nurture.* Philadelphia: University of Pennsylvania Press, 1968.

Withey, Henry F., and Elsie Rathburn Withey. *Biographical Dictionary of American Architects (Deceased).* Los Angeles: New Age Publishing Co., 1956; reprint, Los Angeles: Hennessey & Ingalls, 1970.

Woodford, Frank B. *Parnassus on Main Street: A History of the Detroit Public Library.* Detroit: Wayne State University Press, 1965.

Wortman, Madeline Stein. "Domesticating the American City." *Prospects* 3 (1977): 531–71.

Wright, Gwendolyn. *Moralism and the Model Home: Domestic Architecture and Cultural Conflict in Chicago, 1873–1913.* Chicago: University of Chicago Press, 1980.

———. "On the Fringe of the Profession: Women in American Architecture." In Kostof, *Architect.*

Yeatman, Joseph Lawrence. "Literary Culture and the Role of Libraries in Democratic America: Baltimore, 1815–1840," *Journal of Library History* 20 (Fall 1985): 345–367.

Zboray, Ronald J. "Reading Patterns in Antebellum America: Evidence in the Charge Records of the New York Society Library." *Libraries and Culture* 26 (Spring 1991): 301–33.

Zunz, Olivier. *Making America Corporate, 1870–1920.* Chicago: University of Chicago Press, 1990.

Index

urban libraries. *See* branch libraries; central urban libraries; *specific cities*

urban library boards, 110–20

Utley, Henry M., 181

vernacular architecture, xx

visual surveillance, 107, 120

Warren, Ohio, xxiv, 57, 140–1

Washington, D.C., 56, 95, 100

"Wealth," 10

Weeks, W. H., 60

Welker, L. G., 186

Welty, Eudora, 203, 209

Wetherell, F. E., 60

Whitfield, Henry D., 61

Wing and Mahurin, 60

Winn, Charles Bower, 2, 22

Winn Memorial Library, 3–5

Winsor, Justin, 69

Winston-Salem, North Carolina, 59

women: Carnegie library program and, 134, 165–7; children's librarianship and, 189–92; cultural politics, 65–6; culture of professionalism and, 134–5; feminization of librarianship, 160–5; gender-segregated facilities, 15, 16; librarian skills, 164–5; library design and, 143, 150, 154, 157, 165–73; library function perspectives, xxvi, 65, 135–7; in library hierarchy, 17, 164, 166; municipal housekeeping role, 127, 135, 194; small-town experiences, 193–200; town library site selection and, 137–43

women's clubs, 65, 125–33, 142, 154, 158; Carnegie program and, 133–5; fundraising, 127–9; library establishment and, 125–7; Lillian Gunter and, 194–6

working-class readers, 65–7, 99; branch library design and, 114–9; Carnegie and, 101, 102; children's facilities, 176–7

Xenia, Ohio, 128, 130–2, 203–8

XLI Club, 138, 154, 158, 194–6